"In this book, Doug Luffborough invites readers to share a remarkable and ultimately heartening journey. Prepare to experience a range of emotions as you read this book, including rage, shame, and humiliation as a precursor to compassion, pride, and joy. It is an account of growth and development, the result of which is the emergence of a good man. It is a book worth reading not just because of how it makes you feel, but also because of how it makes you want to be."

—George Reed, PhD, Associate Dean, School of Leadership and Education Sciences, University of San Diego

"From the moment Doug walks into a room, you can feel his energy and the strength of spirit that he exudes—it is captivating. He is the real deal. Present and action oriented, Doug possesses the ability to remain conscious of his past while not allowing it to define who he is as a person. His openness and honesty invite you in from the moment you meet him. Doug not only survived but also thrived, despite the obstacles that he encountered. Doug's willingness to share his vulnerabilities on a visceral level is one of the qualities that allow him to break down barriers and relate to others in a compassionate and genuine manner. His enthusiastic, caring, charismatic approach was contagious, and it is readily apparent that Doug is a man who holds high standards for himself and, in doing so, motivates others to aspire to be better. Doug not only epitomizes effective leadership, but he also transcends it."

—Maria Olson, Former Resident Director, Office of Residential Life, Northeastern University

"A message of hope, hard work, dedication, and never-ending faith . . . For our youth today, and for those of us who work to guide and support them, Doug Luffborough's story provides both inspiration and wisdom. Doug's powerful ability to engage an audience—whether on stage, in a boardroom, or in text—is fully displayed as he shows us that anything is possible, and dreams do come true if you work hard and keep the faith!"

—Kevin E. Baird, Chairman, Global Center for College and Career Readiness

"Doug is the quintessential leader. To have arrived at the level of personal and professional success that he has achieved, given the myriad of obstacles that he had to overcome, makes him a true role model. Others who aspire to create better lives for themselves and their families, as Doug did, can look to him for inspiration. Doug has had the resiliency to persevere, build skills, and then use his innate talents to create positive change both close to home, as well in the greater community. In my thirty-four years of helping countless individuals realize their personal promise, Doug's story is the one that continues to inspire me. His is the success story at which we all marvel."

—Pamela Boisvert, CEO, Massachusetts Education & Career Opportunities, Inc. (MassEDCO)

"Mr. Luffborough's autobiography depicts a riveting story of an abused and frightened young boy evolving into a matured and courageous inspirational leader who befriends President Clinton and has dedicated his life to educating countless troubled youth. This account details the harsh realities many of our young poverty-stricken children face today and offers hope for overcoming our society's ills. It is a sobering, must-read tale for all who are working with our younger generation."

—Dr. Francisco Escobedo, Superintendent, Chula Vista Elementary School District

"Doug works with people who want to be loved back to life and turn their dreams into reality! This is a tall order for a big man who has already delivered. I have known Doug for a short time and hope to know him for a lifetime. He has already done great things and is on a path to be even greater. . . . Be prepared to follow Doug and see the world change."

—Gerry Rose, Life Coach, Integrity Networking Solutions

"This is a stunning story, in and of itself, but there is even more here than that. The book is a case study of how passion drives nonprofit vision and action. It shows us that our contribution is a divine mixture of our own destiny and the mystical intervention of God. Anyone will be better for reading this account."

—Mary B. McDonald, PhD, University of San Diego and St. Vincent de Paul Village

"Everyone loves a good rags-to-riches story, but Doug Luffborough, in this well-crafted narrative of his personal journey, brings this message even closer to home—where the heart is. As Executive Director of Turning the Hearts, a Chula Vista Elementary School Board Member, and a parent of the school community I serve, Mr. Luffborough has inspired me and challenged me through his story to never give up on anyone, including myself. His story will forever be engraved on my heart as I continue my quest for excellence in education for all. God bless Doug Luffborough, and may all who read his story be changed."

—Debra McLaren, Principal, Wolf Canyon Elementary School, Chula Vista, California

"Every man has an opportunity to find his purpose in life, but not every man will embrace it. During the last ten years, I have witnessed Mr. Luffborough strive in pursuing his purpose. His life and who he is as a man has inspired me to grow and change as a father, husband, brother, son, employee, and leader. This book will ignite, motivate, and transform you into the person you are destined to be, as well as challenge you to use the negative events in your life as fuel to propel you forward in reaching your goals. That's what it did to me!"

—Manny Castro, Intervention Specialist and Success Coach, Turning the Hearts Center

"My dad's story will inspire you to become an overachiever and reach your goals. Through this book, you will learn that love, family, and hope are what kept my dad strong and powerful. Watch him rise."

—Micaela Elsa Luffborough, Doug Luffborough's nine-year old daughter

"Doug Luffborough pulls no punches in this autobiography of a fatherless, homeless boy who overcomes more vicissitudes of life than most of us ever face, and he does it by the time he graduates from college and speaks on the same platform as President Clinton. Yes, parts of this story are hard to bear, but we can all learn from its improbable twists and turns that are too strange to be fiction!"

—William R. Torbert, PhD, Leadership Professor Emeritus, Boston College; Principal, Action Inquiry Associates

"In the last eight years, I have had the privilege to work under the leadership of Doug Luffborough. As the program director of Turning the Hearts Center, I have personally witnessed his heart, drive, and passion to be a dream releaser for all who meet him. Amongst the many lessons he has taught me, two have greatly impacted my life. One of them is to 'under promise and over deliver.' In his book, there is a developing theme to live out your words and to keep your word! Another lesson he has taught me is to 'turn your wishbone into a backbone!' Doug has taught me to always rise to the occasion, to live recognizing you have only one opportunity, and to face life's challenges head-on. His book will challenge your perception of what it means to live with purpose, hope, and commitment! It will demand you to stop waiting for life to happen and start pursuing your dreams. Doug's journey to Harvard will compel you to live without limitations!"

—Alejandra Aceves, Program Director, Turning the Hearts Center

"The moment you open this book will be the moment you grasp a fuller understanding of how a champion is processed in life. Doug is not only a graduate of prestigious universities but also a graduate of probably one of the most underrated universities in our time and space: Hard Knocks University. Adversity is no stranger to a champion. In fact, a champion welcomes them as friends. Doug's character, destiny, mission, and purpose in life has mirrored the type of testing and process that a sword must undergo when being prepared for battle—the blacksmith must do this to ensure that when in battle, it will not break. This book will help you refocus your own course in life by challenging you to no longer see your obstacles as problems but as opportunities to maximize your potential!"

—Darius West, Director/Screenwriter

"Very quickly after meeting Doug, I realized what an incredibly talented young man he was. Bursting with potential, I wanted to identify opportunities to develop Doug's skills and abilities—I wanted to invest in him. By leveraging his charisma and developing his leadership skills, Doug's sphere of influence on other young people grew. What began with leading a team of ten grew to a role recruiting and creating opportunities for thousands. This book, Doug's story, will now inspire millions!"

—Nancy Routh, Chief People Officer and Senior Vice President, City Year, Inc.

"If ever a man encountered every possible obstacle to achieving his dreams yet still accomplished everything he dreamt of and more, *this* is that story. Doug Luffborough, with an innate strength empowered by the grace of God and the love of his strong-willed, caring Mama Luff, shows us how to listen to the God within and overcome anything—literally anything—that impedes our way. Read this book and you will be inspired—not by buzzwords or catchphrases, but by the true story of a man who never took the easy way out and found hard work and perseverance as the conveyance to success!"

—Byron Navarro, Doug Luffborough's brother-in-law and aspiring author

Watch Me Rise

Watch Me Rise

From the Streets of Despair to the Halls of the Ivy League

DOUGLAS E. LUFFBOROUGH III

Cristina,
Continue to RISE!
– Douglas E. Luffborough III

Writers of the Round Table Press
PO Box 511, Highland Park, IL 60035
www.roundtablecompanies.com

Publisher: *Corey Michael Blake*
Executive Editor: *Katie Gutierrez*
Lead Editor: *Lizzie Vance*
Director of Operations: *Kristin Westberg*
Facts Keeper: *Mike Winicour*
Cover Design: *Analee Paz*
Proofreading: *Rita Hess*
Print and Digital Interior Design: *Sunny DiMartino*
Last Looks: *Aaron Hierholzer*
Print and Digital Post Production: *Sunny DiMartino*

Printed in the United States of America

First Edition: July 2014
10 9 8 7 6 5 4 3 2 1

Library of Congress Cataloging-in-Publication Data
Luffborough, Douglas E.
Watch me rise: from the streets of despair to the halls of the ivy league /
Douglas E. Luffborough III.—1st ed. p. cm.
ISBN Paperback: 978-1-939418-58-6
ISBN Digital: 978-1-939418-59-3
Library of Congress Control Number: 2014945914

While this book is a true story to the best of the author's recollection,
some names have been changed to protect the individuals' privacy.

This book is dedicated to:

My children. *Faith Lily, Makenna Joy, Micaela Elsa, Douglas Dante, and Meilani Lea. Daddy loves you very much, and by reading this book, you will better understand how I grew up and why I tell you to give life your best, love yourself, and live your dreams. I am so honored to be the father I never had to each of you. You bring me joy!*

My wife, Claire Navarro Luffborough. *Thank you for never letting me go. The best is yet to come for you, for me, and for our children. It was all worth it, and I love you.*

My mother, Elsa Luffborough Mensah. *From the first chapter to the last, you are all over this book as the voice of hope and encouragement that would never let me give up on myself or give up on God. To God be the glory!*

My father-in-law, Dante Z. Navarro. *May you rest in peace, and thank you for the life lessons. You taught me to be the man, husband, and father I am today.*

Contents

Acknowledgments

I was raised to have an attitude of gratitude. No matter how bad life got, I always lived through the lens of a half-full cup. I was thankful for anything—both positive and negative—that happened to me. I have found that a grateful heart opens up opportunities, enabling you to live life to the fullest, with no regrets. Writing this book has been an almost-two-year journey that turned out to be the greatest form of therapy and personal healing I could have ever received.

I have so much to be thankful for—and so many to thank.

First, I would like to thank God for his unfailing love and for being the only one I could talk to during some of the darkest times in my life. Each time I called on him for help, he covered me. Jeremiah 29:11 was written with my name in mind, and the scripture has transformed who I am and the life I am destined to live. My quest now is to love other people back to life and turn their dreams into reality. To God Be The Glory (TGBTG).

Second, I would like to thank my wife, Claire Navarro Luffborough, and my children, Faith Lily (God bless her soul), Makenna Joy, Micaela Elsa, Douglas Dante, and Meilani Lea, for being my foundation and teaching me what it means to "do family." One of my greatest loves in life is being a husband and a father. You all are my everything and the reason for all that I do. I love each of you and live to serve you.

Next, I would like to thank my mother, Elsa Luffborough Mensah (a.k.a. Mamma Luff) for being my inspiration and an unwavering example of what it means to fervently serve God and one's children to the best of one's ability. My prayer is that your life will radically change as a result of the millions of people who read this story. Thank you for the sacrifices you made and continue to make for your children and your grandchildren. The greatest gifts you taught me were to love God and love myself, and to have good home training—priceless. I would also like to acknowledge and appreciate my father-in-law, Dante Z. Navarro (God bless his soul) and my mother-in-law, Lily Cruz Navarro, for being an additional set of parents to me. They are the perfect example of unity, love, and togetherness that my wife and I seek to emulate.

To my siblings, Darrell J. Luffborough, Derrick O. Mensah, Danielle N. Mensah, and Jimmy Barclay, Jr., I love you guys and continue to pray for you and your families. We have gone our separate ways with age, but I think of you often and hope this book brings us all closer together. You are all intertwined in my journey, our crazy journey of doing life together.

There are many heroes in this book (and some who are not) that I would like to acknowledge by name for helping me navigate through life, serving as source of inspiration when I needed it most: Mamma Luff, Mr. Cott, Coach Miller, Ms. Quinn, Ms. G, Byron Navarro, Pam Boisvert, Stephen Bell, Fred Davis, Mr. and Mrs. Incutto, Rosie Colucci, Maria Olson, Laurie Guth, Nancy Routh, President Curry, President Clinton, Mrs. Humphrey, Dr. Willie, Dr. Bempechat, Dr. Nakula, Dr. McDonald, Dr. Galloway, Dr. Hubbard, Dr. Green, Dr. Reed, Dr. Herrera, Alejandra Aceves, Manny Castro, and my best man, Chris Corso. Thank you all.

Finally, I would like to thank my Round Table Companies family for supporting me all the way from the beginning to the end of this project. Special thanks to Corey Blake, David Cohen, Katie Gutierrez, Lizzie Vance, and Kristin Westberg. This is just the beginning of creating real, relevant, and powerful content for the world to read and for lives to change.

Introduction

As I heard the president of Northeastern University say, "Ladies and gentlemen, your student speaker, Doug Luffborough," the world slowed around me. My heart beat like a strobe, flashing intense memories before me: using newspaper instead of toilet paper in the bathroom; helping my mother clean rich people's houses and seeing firsthand the condescending way she was treated; staring down the barrel of a gun. I considered my life without a father or strong male role model by my side. I remembered the tremendous sacrifices made for me to be on this platform. Finally, I recalled being told that I was not college material, that I should stay home and continue working at the local factory. As I made my way to the podium at the Boston Garden, a heat wave of excitement shimmered for the student commencement speaker who would precede the president of the United States, Bill Clinton, live on national television. Some believe that everyone will have their fifteen minutes of fame—and for me, those fifteen minutes would shape the next twenty years.

Since that day, people have asked why I have not written a book about my life. At first, I thought it was my enduring insecurities with writing that stopped me. Then I told myself that engaging help would be too expensive—not that I even knew where or how to start. Now I realize it took me so long because, month by month, year by year, and decade by decade, the story of my life was still evolving. I was still seeking answers to two questions: Who am I? And why am I here?

My mother used to say, "The me I see is the me I will be." In other words, the way you see yourself in life is what you will become. For many years, I saw myself as the child of a housekeeper, a boy who grew up in poverty without a father or a place that felt like home. Becoming homeless during my senior year of high school was, poetically, an outward manifestation of my deep inward struggle to find a home. People say that home is where the heart is, but when you live each day with a broken heart, "home" is self-doubt, depression, and unfulfilled dreams. Home is a shattering loss of hope. At eighteen, my heart's homelessness led me to the edge of a bridge overlooking rush-hour traffic. Jumping seemed like the only way out, but God had a different plan for me, a plan that would eventually lead to the prestigious academic halls of Harvard University—and beyond.

In the end, though, this book is not just about being homeless or graduating from Harvard. It is my journey to find meaning in times of deep sorrow, a personal account of transforming negative situations into moments of strength and triumph. The pages that follow will explore some of the lowest times in my life but also my highest moments of victory. I hope that my story will inspire you to see that quitting is not an option. If what you are doing is not working, change your approach, but never give up on your dreams. Hard work, persistence, and a positive attitude will always pay off.

I believe in measuring success through the stories of lives we change. It has taken me over forty years to build the courage to tell this story, but I believe that relationships will be restored and destinies fulfilled because of it. This book is for everyone: the pregnant teenaged runaway looking for meaning *and* the Ivy League–educated executive seeking to rediscover humanity in a world full of greed, arrogance, and power. This book is for you.

"The me I see is the me I will be," and today I see myself as an international heart-inspired speaker, author, leadership consultant, nonprofit executive, coach, husband, and father determined to become a world changer.

Who are you? Why are *you* here? Thank you for joining me on this journey. Let's discover the answers together.

Chapter 1

Love Does Not Hit

Abusers choose to abuse; don't suffer in silence. You are not to blame.

—Anonymous

Pike Street in Norfolk, Virginia, back in the 1960s was an up-and-coming, middle-class community of predominantly African-American families. They lived in single-story detached homes built perpendicular to a cemetery at the end of the street. There, in the shadows of headstones, was where my mother and father first met. Their beginning before a reservoir of death symbolized the doomed nature of their relationship, which contrasted with the strong sense of living that surged throughout my mother's always-hopeful approach to whatever life brought her. Love and hope never failed to thrive within her heart, even as her union with my father was dead upon arrival.

My mother, Elsa B. Haskins, was the oldest of two children. Her parents were divorced, and her mother made *Mommy Dearest* look like a children's fable. Ma never knew when her mother, frustrated with the realities of life, would kick her down a flight of stairs or tell her she was too dark-skinned, too much a tomboy, to find someone to marry her. From the little I know, my mother endured verbal and physical abuse since the day she was born. It was a hole that gaped ever wider, begging to be filled with love, appreciation, and a sense of self-worth.

She found what she so hungered for in her grandfather, Christopher Bell. Grandpa Bell was a great provider and hard worker, a family man who owned his first home in the 1950s, in the heart of the segregated South. He adored my mother. He took her to the park, bought her pretty dresses and Barbie dolls, and imbued her difficult life with words of affirmation. He told her she was smart and beautiful and that she would do big things with her life. Every time he spoke to her, he breathed hope into her heart. He helped her make important life decisions, such as leaving Virginia because she had no chance of developing as a woman while living under her mother's roof. He took her to appointments when she was pregnant with me and did not have transportation, and helped her with rent or utilities when her bank account ran low. To this day, my mother tears up in reverent sadness when Grandpa Bell's name emerges in conversation.

My father came from a hardworking, educated family. His parents both graduated from college and worked at Norfolk State University. Like Grandpa Bell, my father's father was a great example who built his Pike Street home from the ground up. He was a carpenter and constructed many homes and businesses throughout Norfolk, including many buildings at Norfolk State University, where he taught carpentry and woodworking. As a building superintendent, his name would one day find its way onto a bronze plaque at the home of the university president. His name, my father's name, my name: Douglas Edward Luffborough.

Because Grandpa Bell's house was right across the street from my father's, it was inevitable that my parents met as children. I wish I knew more about their past, but it has long been water under a bridge. My mother—the only one who would be able to talk about it—has no interest in revisiting her younger years, so I'm left to imagine. In my mind, I see Ma coming home from school. Pigtails and all, she drops her backpack on Grandpa Bell's driveway and pulls out thick sidewalk chalk, spending the afternoon hours playing hopscotch with her friends. Meanwhile, my dad pops wheelies on his bike, doing jumps off the curbside right across the street, hoping to make an impression. I imagine they explored the neighborhood playing hide-and-seek and, later, spin the bottle. Maybe they had their first kiss in one of their backyards; maybe it came later. To be honest, I'm not sure what happened first—love, marriage, or me—but my mother was nineteen years old when I was born. She was a sophomore at Old Dominion University, and my father was in the military.

With my father away on deployments, my mom lived the life of a single pregnant woman who was barely scraping by. She lived in an apartment in the Portsmouth/Norfolk area and tried to continue her education, but college was suddenly a luxury she could no longer afford. The military checks my father sent home were few and far between. At a particularly dire time, my mother's aunt offered to lend her some money. The problem was that she was in Akron, Ohio, and my mom was nine months pregnant. Ma had no other choice; with her belly completely distended, and for only a couple hundred dollars, she climbed the steep steps onto a Greyhound bus and settled into a worn gray seat. As day fell to night, she rode from Virginia to Ohio so she could put food on the table for a little while longer. But I couldn't wait. While she was still in Ohio, my mom felt the contractions that said her baby was coming—now! I was born on August 27, 1969, in Akron, Ohio.

Whatever my parents' relationship had been like as kids, their marriage was deeply troubled. My father was a slick character with a conniving spirit. He loved his booze and his women, and he was short-tempered and angry. Everyone around him blamed it on the war, saying he'd come back different, but my mother said the change only revealed his true character.

When I was three or four years old, I hid under my bed to try to mute the banging, screaming, and profanity echoing from the next room.

My mother's voice—*Please! Please stop!*—came as muffled sound through the wall, interrupted by my father's baritone growls and the sickening impact of knuckles on flesh. I trembled beneath my bed, curled in a corner closest to the wall so that if my dad reached for me, he couldn't grab me right away. I thought my father would kill me.

One time, my mother called her younger brother, Junie, for help. Uncle Junie was a big man, someone you would not be glad to see in a dark alley, and I thought he would make things better.

"Elsa!" he yelled, banging on the door. "Open up, let me in!"

Until then, the abuse had been a dirty family secret that no one had seen firsthand, and my dad was enraged that his cover was blown. “Go home, Junie,” he snarled. “This isn’t your business.”

The door shook on its hinges beneath Uncle Junie’s massive fists, but my father refused to unlock it. Finally, Uncle Junie threw his weight into it with fierce kicks until it burst open. He wasted no time before going at my father with his fists, and my father didn’t back down from the fight. He was around five foot nine, a hundred and sixty pounds, while Uncle Junie was one-eighty and well over six feet tall. He could have taken my father out if my dad hadn’t been so filled with rage. Right in front of me, they knocked each other against the walls, grunting as one of them knocked the wind out of the other. I thought for sure someone would get killed that night.

“Stop it!” my mom yelled. “Junie, you quit it right now!”

She squeezed her body between them, but they tossed her aside as if she were a child. In one breath, she yelled at my dad to stop hitting my uncle; in the next, she was shrieking for Uncle Junie to stop, saying that he was going to kill my father. I didn’t understand why she was defending both sides when she was the one who’d called Uncle Junie to begin with. Who was wrong here? And what was *I* supposed to do? Paralyzed with fear, I screamed and punched my own legs because I wanted to help but knew I couldn’t do anything. I felt completely powerless and overwhelmed with the reality I was witnessing.

My mother wasn’t the only one my father beat. My skin reddened under his palms just as regularly as my mom’s did. He hit me like a grown man would hit another man, not like a father would discipline a three- or four-year-old boy. Anything set him off, and he slapped me on the face or punched my chest when he was upset, never showing any signs of apology or remorse afterwards. Eventually, the situation escalated to involving the police. That was the beginning of the end of my parents’ marriage.

My mother divorced my father when I was four or five years old and my brother, Darrell, was two or three. We moved in with my mother’s father and stepmother. They lived in a one-story, three-bedroom house on a corner street and had a kennel of half-breed, wolflike dogs that lived in cages in the backyard. The dogs were neglected, malnourished, and mean, snarling at us through the rusty brown chain-link fence. We didn't venture close to them very often.

My brother was too young to fully comprehend the change in our lives—a fissure that was about to deepen. Soon after we moved in with my mother's parents, Grandpa Bell passed away. At that point, having lost the only person she felt truly loved her, my mother had no more soul ties to Norfolk. She carried deep scars from the abuse she'd suffered from her mother and husband, and she thought maybe she'd be better off somewhere else, where she would not be judged for her mistakes or shortcomings. My father wasn't interested in playing a role in our lives, so Norfolk may as well have been a ghost town to her—nothing worth missing or coming back to.

Darrell and I shared a bedroom at our grandparents' house, and Ma came in one afternoon to tell us her plan.

"I'm leaving you with Grandpa and Grandma for a while," she said. "Just until I get some work and a place for us. I need to get on my feet again, and then I'll come back for you."

Darrell and I looked at each other, stricken. We had already seen things that we should not have seen, heard things that boys our age didn't need to hear. Just as my mother felt when Grandpa Bell died, we felt now: our number one advocate was leaving our lives, and we were convinced it was forever.

"Don't go, Ma," I cried, wrapping my arms around her neck. Darrell crawled into her lap, and she held us both as we cried.

"You boys be strong and behave yourselves," she said.

The next day, my mother was gone.

Darrell and I spent many nights supporting each other as best we could in our mom's absence, but mostly we cried ourselves to sleep. Children need parents in their lives. Having caring adults helps, but nothing takes the place of a loving mother or father. And though our mother had promised to return, we couldn't help but doubt her. What if she was happier without us? Deep in my broken heart, I feared she had abandoned us just as surely as my father had.

We stayed with our grandparents for a year or so while my mother transitioned to Massachusetts. There, she met another guy named Greg, who was also in the military and was doing some work in Worcester, Massachusetts.

We knew very little about Greg or what he did for a living, but when Mom called every other month, it seemed as though she was happy. She said she wanted to get settled with Greg and then would send for Darrell and me. I was happy for her, hopeful she'd found someone who loved her. Still, I missed her presence and remained fearful that my father would hurt Darrell and me or just come by and take us on a whim. I needn't have worried about that. In the one year we stayed with our grandparents, my father took us out no more than twice.

On one of those times, he drove us to McDonald's for dinner. He paid for our Happy Meals and sat at a table with us, but he didn't try to engage us in conversation. Darrell and I were afraid of him, so we sat quietly in the vinyl booth, speaking only when spoken to. I watched my dad from the corner of my eye as I ate my nuggets. His eyes roved over every woman who passed our table, a long up-and-down appraisal he didn't bother to hide. He showed no interest in who we were becoming in his absence. After dinner, he dropped us back off at my grandparents' house, and that was that.

My grandparents gave us a roof, but our time with them was not easy. My grandfather was a mean, strange character, a rough old man who pushed us around too much. He pulled on our ears, pinched us, and slapped us upside the head for no reason. Sometimes he pushed us to the ground and sat on us until we cried because we couldn't breathe. Worst of all, he often put on a wolverine-type mask and scared the heebie-jeebies out of my brother and me when we were sleeping. We never knew when he would do it, but he snuck into our bedroom late at night and roared at us, terrifying us out of sleep. One time, I wet myself, and my brother nearly fainted with fear. What I recognize now as a form of torture went on for the entire time we lived with our grandparents. I had no explanation for it then. Now I see it as a way of showing us who had the power. It wasn't unlike the abuse my mom suffered at my dad's hands.

"Grandma, please tell him to stop," we begged, clinging to her sturdy thighs.

Grandma was a typical, nurturing Southern woman who cooked a lot of food, loved going to church, and took care of all the domestic affairs throughout the home—she did the laundry, cleaned the house, and made a mean sweet potato pie.

Grandma laughed gently. "He's just playing around, honey." She gave Grandpa a lightly reproachful look. "But you take it easy on these boys."

Looking back, I'd be surprised if Grandma wasn't also scared of Grandpa. Her soft words had no effect on him. He just grunted and walked out of the room, giving Darrell and me a glance over his shoulder that meant nothing had changed. As much as I wanted to tell Ma what was happening, I didn't want to worry her or risk where we were staying. We just had to be patient. She'd come back for us one day.

"Are you sure?" Darrell whispered in the darkness of our room.

I sighed in bed, pulling the covers up to my chin. "Of course," I said.

That tenuous hope was all we had to hang on to.

Chapter 2

In the Land of Fire, Leaf, and Snow

Real fatherhood means love, commitment, sacrifice and a willingness to share responsibility and not walking away from one's children.

—William Bennett

Almost a year to the day my mother left us, the doorbell rang. We weren't expecting anyone, and I flung open the door full of curiosity. There, with a big smile on her face, stood my mom.

"You're back!" I cried, diving into her arms. I buried my face in the warm skin of her neck as she wrapped her arms around me.

She laughed. "Well, of course I'm back! What did you think, boy, I was leaving forever? Where's your brother?"

"Darrell!" I shouted. "Ma's back!"

Darrell rushed from the living room, his eyes wide. He stopped at the entry, staring in shocked happiness, and Ma opened one arm so he could run to her. We were half in the house and half out, burrowed into Ma's coat. I had never been so happy. The smell of her perfume filled me with a dizzying swell of comfort, reminding me of her protection, presence, and love for us. Ma was only in her twenties but had already lived a life of someone ten years older. You could see wisdom and the regret of past mistakes in her dark eyes; you could hear it in her always thoughtful choice of words and careful tone. She had a way of teaching without telling, of convincing without forcing. She was wise beyond her years.

"Have you boys been behaving yourselves?" Ma asked.

Darrell and I exchanged glances over the collar of Ma's coat. We hadn't said a thing about Grandpa's roughhousing or midnight scares, and we didn't intend to. Ma was back and, with her, a sense of shelter, safety, and security. *There is no place like home*, the old saying goes, and for me, "home" was Ma. There was no point in rocking a boat we were about to abandon anyway.

"Where's Greg?" I asked, changing the subject. I stared over Ma's shoulder. There was nothing and no one in the front yard, and Ma had only one small, worn bag beside her.

"Greg and I aren't together anymore," she said, kissing my head. Then she stood up, groaning a little as she stretched her legs. "He wasn't going to be a daddy to you boys. We didn't need that."

During the time we'd stayed with our grandparents, my mother had come to visit only once. Greg, a medium-sized white man with a mustache, was with her. He smiled at my mother a lot, eyes twinkling, but he was standoffish toward Darrell and me. He never tried to engage us in conversation or play, which made me feel awkward and out of place. If my mother were just a single woman—and not a single mother—they might have stayed together, but it takes a special man to embrace a divorced twenty-something-year-old woman with two kids. Thankfully, though, my mother's priority was her children, and she didn't try to keep Greg from walking away.

"I met someone else, though," Ma said as we walked inside, shutting the door to the cooling fall air. "His name is Joe. He's going to be waiting for us in Worcester."

We were young and far too self-involved to ask Ma any questions about Joe, but I later found out he was from Ghana, Africa, and was going to school to study business. Ma had met him after Greg left her and she found a room at the YWCA in downtown Worcester, with a job across the street at Filene's clothing store in the mall. Though I'm still not sure how their paths crossed, they quickly moved in together. A simple justice of the peace marriage followed. Unlike Greg, Joe seemed open to Ma *and* her children.

In November of 1975, Darrell and I squashed our paltry belongings into a couple of bags, and we all piled into Grandma and Grandpa's station wagon. The drive to the Greyhound station was quiet and unemotional, our goodbye bittersweet. My grandparents' house had been safe and unstable at the same time, a strange mix of my grandmother's Southern comfort food and my grandfather's unpredictable mood swings. It was sweet potato pie and pinching, fried chicken and slapping. I wasn't sure if I would ever see Grandma and Grandpa again, but I was thankful to be heading to a new life in a new community with another chance to start over. Even the caged dogs in the backyard had barked as if to say, "Good for you . . . don't come back."

When we arrived at the bus station in Norfolk, "Massachusetts," by the Bee Gees, played over the PA system: "Feel I'm going back to Massachusetts / Something's telling me I must go home." Among the sharp smell of exhaust and rush of travelers, the song seemed like a good sign, a hint that a new life was ahead of us. I was naively thinking that my mother had found her knight, a shining king who had come to rescue his queen and her children and give them a life of royalty and prosperity. Finally, I thought, my brother and I would be able to be with my mom and live a normal life, with a man who truly loved us. We'd live in a colonial house with a white picket fence, a golden retriever, and enough bedrooms for each of us. Most importantly, there would be no more family drama, no more violence and abuse. Such were the thoughts of a little boy who, like all children, only wanted happiness in his life.

It was a long trip. As we headed north on Interstate 95 to the Massachusetts Turnpike, the weather became colder and colder. It was autumn in New England, and fall foliage was in full bloom, with flame-colored leaves burning out the disappearing green boughs. The collage of colors was stunning. I pressed my face to the window, gazing at the multicolored trees. They represented a new land of opportunity and individuality, a chance for us to discover a new path in our lives. The farther north we rode, I felt this was exactly why my mother had left Norfolk for Worcester—to develop a new identity as a family, leaving behind the bruises and neglect of the past.

When we arrived at the Greyhound station in Worcester, there was snow on the ground. It was the first time I had ever seen snow. It was strange to see so much white after all of those fiery leaves. As my feet touched the ground, the cold air pricked chills up my spine.

I zipped up the only jacket I owned, a light spring windbreaker, as the bus driver hauled our luggage from underneath the bus. My breath smoked with every exhalation, and Darrell and I competed to see who could blow the biggest puffs of white.

"Douglas, you and Darrell need to hurry up now," Ma said, grabbing two bags and bouncing up and down on her toes. "I don't want you to freeze to death!"

I followed Ma's lead and grabbed my bag. The tips of my fingers were white, and I could not feel the pressure of the handle against them because of the cold. We dragged our bags behind us and followed Ma up to the station. A wave of heat washed over us as soon as we opened the door, and I shivered with relief. Joe waited outside, his rusted-out car idling, puffing out plumes of heat from the back end of the parking lot. When Ma spotted him, she went quickly up to him, gave him a hug, and then turned to my brother and me. "Kids, this is Joe, and Joe, this is my oldest son Douglas and his little brother Darrell. Okay, let's go!"

And that was that—not quite the introduction I had built up in my mind, but I was still optimistic about our future.

The apartment we moved into was a tiny one-bedroom—simple, dark, lived-in. Ma and Joe stayed in the bedroom, and Darrell and I slept on a foldout couch in the living room. We did not have much space, but at least my brother and I weren't tormented by my grandfather anymore.

Joe grew up playing soccer with many brothers and sisters in Ghana. His English was broken, since his first language was Ga, the national language of Ghana. Joe talked on the phone often with family members in the States and back home, and the foreign language cut through our small apartment in sharp, mysterious fragments.

I never did find out how my mom met Joe or even what made them get married so quickly. Joe was on a student visa, so perhaps he was hoping for a green card. Whatever the case, he always seemed to have a box of Marlboros in his front right pocket and an opened can of Schlitz beer in his left hand. Except for physically inhabiting a house with a woman and her kids, he lived the life of a bachelor: he woke up, got dressed, had a smoke, and went to work at a factory. When he got home around five, he made himself a meal out of food he'd purchased from a local African grocery store and ate it apart from us, using African customs like eating only with his hands. Then he had another cigarette, slammed down a six-pack of Schlitz, made a move on my mother, and eventually passed out. Very rarely did he engage as a father figure with my brother and me. Like my father and Greg, Joe seemed to want the attention of my mother without the responsibility or privilege of becoming a father to two boys desperately seeking love and attention. Joe rarely did fatherly things with me, and I never called him Dad.

Fridays were differentiating days in our house. Joe didn't have to work the two days following, so we never knew what would happen, but we knew we would have a story to tell in the morning. One Friday night, I woke up to Joe speaking in Ga, laughing and joking in the wee hours of the morning. When I told him I was trying to sleep, he let loose a furious stream of Ga. It felt as though he was telling me how he really felt about me. The next morning when I went into the kitchen, I found him passed out on the floor with a spilled can of Schlitz by his side. That was the regular weekend cycle: first the smell of dead lamb searing, then one cigarette burning after the next, then the case of Schlitz on the kitchen counter, then the loud African music and Joe singing in Ga, then the midnight conversation with friends, and then the taunts and aggravation toward my mother. The more he drank, the louder he became. The yelling and screaming went on until he passed out, always about trivial matters. He never apologized in the morning for things he'd said or done the night before—mainly, I guessed, because he didn't remember.

I realized after watching how Joe and Ma interacted that their relationship was not the example I wanted to follow. Ma was young, looking for love in all the wrong people, and Joe was opportunistic. However, I never said anything about the injustices I saw, for I was raised to be thankful for the little I did have, as well as to respect the authority over me. So for most of my childhood, I grew up thinking it was okay to treat women a certain way, to be the "man of the house" but not take care of your children. Children learn what they see, and my only models of fatherhood came from men who refused to fill those shoes.

Ma was a housekeeper, and Darrell and I often went with her to clean homes. Some of the houses were big—two-story homes filled with granite countertops and crown molding. They were completely loaded compared to our tiny one-bedroom apartment with linoleum floors. My mom worked long days and had a fierce work ethic, even though she didn't make more than seven thousand dollars per year for most of my life. It was hard to watch her on her hands and knees, scrubbing other people's floors and toilets; it looked so degrading, but at the same time, I saw her pour all her energy into making sure her job was done well, with a spirit of excellence. I took away from this experience two powerful things: first, I learned the importance of working hard, of always putting forth a strong effort. Second, I caught a vision of the type of home I hoped one day to live in. When I helped my mom clean houses, I thought, *One day, when I own my own home, I want to have granite countertops and crown molding. I want to have a big king-sized bed with plenty of food in the cupboards and plenty of toilet paper.*

Many times, Ma's customers made condescending remarks like, "Elsa, make sure you take off your shoes before you enter my house, and don't steal anything on your way out, you hear?" Ma always responded with a "Yes, sir" or "Yes, ma'am." I knew stealing was the furthest thing from Ma's mind. But one time, we had no food in our cupboards and no toilet paper in the bathroom; Joe had his own food and was not the least bit concerned about our wellbeing. He did not even see the necessity of toilet paper. We had to rub newspaper together until it was soft enough to use to wipe ourselves. (To this day, I will never understand that!) So just once, my mom stole one can of ravioli and one roll of toilet paper from one of her homes. She didn't say anything when she walked into our kitchen—just quietly slipped the provisions from her bag. I knew what she'd done and that it was wrong, and I saw the shame on her face, but I was hungry and not looking forward to wiping myself with newspaper again. Ma immediately emptied the can of ravioli into a small pot on the stove, and Darrell and I waited impatiently for it to fill our bowls.

We moved a lot when we got to Worcester—three times in two years. Ma and Joe looked for the cheapest place they could find, with the least expensive living costs. With all the transition, I did not receive the benefit of the intensive, quality kindergarten education every five-year-old deserves. I was at a disadvantage from the start of my schooling, and I had a hard time getting along with or trusting others. Only now as a Ph.D. student am I truly able to face my fears and inadequacies in reading and writing.

My most vivid early school memory was at Elm Park Elementary School. I was in kindergarten and being bullied every day by one behemoth sixth-grade white boy. Every day, he grabbed me by the shirt, punched me in the chest, or slapped me upside my head and demanded that I give him my lunch money. He reminded me of my father and grandfather, who victimized me freely without fear of repercussion. I hated going to school and did everything I could to avoid being alone on the playground. When the bell rang, I ran as fast as I could to my classroom. Carl Lewis, former Olympic gold medalist in the hundred-meter dash, had nothing on me.

One day, as the school bell was about to ring, I peeked around the corner to see my bully. He was scanning the schoolyard, clearly looking for me. I ducked back against the building, heart pounding. At this time, we lived less than twenty yards away, right across the street from school. Ma was washing dishes and caught a glimpse through the window of me holding up the walls of the school. She yelled, "Douglas, what are you doing, boy? Get your butt to school; you don't want to be late!"

I put one shaking finger over my mouth, but it was too late. There he was, yanking my finger away from my mouth, grabbing me by the shirt, slapping me upside the head, and rifling through my pockets for my lunch money. I burst into tears and fell to my knees, but that day, the right person saw everything. In what seemed like seconds, Ma ran out of our apartment in her robe, hair uncombed, wielding a broom over her head. She grabbed my hand and ran after my bully on the playground. Without a second's hesitation, she whacked him with the broom, yelling in rhythm with each hit, "Don't you *ever* put your hands on my son or take his lunch money! Do you hear me?" She let him have it. I watched in awe, thinking, *Serves him right, jack this fool up, Ma!*—though a part of me worried he might turn his wrath on her.

My bully threw his arms up to block the thrusts of the broom. "Stop it!" he cried. "Get off me!" At one point, I even remember him saying, "Here, take the money back, take the money back!"

Later on that night when I was at home watching television, my mother came into the room with a determined, angry look on her face. She looked me intensely in the eye and told me to never back down from someone trying to get one over on me—even if I knew it was a losing fight.

"I did not raise no chump, no sucker-punk of a son," she said. "You go down defending yourself. You may not win, but you will gain the respect of many. You hear me?"

I nodded, and something in me rose to the surface—some feeling of strength or pride, a resolution never to let others push me over again.

After that day, everyone knew the son of Elsa Luffborough Mensah. We spent the rest of the week meeting with school officials and my bully's parents to try to resolve the matter. Ma was the nicest lady you could expect to meet, but if you messed with her children, she turned into a feral beast. She was as unforgiving of my bully's parents as she was of him, making it perfectly clear that their son was to stay far away from me. To my surprise, it turned out I was not the only one he was victimizing at school. In fact, many other students and parents came forward with similar tales once my story was out. From that day forward, my bully never bothered me again.

I learned a lot from my mother that day about standing up to others in moments of adversity. I learned about courage and facing my fears head-on. My mother was the type of woman (and still is, for that matter) who carried the Bible in one hand and a belt in the other. She lived a crazy life, and those who knew her knew not to mess with her. She had to fight for everything she had, and that was one thing my mom was good at—fighting for the right to live a life she deserved, the lives her children deserved. I vowed to make her proud.

Chapter 3

The Grass Is Not Always Greener

Mama told me I could be a lawyer, a doctor, or even the president, but then I had a bad teacher.

—Doug Luffborough

After I left Elm Park Elementary on the east side of town, we moved to Tatnuck Square, a village in the western part of Worcester nestled at the base of Worcester Regional Airport. *Tatnuck* is a word derived from the Nipmuc Indians meaning "at the great hill," and we grew up calling the area "The Hill."

We lived upstairs in one of four duplexes on High Ridge Road, the only privately owned dirt road in the community. This was a bigger apartment, with three bedrooms: one for me, one for my brother Darrell, and one for my mother and Joe . . . and our newborn brother, Derrick.

Darrell and I were happy to have a new brother. At first, Derrick's birth promised a new start for my mom in Massachusetts. She seldom talked about her time in Norfolk and even said to us, "Boys, isn't it great to have a new brother and a second chance for us to start over as a family?" Even Joe seemed happy. At first, he helped out more around the house, but the help was only temporary; over time, his presence slipped from Derrick's life. I can't recall Joe ever changing Derrick's diaper, mixing formula into a bottle, rocking Derrick to sleep, or giving him a bath on his own. He still sat around smoking cigarettes and drinking beer all day; it was as if they were the only children he cared for.

Meanwhile, my mother busied herself washing clothes in the bathtub with a bar of soap and a stick because we did not have washer and dryer machines. I think she enjoyed having us play outside because it gave her space to escape her reality of being a full-time mother and father to us.

Ma's only request back in those days was that I come home once it started to get dark. I loved our new neighborhood. The homes were not on top of one another, and we had a thickly treed area in the backyard that we called "the woods," with a man-made fort I spent as much time in as I could. Plus, there were many families in the neighborhood with children my age, so there was always something to do and plenty of children to do it with. From sunup to sundown, we dominated our two-on-two fast-pitch Wiffle ball tournaments, or tick-tacked from one side of the road to the next on our skateboards, or played stickball in the streets, or threw a tennis ball from one rooftop to the next—not to mention the large co-ed neighborhood kickball games. Ah, to be a kid again!

There was only one other family of color in our community, and though kids our age didn't care about ethnicity, some of their parents did. One of our friends always came to our house to play; one time, I suggested we go to his house instead. He tossed a baseball from one hand to the other, avoiding my eyes. "Nah," he said. "I don't think that's a good idea."

"Why not?" I asked.

He shrugged. "My parents would rather I come play with you, not the other way around."

I was taken aback for a second but didn't think too much of it. My biggest concern was just getting out of *my* house.

Saturday mornings in the late seventies and early eighties found me riding my Huffy bike down the uneven, rocky, slanted dirt road pretending I was a professional BMX biker racing for the gold. I imagined that every race I started, I finished in first place. Then I went into the woods to daydream about what I would do with my prize money. I'd buy my mom her first home with its own garage, enough rooms for everyone, and—most importantly—her own washer and dryer. I fantasized about buying myself a reliable car (even though I was too young to drive it) and even a real father who loved me and wanted to spend time with me.

As fall approached, my mother enrolled my brother and me into a different school called Tatnuck Elementary, just under two miles from our home on High Ridge Road. My brother Darrell and I were expected to walk to school together, but on our first day, Ma walked with us. Together, the three of us met with the principal, who walked us to what would be my third-grade class. The rows of desks were all occupied by white kids; you could count the students of color in the entire school on one hand—including Darrell and me. Our entrance interrupted the teacher, and she scowled as she walked over to us.

"This class is full," she said, crossing her arms. She squinted at us over the rims of her square reading glasses, a pencil jutting out from her severe bun. "I can't accept any more students."

Almost in unison, Ma, Darrell, and I looked at the last row of seats and then at one another: there were three empty desks, right in front of us.

"Take him to the other third-grade class," the teacher told the principal.

The principal, who wore gray slacks, a blue blazer, and a stern expression, was as surprised as we were. "Will you excuse us for a second?" she asked Ma. To the teacher, she said, "May I have a word with you, please?" They stepped outside the classroom, leaving us as spectacles by the door.

I didn't look the other kids in the eye. How could I? The feeling of rejection that I felt from my father and from being bullied descended on me like a cloud covering up the sun. I saw a fog of darkness roll into my mother's eyes as well as she lowered her head and looked away from both me and the other students.

After a couple of minutes (that felt more like an hour), the teacher came back into the room and reluctantly announced that I would be a new student.

"Go take a seat in the back," she said.

I made my way to the back of the classroom, head ducked in embarrassment. No one welcomed me. No "hello" or "glad to have you with us." Not even a smile or nod of greeting. The students seemed to take their cues from the teacher and mimicked how she felt about having me in her class. As my mother left with the principal, I knew that I was in for a difficult year.

Besides asking me to take a seat in the back, the teacher didn't acknowledge my existence for the rest of the day. Neither did my classmates. I took the long way home that afternoon and went straight into my bedroom, jumped onto my bed, placed a pillow over my head, and cried like a baby. I screamed as loud as I could, hoping the pillow would muffle the sound.

I thought the next weeks would be better, but each day was more of the same: the teacher ignored me in class, and no one played with me during recess. The other students made fun of me because I was only one of a few students who received a free-and-reduced lunch, wore oversized, grandpa-like hand-me-down clothes, and—because we could not afford to buy boots in winter—wore run-down, holes-in-the-soles sneakers all year round. Each day, the teachers and students reminded me that I did not belong and reinforced my feelings of inadequacy.

When school ended in the afternoons, I avoided my homework like the plague and played outside until it was nighttime. The house was dark when I walked in—no one ever changed the blown-out light bulbs—the countertops were dirty and covered in crumbs, and days-old dishes were piled up in the sink. The carpets had stains from spilled soft drinks and Joe's beers, dirty clothes accumulated in the corner of the kitchen near the bathroom, and most of the bedrooms were in total disarray. The smell of depression was enough to make me want to stay outside or go to my room and try to sleep the dankness away.

It wasn't just me who felt this way. I could see it in my brother Darrell, I could see it in my mother, and I could see it in Joe. We weren't a family; we were just a group of people living together with no direction, no purpose, and no vision for our future. I even second-guessed the decision to leave Norfolk and thought that perhaps I was better off staying with my grandparents; at least there, the house was clean and you knew someone lived there. At least there, we sat down as a family unit for breakfast, lunch, and dinner and went to church together as well. In Massachusetts, that virtually never happened. As time went on, I became more and more isolated and disconnected, and I developed a bad attitude about school and the people around me. I had a chip on my shoulder and was ready to lash out at anybody that challenged me. That day came sooner rather than later.

At school during recess, the boys were playing kickball and needed an extra player.

"I'll play!" I darted forward.

One of the bigger boys from my class sneered. "We don't play with niggas, and besides, your momma looks like a German shepherd."

Oh, no, he didn't! I thought. The next thing that came to my mind was what my mother had told me at Elm Park: "Never let someone try to get something over on you. Defend yourself—Mama didn't raise no sucker-punk for a son." And before I knew it, with the same fierce rage as when I'd witnessed my father punching my mother, I leaped forward and tackled the boy. My fists landed wildly, some punches catching him square in his face and others hitting the ground. I had no control over myself. It was as if I were taking out all of my life's pain and frustrations on this kid's face and body.

"Break it up!" my teacher yelled. "Someone, break these boys apart!"

She hung back until two male teachers pulled me off the other boy. Before then, I had not realized how enraged I was, but I screamed and kicked as they escorted me to the principal's office. "Get off me! I hate you, and I hate this school!" I yelled hard enough to hurt my throat. My voice bounced against the lockers, filling the hallway of the school.

Because this was the most action the school had ever seen, the principal had already heard what happened and was on her way to meet me directly. Her face was set in rigid lines, with no hint of the sympathy—or at least civility—she'd shown on my first day.

"Get into my office!" she yelled. "I'm calling your mother."

That stopped me cold. "Wait," I said. "Please don't call her."

My mother made no more than seven thousand dollars per year and did not own a car or even have a driver's license, so she walked or took the city bus everywhere she needed to go. That not only meant it would take her a while to come to school but that she would lose a day of pay from housekeeping. That was thirty or forty dollars for between five and eight hours of hard work. I never wanted to cause my mother trouble or, worst of all, to lose the limited funds that we had.

"There are consequences to your actions," the principal said, picking up the phone.

When my mother arrived, she was quiet and cordial to the principal. But I could see from the tense set of her jaw that I was going to get it later.

"I'm sorry, Ma," I said. "But he started it." I told her and the principal what had happened, and though neither of them was happy with what I'd done, I did not get into much trouble besides apologizing to the boy and staying after school for detention for a week. What I *did* get was recognition—just not the kind I was searching for. I yearned for a sense of belonging, but what I got was a label of misfit. Everyone knew who Doug Luffborough was, but nobody wanted to be his friend. The more alienated I became, the more I wondered what was wrong with me and why I turned out this way.

It wasn't just socially that I was struggling. I started to fall noticeably behind academically. Each day, I was the only student who was pulled out of class to receive one-on-one remedial intervention for reading and math. I felt like the only student who had to ride the short yellow bus to school because I was not good enough or smart enough for the regular bus. As if that weren't bad enough, my teacher exploited my challenges in front of the entire class.

"Doug," she said, "please recite the passage on page twelve for the class."

I opened my mouth to start reading.

"Up front, please."

My heart in my throat, I shuffled to the front of the classroom. The book trembled in my hands. I did the best I could to sound my way through basic words and phrases, but as the snickers rose among my peers, my desire to do well faded. I became paralyzed with fear, started crying, and ran out of the classroom. Eventually,

I developed a recurring, stuttering speech impediment any time I had to speak out in class or anywhere in public, for that matter. They say sticks and stones may break your bones but names will never hurt you, but the names other students called me—stupid, retard, nigga—stayed with me until my adult years. I let what people said about me *become* me to the point that I felt I deserved that humiliation.

At the end of the school year, my mother was asked to meet with the principal and my third-grade teacher. I felt an immediate sense of foreboding when they called me into the office.

"Douglas," my mother said, "we've been talking about your progress this year . . . and they feel it would be best if you were held back next year."

"What?" I asked, aghast. Thankfully, the teacher had left the room, because tears instantly streamed down my face, and I stuttered uncontrollably on my next question: "Are you k-k-k-k-kidding me? Y-y-you mean—d-d-do the third g-g-grade again?" I couldn't imagine anything worse than reliving the previous year.

"We think it would be better for you," said the principal. "You'll stay with the same teacher, since she already knows you."

I looked between the two of them and, without warning, broke down. I sobbed uncontrollably, wrenching my shoulder away from my mother when she tried to touch me. How could this be happening? How could I endure another year of being overlooked, undervalued, and unappreciated? I fell to the ground in total defeat. I felt like my mother had betrayed me by letting this happen.

That summer was the worst. Instead of playing outside like most kids my age, I was so depressed about staying back in the third grade and having to face the same teacher again that I spent most days in my room, sleeping and listening to music. My Huffy bike collected cobwebs. When my neighborhood friends came to the door, I told them that my mother would not let me play with them anymore. "Just leave me alone," I said quietly, shutting the door.

The saddest point of my summer came when my mother was supposed to attend her stepsister's wedding. Several months earlier, I had overhead my mother talking with Joe about her stepsister wanting her to be in the wedding. "Do you think you could give me money to buy a dress?" she asked. "And help me get to New Jersey?"

Joe was already messy on Schlitz, and he stroked her arm with a big paw. "Sure, baby," he said, "if you help me out a little, too."

As the months until the wedding became weeks, and then the weeks became days, Joe, sober, withdrew his promise. "No, I will not buy you that dress for that wedding, and no I will not give you the finances to go to New Jersey. Figure it out on your own."

Like I had in the principal's office, my mother dropped to the floor. Tears streamed from her eyes like rapids from a breached dam. Between moans, she rocked her body back and forth and prayed, "Lord, have mercy. Jesus . . . Jesus . . . Jesus." In total desperation, she pulled on one of his pant legs and begged him to help her. He looked down at her with a sense of pity, cracked open a can of Schlitz, lit up a cigarette, and walked out back to have a smoke. It was like a scene out of *The Color Purple*. In my entire life, I had never seen my mother so broken, so painfully defeated by life's disappointments.

My mother stayed on the floor for some time and then slowly rose and picked up the phone. "Doreen, I'm sorry—I won't be coming to your wedding after all."

For the next few weeks, my mother spent most of her time lying down in her room, sharing only one or two words of conversation and sleeping off the pain and disappointment she was feeling. It was as though this event had stolen all the joy from her heart. Sometimes, she sat in the room all by herself reading her Bible and talking with God about things only they could understand.

After that, my mother turned to the Bible more and more. She carried her Bible, worn and tattered, everywhere she went—cleaning homes, at the grocery store, on the bus, and even to social gatherings at our school. She talked to God out loud, not caring who else was around, and started sitting Darrell and I down for weekly Bible studies. One Sunday evening, she shared that since we did not go to church on a regular basis, she wanted to bring church to our home.

"I want you all to know God's word, and the best place for me to start with you is in the book of Proverbs," she said.

I thought, *Proverbs, why this book?*

"Since your dad is not in your life and Joe is doing his own thing, let Proverbs be your Father," Ma said. "Let it give you spiritual guidance, wisdom, and insight on how you need to live your lives."

So we all sat down once a week and listened to my mother explain the book of Proverbs to us. She pointed out that we needed to live a life that honored God, pay attention to our actions toward others, and ask God for wisdom and discernment in all we did. Joe was never interested in our Bible studies. He just snickered at us as if we were crazy. On some occasions, even *we* thought my mother was crazy, all her out-loud talk to a God she could not see but so desperately believed in. There were so many times growing up that I questioned whether God was really there and if he really heard my mother's cries for a different life. I see now that he was there, listening, and my siblings and I have become the answer to her prayers, but back then, it was my mother's way of keeping a positive perspective in the midst of deep sorrow.

On the heels of my mother's prayers, I got ready for my second year in the third grade. I just wanted to stay home with my mother. I passed the time by praying for a new teacher or praying that I would be transferred into another class, but neither of those things happened. It was back to the same room, the same row of desks lining the back wall. As the year started, I still had a lot of anxiety, but I was a year older, wiser, and stronger, and was mostly able to hold my own. By no means was I the star student, but the previous year had taught me what the teacher was all about and how to work the system to just get by.

About midway through the school year, my mother started talking to me about playing the violin. Maya Angelou once said, "Music was my refuge. I could crawl into the space between the notes and curl my back to loneliness." I think my mother hoped music would be *my* refuge—a way to cope with my family, academic, and social challenges.

"I know you two aren't going to become concert violinists," she said to Darrell and me, "but I want you involved in the arts so you stay out of trouble and learn discipline." I think she also hoped we would process our anger, fears, and frustrations in a positive way through music.

Of course, as someone trying to build confidence and self-esteem, it was hard to look cool walking down the hall carrying a violin case. However, reluctantly, once a week my brother and I practiced as a part of our elementary school's orchestra. My mother believed so strongly in us playing the violin that she asked our teacher, Mr. Cott, if she could pay him to give us private lessons once a week. He took the job with a smile.

Mr. Cott loved playing and teaching others how to play the violin. He was always on time and never hesitated to share words of kindness and encouragement. "There you go," he'd say, listening closely. "You hear that? That note's just where it's supposed to be. Great work."

It was a tremendous sacrifice for my mother to pay for violin lessons. One day of cleaning homes was the amount needed for one lesson, but my mother believed in it so strongly that she worked six to eight extra hours to afford the luxury.

Each week, we practiced the violin for an hour at school, during private lessons at home, and by ourselves. Still in third grade, I was practicing one afternoon in my room and found myself making up a song. I worked on finding the right notes to express each part of the song and sang the lyrics as well. When I felt I knew the song by heart, I called my mother into my room.

"I have a new song I want you to hear!" I said, bubbling with enthusiasm. It was called "You're a Loser!"

"You're a loser, and you know it," I sang. "You're a loser, and you don't want to show it."

The joy in my mother's face turned into sadness and then into anger. Before I could even finish the song, she cut me off and told me never to write a song like that again. She left my room in a huff of displeasure.

Confused and wondering what I had done wrong, I looked at my violin. Maybe the sound wasn't good enough. I could make it better. I picked up the violin and started singing and playing the song again: "You're a loser, and you know it. You're a—"

Right in the middle, my door flew open. "Stop playing that song!" my mother yelled. "You are not a loser, and I refuse to let you feel that way about yourself. Now put your violin away and go play outside."

I was shocked. Until that moment, I hadn't realized the song was about me. Not wanting to further upset my mother, I put my violin away. My mom's eyes were filled with sadness and hopelessness as I made my way outside.

My brother Darrell and I did not have the best relationship growing up, and sometimes even now it is a struggle, but I enjoyed playing the violin with him. It was the only time, besides sports, that we bonded. (Besides, sports often became too competitive and led to all-out fist fights—even rock fights.) One of our favorite songs to play together told the story of a bumblebee with an upbeat tempo. Then we slowed it down with a Mozart's duet. But the best piece we played together we called the "upside-down piece." I sat on one side and my brother on the other, and we played from the same sheet of music. The upside-down piece was a metaphor for how each of us saw the world we were living in. We played from two very different perspectives, but once we came together in the right spirit, we became one.

Our family and friends loved watching and hearing us play together. I remember going back to Norfolk and my mother making us take our violins so we could perform for our relatives. I came to find out my grandfather on my father's side, Grandpa Luff, also played the violin, and vaguely remembered hearing him play. My father, even though he was not in my life, also played an instrument—the trumpet. It seemed as though music had always been a part of my life.

As time went on, my brother and I started playing for school concerts and community and church events. We both auditioned for and were accepted in the Worcester Youth Symphony Orchestra, with whom we practiced and then performed throughout our city. The competition was fierce, but Darrell and I had each other and held our own. We were usually in the violin second section, seats one and two. Considering everything we had been through, it felt great to sit next to my brother. If folks only knew . . . For us to stand on that stage with our violins was a test of resiliency. It was a testament to the hours spent practicing, the financial burden placed on my mother, and the many homes she cleaned in order for us to have private lessons. But, as our music brought crowds to applause, the sacrifices seemed to be paying off.

Chapter 4

Coach Miller

The way I figured it, I was even with baseball and baseball with me. The game had done much for me, and I had done much for it.

—Jackie Robinson

Along with playing the violin in elementary school, I also started to play baseball. In the fourth grade, one of my friends played and told me that I should sign up with him and that his mother could give me rides to practices and games. We had a car, but Joe was not reliable; plus you never knew if he would be coming off or going on one of his weekend benders. My mother sometimes cleaned my friend's parents' place and was happy to hear that they were willing to give me a ride, so she signed me up to play on a minor league baseball team for eight- to-ten-year-olds. I could not afford a glove, but my friend's father gave me a hand-me-down glove. This would be my first time playing organized baseball.

The first year was a learning one, and though the coaches didn't seem too interested in teaching me, I got through it. When I was ten, I had a choice: I could play another year in minor league and then move up to Little League, or I could try out for Little League and see what happened. When I told my minor league coach that I was thinking about trying out for Little League, he chuckled.

"What, you think you can play Little League all of a sudden?" He hit an assistant coach on the shoulder, both of them enjoying a laugh at my expense. "You're not good enough for Little League, boy. Just do one more year of the minor leagues, work on your fundamentals, and try out after that."

I nodded and walked away, deflated but also a little indignant. Why was it such a bad idea for me to just try out? After all, if I didn't make it, I would just spend another year in the minor leagues. But what if I did make it?

The day for Little League tryouts came, and I decided that despite my minor league coach's advice, I was going to give it my best shot. I was trying out with other ten- to twelve-year-olds, and there was a nervous rumble in the dugout as we all waited for our names to be called.

"Douglas Luffborough!"

I bolted up, and they asked me to take the infield position that I wanted to play. I ran over to third base, ready to field ground balls and throw them to first. Just behind home plate, I could see my minor league coach with his arms crossed, shaking his head. His presence intimidated me so much that the first ground ball went right through my legs. The laughter that ripped around me made something in me come alive. I punched my glove. *Bring it on!*

I fielded the second ground ball cleanly and made a strong throw to first base. I made the next play and the next, and then they timed me as I ran the bases. I liked running and could take any kid my age in a race (chalk it up to those bullied days), so the Little League coaches were impressed with my speed. Then came hitting. I was not the best hitter, but I took big cuts at the ball and was not afraid to go down swinging. At the end of tryouts, I walked off the field satisfied with my performance but not sure if it was enough. Was I Little League material?

When I got home, my mother was in the bathroom washing our clothes in the bathroom tub. With wet, sudsy hands, she stuck her head out of the bathroom when she heard me arrive.

"How'd you do?" she asked, smiling.

I shrugged, scuffing my feet on the floor. "I gave it one hundred percent, but I don't know if it was good enough."

In her gentle manner, Ma said, "It's in the Lord's hands now, son. You did your best, and that is all you can ask for; let God do the rest."

I did not hear from anyone until the day of my minor league team practice, which I did not attend—because on the phone talking to Mama Luff was Coach Miller, a former professional baseball player with the Baltimore Orioles. He had a son my age and was looking to start a Little League team of players that he could coach for a few years. He'd watched me during the tryouts and said that I had heart—and that he would be honored if I joined his team. My mother was all smiles as she gestured for me to take the phone. "He's right here," she said, all but wrapping my shocked fingers around the device.

For a couple of seconds, I was amazed into silence. The feeling of being wanted consumed me. I had made it. I was good enough. I did have what it took to play Little League. What I remembered from our conversation was that Coach Miller was direct, straightforward, and had big expectations for the new team. Our conversation was brief and matter-of-fact, but I was excited to speak with him.

When I hung up the phone, I realized a valuable lesson that I live by today, an echo of what motivational speaker Les Brown once said: "Never let someone else's opinion of you become your reality. Only you can determine that!" I was so glad I had not let the voice of my minor league coach become louder than my inner voice that insisted, "You can do this!"

The first practice came up, and my inner battles of insecurity and low self-esteem started to once again consume me. I arrived early to see what was going on but kept to the outskirts of the field until more people arrived. There is something vulnerable about showing up first, and I was worried about putting myself out there. I wanted to scout out what I considered the competition to see if I would fit in. The savage, scared voice in my head was saying, "*You are not good enough to play Little League. You don't deserve to be here.*" So I watched the other players to see if they looked like me: were there any kids of color? Would I fit in? Or were they all white kids from affluent families? My heart sank when I saw no one resembling the person I saw in the mirror. I then turned to analyzing the way they played ball; even if we had different lives, different stories, could I match their skills?

I loitered in the background until the entire team arrived and formed a circle around the pitcher's mound. Coach Miller stood in the middle of the circle, welcoming his young crop of players.

He looked like a clean-cut baseball player with a permanent tan, dressed in our team baseball cap, an orange polo shirt, black slacks, and a black jacket. He had a square face with a strong jaw, and later I'd discover he smoked cigarettes in between practices and games. As I approached, he stopped what he was saying and turned to me.

"Luffborough," he said gruffly, "I was just talking to everyone on the team about the importance of showing up early in life. If you are fifteen minutes early, you are on time. If you are on time, you are late, and if you come late without calling me, you run—so put down your gear and start doing laps around the field. I will tell you when to stop."

My heart sank. The last thing I wanted to do was to disappoint someone who believed in me, someone who was giving me an opportunity to play Little League. I had been there early but let fear and intimidations overwhelm me. What a horrible first impression I'd made. Never again, I vowed.

The first practice for me was more like track practice—I never even used my glove. Immediately afterwards, I spoke with Coach and apologized for being late. His response was short and sweet: "Luffborough, you are not in the minor leagues anymore!"

I left practice defeated and angry with myself. I did not want to sabotage this opportunity because of my insecurities, but up until now, assuring myself of my unworthiness was the only way I knew how to deal with new situations. It gave me a backwards sense of comfort; after all, if I told myself I wasn't good enough, didn't stack up, then I didn't have to put myself out there and really try. When I got home, my mother asked me how practice had gone and I told her it was fine, but I needed to make some adjustments.

The next day, I arrived to practice thirty minutes earlier than needed because I wanted to warm up and run before the rest of the team arrived. To my surprise, many of my teammates were already there doing the same thing. I had never seen that level of commitment from my peers before, but as Coach had said, I was not in the minor leagues anymore.

When Coach arrived, he greeted everybody, and we started running as a team. If one person started to lag behind, he had the stronger runners run backwards so we all stayed together. Coach

Miller was intense and managed us as if we were professional baseball players. He had a spirit of excellence and expected 110 percent from each player, regardless of talent and natural abilities. Coach despised laziness and laid into anyone who took a laissez-faire approach to practice or games. He led through fear and intimidation at times, but that was motivated by a desire to help us be the best we could be. His presence demanded it.

One moment that stood out to me was when we were playing a game and our pitcher was falling behind in the count. He seemed hesitant to throw the ball hard, and Coach called time-out. Breathing hard, the entire infield gathered at the pitcher's mound. There, Coach grabbed the pitcher by his shirt. "Throw the fucking ball hard and grow some balls," he said. "Stop being a fucking pussy and man up!"

Coach Miller did not play around.

After our huddle, you could tell that our pitcher was deeply affected by what Coach had said. His face reddened and he kept rubbing his eyes one at a time to try to shake off what Coach had just said to him. On the very next pitch, he threw the ball as hard as he could, striking the opposing player on the front of his helmet. From the sidelines, I heard Coach say, "If that is what it's going to take for you to throw hard and put all your heart into it, then so be it!"

"Time out!" the umpire called.

Both coaches approached the umpire, who accused Coach of deliberately advising our pitcher to hit the next batter. We knew that was not the case. From my point of view, our pitcher was both hurt and motivated by Coach's words and needed someone to take his frustration out on. For him, it wasn't the batter at whom he was throwing the ball; it was Coach Miller.

For the next practice, we met at Worcester State College, where Coach Miller took all of us into a vacant classroom. He spent the entire practice going over plays on the board and teaching us the fundamentals of baseball.

"Okay, Doug," he said. "Man on second and the batter hits the ball into right field—where does each of the players go in the infield?"

And over time, we all learned that the pitcher goes behind home plate to back up the catcher, the first baseman is the cut-off man for the right fielder, the second baseman covers first base, the shortstop covers second, the third baseman covers third, and everything after that. Coach taught us to have pride in our appearance, showing us how to properly wear our baseball uniform—hats straight, shirts tucked, and pants on in the precise way that allowed our socks to show correctly. He instructed us to shine our baseball helmets with our names on the back. Everything you needed to know to play in the majors—we learned it.

He also encouraged us to one day play college baseball. He talked about the importance of going to college and his experience playing and coaching college teams. He shared that if we were good enough, we could even get a full-ride college scholarship for baseball. With finances always an issue in my life, I thought that would be one way for me to go to college. Ma was always talking to us about our goals and dreams during that time, and college was one thing she wanted for our futures. One day, she told me to think of three goals that I wanted to achieve most in this world. She instructed me to write them down on an index card and to always keep the card in my wallet as a constant reminder of what was worth going for in life. The three goals that I wrote down were (1) to make my mother proud of me, (2) to graduate from college, and (3) to make it in life so that my mother never had to work again. When Coach talked about baseball as a means to college, I saw a way of making all three goals come true.

The next practice, we were off to Coes Pond with instructions that we were not to bring our gloves. *Coes Pond? What is he up to now?* I wondered. Coes Pond was a half-mile stretch of stagnant water between a highway on one side and the projects on the other. Affluent families stayed away, but poor families cooled off in the questionable water. What were *we* doing there? Was he going to have us swim? In the back of my mind, I rehashed stories I'd heard about people needing to be rescued; one had even died trying to freestyle from one side of the pond to the next.

Coach started us off running the beach. Our cleats threw up sand as we raced along the water's edge. Then we spent the entire practice learning how to do pop-up slides and suicide slides face-first, as well as when *not* to do them. We had a game soon after that practice in which I hit a ground ball to the infield. The fielder bobbled the ball and then threw it over to first base. A hunger to win came over me, and without even thinking, I dove headfirst into first base—a cardinal no-no. When I went back to the dugout, Coach did not reprimand me; he hit me on the butt and said, "That-a-boy!" I basked in the glow of Coach's praise. That was when I realized that I might have come from a poor, dysfunctional family, but I had the heart of a champion that many of the other players around me—especially on opposing teams—lacked. I developed an eye-of-the-tiger approach to winning not just on the field, but also off. My grades were improving in school, and I was getting better at playing the violin, with opportunities to perform in public recitals.

Before the start of our last game that year, Coach led us through a visualization exercise to condition our minds, bodies, and souls for what lay ahead. He had all of us lie on the hard-packed dirt, our prone bodies forming a circle. Coach stood in the center.

"I want you to picture yourself playing on your favorite baseball team," he said. I immediately thought of the Boston Red Sox. "Against your number one rival." The New York Yankees, of course. "—with the bases loaded, bottom of the ninth inning, two outs, losing by three, and the number one reliever—" Goose Gossage. "—has just been called out of the bullpen to pitch to you. At first you can't believe it—this guy throws over one hundred mile per hour fastballs and is one of the best pitchers in the entire league. You're so preoccupied with his presence that the first pitch goes right past you. The second and third pitches are balls (2–1 count); then the next pitch, you see the ball and foul it off (2–2 count). The next pitch is high and outside for ball three, so now it is a 3–2 count with the bases loaded, two outs, bottom of the ninth, with you being the winning run at the plate."

Coach paused. I was swept up in the game in my mind, feeling the ground beneath my feet, the sweat at the base of my helmet, the quickness of my breath. This was it—the moment to win it for the team.

"You take a step out of the batter's box and you tell yourself that you were meant for this occasion. Then you step back into the batter's box and you pretend that the ball is the size of a beach ball, so big you can count the seams on each of the sides. There is no way you can miss the ball. It's thrown right down the pike, and when you make contact, you already know you've won the game. Sure enough, that ball flies out of the park—it's a grand slam home run."

I grinned, imagining how the spectators would jump out of their seats in astonishment, applause thundering in the bleachers. I imagined the joy of my teammates as we all ran to each other and the satisfaction of shaking the other team's hands, knowing that I was responsible for that moment of victory. I could feel it as vividly as though it had already happened, as though it were happening right then.

After our visioning session, we went through our normal pregame activities. Since it was the last game of the year, many parents came out to support the team. My mother was not able to come to many games, but when she did, she carried sleigh bells that she rang throughout the stands in support of the team. Everyone remembers my mother with those bells. Joe never came to my games, but just as we began to take the field that day, he showed up. On the sidelines, I could hear my teammates murmuring, "Who's the guy over there drinking and smoking, yelling and causing such a ruckus?"

Without even looking, I knew it was Joe. When I finally turned to look in his direction, there he was—cigarette in one hand, can of Schlitz in the other, barely able to stand without support from the fence along the field. My mother, who had not even known Joe was coming, tried to tell him to calm down, but her words just incited him even more. I wanted to curl up and disappear. I knew he was there to support me, but it did not strengthen my relationship with him. In fact, that was when I started disconnecting from him and his place in my life; he was my mother's husband, but he would never be my father.

As soon as I took the field, my focus shifted from Joe's shenanigans to the game. It was a back-and-forth game that came down to the last inning. I was batting with the bases loaded and we were losing by three; I represented the winning run. I couldn't believe that just a year ago I had been in the minor leagues, desperate for my coach's approval. As I walked into the batter's box, the visioning exercise we had done just before the game rushed to mind, and the next thing I knew, I had a 3–2 count with two outs: the game was mine to win or lose.

I stepped out of the batter's box and looked at Coach Miller. He had a stoic, determined look on his face as if to say, "I have all the confidence in the world in you. Do as I have taught you." Just off the third base line, I saw my minor league coach standing on the sidelines with his arms folded, shaking his head the way he had when I'd tried out for Little League. Not too far from him was Joe, downing the six-pack he'd brought with him to the field, and not too far from him was my Booster Club, Christmas-bell-ringing mother cheering me on. In my mind, I saw my father abusing my mother, the bully taking my lunch money, the principal telling me I was being held back in the third grade. All these images crowding my mind, and when I saw the pitcher on the mound, it was as if he was really Goose Gossage and I was in the big leagues playing for the Boston Red Sox. As the pitcher started his release, I envisioned that the baseball was the size of a beach ball and I could count the seams on each side. The ball was thrown high and in the middle of the strike zone and with all that I had, I swung and hit the ball into left field and watched the left fielder look at the ball as it went over his head and out of the park for a grand slam home run.

We won the game by one run.

As I approached third base, Coach Miller hit me on the butt again but did not need to say a word. Then, with his stumbling gait, Joe came up to me.

"Good game," he slurred, clasping my shoulder.

I mumbled a thank you and shrugged off his hand, wanting nothing to do with him. My mother was next to approach me. She enveloped me in her arms, squeezing tightly as she told me how proud she was. Soon after, she went home with a friend of the family, and my minor league coach vanished into the crowd without saying a word to me. Still buzzing with pride and disbelief, reluctant to go home, I grabbed a hotdog and soda and stayed at the field to watch the next game. I had learned to play to win and to face my fears head-on despite the distractions around me, and I wasn't ready to let go of this feeling.

We ended the year around .500, winning half our games, but I had made an impression on Coach Miller and was excited to come back the next year and the year after that. We had an end-of-the-year cookout with all the players and our families. No one from my family was able to attend, but I went anyway. During the awards ceremony, I won my first trophy for being the only ten-year-old player in the league to hit a home run.

Each year, our practices got tougher and tougher; we got to the point where Coach had us take infield without using our gloves. We had to get to the ball, knock it down, and make the play, and Coach started to call me Magic because no matter where or how hard the ball was hit, I did whatever was necessary to make the play. *Magic!* I can still hear his gruff yell across the field and feel the surprised rush of happiness to realize he was talking to me. Someone thought *I* was magic. The feeling of worthiness was new and addictive. It hit me that baseball was the great neutralizer. It didn't matter if you came rolling up in a Range Rover or Joe's old two-tone panel brown station wagon—if you couldn't play, you were out.

We started learning trick plays and advanced baseball fundamentals, such as catching the ball on the outside of our gloves in order to better turn double plays. One game when I was on third base, Coach noticed that after every pitch, the pitcher casually caught the ball from the catcher and turned his back to third base, facing first base. Simultaneously, the catcher was looking around the stands or in the dugout, losing focus, so Coach leaned over to me while I was on third and said, "Watch the pitcher and the catcher." He chose his words wisely so I knew exactly what he was saying to me. I simply looked at him, and he added, "If you think you can take it . . . take it." Like clockwork, after the very next pitch, the pitcher caught the ball from the catcher and casually turned to first base. At the same time, the catcher was talking with the umpire. That was it—*bam!* I took off. The spectators, parents, and players yelled and whooped in surprise, and in total confusion, the pitcher just held onto the ball as I slid head first into home plate. The place exploded. Many could not believe that I had just stolen home plate, but for each of us on the team, it was business as usual. Coach Miller demanded that we give 110 percent every time we came out on the field, regardless of what was going on in our life outside baseball. In fact, he seemed to push me harder when things were difficult at home—and I responded; I took all the frustration and anger and loneliness and channeled it into the relationship between bat and ball, feet and ground. Coach Miller taught me there were no excuses not to give life my best.

During the off-season, as snow collected on the ground, I honed my skills and grew another five inches. At eleven, I could not wait for the next season to start. Coach Miller gave me a call over the break.

"I'm proud of you, Magic," he said. "I want you to step up your role as one of the leaders on the team."

My heart thudded with excitement and nerves. "What do you mean, Coach?"

"I've decided to move you from third base to short stop." He paused, and I could feel his grin from across the phone line. "What do you think about that?"

"Wow, Coach!" I said. "That's great, but . . . you really think I can play shortstop?"

He laughed. "Let me be the coach, and you just stay hungry to play ball." That was not a problem for me because I loved playing baseball and having Coach Miller as a mentor.

When the season started, I was ready to play and play hard. I showed up thirty minutes before practice to warm up. When everyone else arrived, I was as drenched with sweat as if I'd run a marathon. My phone conversation with Coach motivated me. I was hungry to be the best and serve as a leader and role model for my new teammates.

Most of the new guys showed up late for that first practice. True to form, just as he had a year earlier with me, Coach called them by their last names. Fervently, he let them know: "If you are fifteen minutes early, you are on time. If you are on time, you are late, and if you come late without calling me, you run—so put down your gear and start doing laps around the field. I will tell you when to stop!" I couldn't help but laugh, not at the newbies but at the moment of *déjà vu.*

Being a new player on our team was quite a transition for the players and their families. Many of the new parents questioned Coach's tactics and techniques for teaching the game, but Coach didn't back down. Once, he told a new parent, "If you don't like the way I coach, then take your child to another team." He was confident in his abilities and did not do well with distractions—which didn't sit well with the parents. Some of them even went to the board of directors of the league to reprimand him for some of his coaching practices; they went so far as to try to kick him out of the league. However, we also had a group of parents who idolized his teaching practices, so none of the complaints amounted to anything. Coach Miller continued his unorthodox ways by having practices in the winter with snow on the ground, going to the lake for sliding practices, staying at the indoor batting cages until midnight, and renting out a room on a college campus to go over fundamental plays on the chalkboard. No other teams were doing this, and that became our competitive edge.

The most extreme tactic he used this season was when Coach called infield practice with no gloves. *What is he up to now?* I wondered. *He is not going to hit us the ball, is he?*

"Luffborough, stop the ball," he said. And without warning, he hit a major league ground ball in my direction. At first, I panicked and moved out of the way of the ball, but quickly realizing what I was supposed to do, I begged him to hit me another one. This time, I aggressively went after the ball with my bare hands. It took a short hop right in front of me and hit me right in the nose. Blood immediately streamed all over my face, but I knocked down the ball, picked it up, and threw the bloodstained ball to first base. The other players looked at me with amazement when I finished the play. Even Coach seemed surprised by my actions.

"Luffborough, great job," he said. "Now come in and let me take a look at your face."

I was not the only player who bled that day, or any time we had practice without gloves for that matter, but Coach was teaching us how to have heart and be aggressive players.

Toward the middle of the year, I was comfortable fielding ground balls without my glove and making clean plays in the infield. Coach and other teammates continued to call me Magic and I developed great intuition and a love for understanding the psychology of baseball. I was not the only one that felt this way—you could see the same investment on my teammates' faces.

Coach was just as serious about our character off the field as he was when we were on; he required our report cards every semester and sat out players whose grades were not As and Bs. I was not a strong student, but this motivated me to seek out extra tutoring so I could play baseball. I stayed after school and received tutoring from local high school students, and my grades improved enough to increase my confidence in myself academically. It was a period of positive growth and change, collected within the framework of baseball.

It truly was amazing to see our team in action back in those days. From suicide bunts, to double steals, to completing double plays, our team acquired the name "Orange Crush." The color of our uniforms was orange, and most of the time we blew teams away. It was normal for our team to have four to six home runs, with some players hitting two or three home runs in just one game. We sometimes won by ten or twelve points, and shut-outs and no-hitters were commonplace. We were a sight to see! When we won, we huddled up and chanted, "Orange Crush, Orange Crush, Orange Crush!" We drank Orange Crush soda before, during, and after games as well. We embodied the spirit of our team.

The flipside of our fierce drive to win was that coaches, players, and parents from opposing teams complained about our aggressive play and "lack of sportsmanship." They felt that Coach Miller had too much of a *win at all cost* style of play and teaching. They felt that he was an arrogant coach who was creating arrogant baseball players. This perception hit close to home for me when we had an assistant outfield coach working with us. He was a student from

Worcester State College, and between plays at one practice, he came right up to me and told me that I had delusions of grandeur.

I looked at him blankly. "What does that mean?"

With other players hanging around, he repeated, "You have delusions of grandeur—you think you're better than you actually are."

Some of my teammates laughed, some turned the other way, and a few walked away. I was stunned. I wanted someone to come to my defense, but because no one did, I wondered if they agreed with what the assistant coach said. I couldn't help thinking of my third-grade teacher and the beating my self-esteem had taken in her classroom. For so long, I'd thought of myself as a loser. A nothing. Now I was being told I thought I was better than I was? I was hurt and confused, but I knew that Coach Miller believed in me, and his point of view was all that mattered. I looked back at the assistant coach in silence and never talked to him again.

I realized that day that not everyone wanted to accept what I was becoming. The assistant coach left shortly after this, but I will always remember what he said to me. There will always be people in your life who want to steal your joy. Don't let them.

By the end of our second season, we lost some games but ended up in first place overall. It had only taken one year for us to become the best team in the league, and the majority of us still had one more year to play. This record was almost unheard of for an expansion team.

Our reputation as a bad-boy team continued, and we did whatever we needed to do to win. In my last year under Coach Miller, Orange Crush went undefeated (12–0). Many critics were astounded at our level of play and competition. Looking back, I believe that our team could have competed in the Little League World Series; we were that good. And there are no delusions of grandeur behind that statement.

I may not have made it to the big leagues, but during an All-Star game with other leagues throughout my city, we faced one of the best pitchers to come out of Worcester during that time. His name was Tanyon Sturtze, and he had one nasty curveball. I found myself again with the bases loaded and a 3–2 count. He threw one of his vicious curveballs, but my training taught me not to move, to wait until the ball broke, and I hit the scoreboard in center field, another grand slam home run. Almost twenty years later, I'm watching the Red Sox take on the New York Yankees, and the Yankees go to the bullpen to bring out one of their relievers, and out walks Tanyon Sturtze! He had become a relief pitcher for the New York Yankees.

Someone once told me a story about Larry Bird, who was a star basketball player for the Boston Celtics throughout the 1980s. He was shooting a commercial where he was supposed to take a bite out of a candy bar and then miss a free throw. It took Larry Bird nine takes just to miss the basket, because he was conditioned to get the ball in the hole. He was conditioned to win. Coach Miller conditioned each and every one of his players to win. He was an out-of-the-box coach who incorporated real-life issues into the game of baseball. He taught me how to win, how to compete, and how to be extremely aggressive toward my life goals.

I was not sure what my life would be like after playing for Coach Miller. Deep in my spirit, I sensed that I would never have another coach—or role model—like him again. In many ways, I was right. As I moved forward into middle school, my interests started diverting, and the voices of my friends became louder than my own.

Chapter 5

Breakdancing

The floor is milk. Churn it and make it butter.

—Crazy Legs, Rocks Steady Crew

There was a large hole missing in baseball without Coach Miller. The entire game lost its intensity—the players, the coaches, the fans . . . everyone seemed to be going through the motions. With Coach's gruff voice in my head and *Magic* ringing in my ears, I tried forcing myself through the inertia, but my fire was burning out.

I played with older guys who liked chewing tobacco, and one time I thought I would follow the crowd and put a wad of Red Man chew in my mouth during a game. The veteran chewers neglected to tell me that you are not supposed to swallow the juice. Later in the game, I felt high and loopy, the ground swelling and dropping like waves beneath my feet. Then, giving me little time to react, a batter hit a thunderous line drive right to my head. I threw up my glove, caught the ball just in time, and swallowed the wad of Red Man—chew-leaves and all. I gasped and choked as my face turned different colors, and my stomach jerked as if I had food poisoning. The other players and coaches laughed at me. No one came to my aid. Finally, with one particularly violent churn of my gut, I ran off the field, grabbed the rest of my belongings, and started running home. I only made it five hundred yards from the field before vomit rose to my throat. I threw up tobacco leaves while diarrhea dripped down my legs underneath my baseball uniform. And this experience mirrored my Babe Ruth debut without Coach Miller: not one that was enjoyable or lasted very long. After just two seasons, I quit baseball altogether.

In the early eighties, I put my John Mellencamp and Air Supply albums to rest and picked up rap music. The first record I played over and over again was "Rapper's Delight" by the Sugarhill Gang. This was the first rap song to go worldwide, and the long version was over fourteen minutes. I remember putting the needle to the record in my room and being astounded by what I was hearing. *That's not a song—that's a short story!* I had no idea music could evoke a world I recognized.

When I was thirteen, I was at home with my brothers watching music videos on MTV. That was when I first saw Lionel Richie's "All Night Long" video. All across the screen, people were popping, locking, and breakdancing, exerting total control over each individual limb. I was especially mesmerized by two little African-American boys, around ten years old and commanding their bodies along with the rest of the dancers. I instinctively felt I had more in common with them than I did with my middle school classmates. My elementary school had become a K–8 school, and now that I was in seventh grade, there were still less than a dozen kids of color in the entire population.

I was the only one in my family who seemed captivated by the growing urban phenomenon called breakdancing—and captivated I was. I sat in front of the TV for hours, just waiting for the video to play again. Then I jumped up, suddenly alive with adrenaline and eager to imitate the motions I saw on the TV, desperate to feel as though I were a part of that community—of *any* community. At night, I stayed up until midnight waiting to listen to the only local college music station that dared to play rap music. "Planet Rock," "Jam on It," and "Rock It" brought me to life in a new way.

In that same year (1983), I came across Motown's twenty-fifth anniversary special on TV. Out walked Michael Jackson to perform "Billie Jean." Michael Jackson in the eighties, of course, was like the Beatles in the sixties and Elvis in the seventies. He was the King of Pop, and all eyes, all over the world, were on Michael that night. When I opened the window and craned my neck out, I could see and hear other families gathered in their living rooms watching the once-in-a-lifetime performance. Whenever Michael Jackson took the stage, you knew something magical was going to happen. That night, everyone in my house watched in amazement when he displayed his signature moonwalk. My jaw dropped. It was the same moonwalk I saw the two African-American boys do in the "All Night Long" video. That was it. I was hooked.

Almost every day after school, I retreated to the attic in our apartment to practice breakdancing. I did it alone at first, because I was somewhat embarrassed to show others that I was stepping out of my comfort zone. Then, as I started catching on, I recruited three or four friends from school to join me. Even right up to this moment, the song that sent me into a trance was "Planet Rock" by Afrika Bambaataa and the Soulsonic Force. When that song played, it did not matter who was watching—I just had to move my body and break.

At the time, my mother worked as a housekeeper at two Catholic churches and brought home information regarding their youth programs and activities. Every few months, the churches held a Friday night dance where all the boys stood on one side of the room and the girls on the other. No one danced until one or two songs came on. One was always a Michael Jackson song, and the other was usually the last song of the night—"Open Arms," by Journey. In between Michael Jackson and Journey, the DJ occasionally went out on the edge and played what was considered a rap song. Invigorated by "Planet Rock" or "Rock It," the local breakers drew into a circle to perform. During one of these dances, I decided to go for it: I cut into the middle of the circle and let it rip. My peers, many of whom had never seen these moves before—let alone from *me*—cheered me on, and their cheers fueled my confidence. Then I really cut loose.

Not long afterwards, I heard about a dance that students from different schools would be attending. They knew how to breakdance and wanted to see what I had to offer. I still considered myself a novice, but to those who went to these church-hall dances, I was a pro! Back in those days, our lives were sheltered, and we were all waiting for that freeing, footloose experience. Perhaps breakdancing was it.

The Friday night came, and I hitched a ride from a friend to another church-hall dance in a different community. Beneath the sanctuary, the room was cavernous—it could easily fit two hundred people. There were no decorations except for pictures of the apostles and various saints on the walls. When the dance started, all of the lights were turned down except the stage spotlights, which illuminated the DJ area. As usual, most of the kids there were white, and true to form, the boys lined up on one side of the room and the girls on the other. No one took to the dance floor until a Michael Jackson song rang out. Then, as the dance progressed, the tension rose as various song requests were made so that a breakdance competition would take place.

Finally, without warning, the beat dropped. All the wannabe breakers circled around one another in the center of the dance floor. The energy in the room was friendly, inviting, and exciting—we all wanted to see others express themselves. Since I had already put myself out there at the other dance, I had to strut my stuff here as well—but, as with my first baseball practice, I sat back to check out the competition first. The majority of the crowd was white, and though some of the kids were in my circle, others were distant acquaintances with whom I never thought I had anything in common. I clapped and cheered along with the rest of the crowd as the dancers busted out their best moves. That was when I saw a familiar face in the middle of the circle: Richie Miller, Coach Miller's son. Richie had played baseball with me; it had been around two years since I had seen him.

"Richie!" I exclaimed, cutting into the circle.

"Magic!" he called back. He laughed, and we united on the dance floor, showing each other our signature moves. For the next ten minutes, we imitated our favorite dancers, cheered at each other's moves, and sweated out all our teenage energy. The adults there looked on with a mixture of entertainment and caution—worry flashed in their eyes when our bodies hit the ground and some darted forward with concern when a dancer attempted a head spin. But for the most part, they left us alone. It was harmless, wholesome fun, and toward the end of the dance, some of us exchanged numbers and promised to get together to practice our moves. Maybe we'd even put together our own crew.

Each day after school, I waited for my two friends to join me in the attic so we could practice our routine. The musty area of the attic was cluttered with old boxes that we'd stored there from our last move and even older boxes from previous tenants. It was an unfinished space with no air conditioner, heat, or insulation panels—just bare wood beams firmly holding up the roof. What was so great about the attic was the twenty-by-twenty-foot space in the middle. Its linoleum floor was the best surface to practice hand spins, back spins, head spins, moonwalks, earthwalks, and windmills. Many times, Joe and my mother heard and felt loud thumps and crashes as if the ceiling were caving in and asked me to stop banging on the floor so much. My mother thought I was crazy and that breakdancing was very dangerous.

"Boy, you need to stop smacking your body against the ground so much. Why do you like doing that anyway?"

I just rolled my eyes. "Oh, Ma, it's fine," I said. "This is how teens express themselves."

What I really meant was that it helped take my mind off our unhappy issues at home. It added a different dimension to my life, showing me that I had more than just one talent. Baseball was a sport of discipline, but breaking was a form of self-expression.

Each time, Ma lifted a skeptical eyebrow; clearly, she was not buying it.

The crew at the time was just three of us: me, Jerry (we called him Kaz), and Will (we called him Web). We were an unlikely grouping: me, a slim and tall African-American with a jacked-up Afro; Web, a skinny and short Colombian who looked like a little person; and Kaz, a short and stalky, curly-haired Armenian. If you saw us walking down the street together, you would think, *What do those three have in common?* The answer was breakdancing. Every day we got together to practice. In my linoleum-floored attic or one of their basements, we honed our skills until others around us took notice.

After just a few months, we had a number of friends who looked forward to the church dances so we could get together and breakdance. At the end of one dance, some adults asked some other breakers and me to enter an upcoming talent show at the church.

This would be the first time I would perform in an organized event with different acts, and we would be the only breakdancing act. Eager to continue doing what we loved, we enthusiastically said yes.

When the night arrived for the four of us to compete—Richie was performing with us that night—we were nervous but excited. I stood behind the curtain before show time, amazed at what I was about to do. We were in the church hall where I'd first seen Richie, and he peeked through the curtain to see the crowd. They were all amateur dance mom types, supporting their little five- to ten-year-old girls. Some of their acts included a lip-synched Michael Jackson performance and a ballet routine. We were the bad-boy group, and we had each scraped together enough money for matching outfits—monogrammed red sweatshirts, black pants . . . and stage names like Chilly D, which was mine.

"And now, ladies and gentlemen, please welcome to the stage for the first time Doug, Will, Jerry, and Richie!"

The curtain slowly opened, and all I could see were the spotlights. I could only make out the first couple of rows, but the church hall was filled to capacity, with people standing in the aisles. As we emerged on stage, there was an odd silence in which you could hear a pin drop, and then *BOOM!* "Let the Music Play" by Shannon came on, and we began.

As I started breakdancing, lost in some funk-a-delic trance, I was in my own world, as comfortable as if I were just practicing with my friends in my attic or their basements. The cheers were affirmation that the audience liked what I was doing, and it was an intoxicating feeling that made me feel appreciated and not just tolerated the way I'd felt in the third grade or sometimes at home living with Joe. I had found a natural talent—something like baseball that I did well and others wanted to see. The audience was stunned the way I was when I watched the two boys in the "All Night Long" video, and after our performance, kids and adults alike asked us what we were doing and how we had learned how to do it. I talked about "All Night Long" and practicing seven days a week.

Someone once told me that if you do what you love, the money will follow. A couple of weeks after the talent show, I got a call from Richie.

"Hey Doug, how would you like to teach breakdancing and get paid for it?" he asked enthusiastically. It turned out that a nearby dance studio was looking to hire young teens to teach breakdancing classes. Richie had made the connection through someone at church, and he was raring to go.

"Dude, for sure," I said. "Let's do this."

I had walked by the Charlotte Klein Dance Studio in Tatnuck Square almost once a week but never thought I would be going there to interview for a job. *Wait until the dance moms with their petite blond-haired princesses see me*, I thought. I knew nothing about jazz, ballet, or tap, but I loved expressing myself through music. I must admit I was excited about being one of very few boys totally outnumbered by pretty, young, and fit girls interested to learn the form of street dancing about which we were so passionate. Sure enough, as I opened the doors to the dance studio, girls my age dressed in formfitting black leotards passed me with curious smiles. *I think this is going to work out really well for me.* I stood out like a sore thumb, but I did not mind it one bit.

Then Charlotte Klein walked out from behind one of the doors. She spoke with me briefly about her vision and asked me to perform for her in one of the studio rooms before signing a small contract to be a part of the Charlotte Klein Breakers (CKB). I found out that I would be part of a crew that would perform at local, state, and national competitions with the studio, and I'd be teaching breakdance classes for ten dollars a session, plus all travel expenses associated with recitals and competitions. I was only fourteen and excited to be getting paid (albeit not very much) for doing something I loved to do.

Even though I was young, I realized I had strength for teaching others—no matter who they were. I taught a one-hour class in popping and locking to a grandmother and her granddaughter at once. The generational gap between the two was awe-inspiring. At first, I was somewhat intimidated by working with adults as old as my grandparents, but eventually I realized they were looking to me to teach them. I also discovered that, as the oldest in my family, I was a natural working with children. After some time, I had it down: "Wrist, elbow, shoulder, chest, shoulder, elbow, wrist, out." I organized the hour-long class with a fifteen-minute warm-up, thirty minutes of instruction, and fifteen-minute closing freestyle session. At first, I had just one class a week, but over time, it moved up to three to five classes per week at studios in Worcester and Westborough. What I liked most was that I was teaching something I loved, and I got to see other people fall in love with it, too. Once, I had a brother and sister who got the hang of it enough that they made up their own routine and performed it during my class. Even better, the experience got me out of the house and away from the domestic drama I had faced all my life.

Each month, as the classes grew and breakdancing became more popular, the dance studio received requests for us to perform all throughout New England. One memorable performance took place at Quinsigamond Community College, where our crew—the CKB—performed before a packed house honoring former world boxing champion Sugar Ray Leonard. After the presentation, one of the managers leading our group came backstage and told us that Sugar Ray wanted to come back and congratulate us on our performance. *Wow, Sugar Ray Leonard has something to say to me,* I thought. *He must have really liked our performance.* I thought I would meet a big, aggressive brawler, but the person who joined us backstage was a skinny, mild-mannered, pretty boy genuinely excited to meet each of us and hear how and why we'd started breakdancing. I was so surprised that the professional boxing champion standing before me was so down-to-earth; if you'd never seen him in the ring, you would never believe he could knock anybody out. That day, I learned a very valuable lesson: never judge a book by its cover.

When we weren't breakdancing at studios or for competitions, we went to the malls or street corners to breakdance for money. All we needed was a large square of flattened cardboard and a boom box with enough D batteries and we were in business. The mall was great because it had the most people with money in their pockets. Of course, we didn't make millions, but it was another way to show off our talents, and my mom appreciated it because after we split the tips, I bought milk, juice, and toilet paper for the family. The problem was that the police considered what we were doing as a form of loitering. At the beginning, they just told us to leave, but as breakdancing became more popular and more crews did it for money, the police (or what we called the 5-0) started arresting teens they found breakdancing at the mall. Moreover, they profiled anyone who dressed, talked, or walked in a certain way, or who was with a large group of other teens. This type of profiling continues today, and when I speak, I tell young people to think about the images they project to others through the way they dress and carry themselves. That was a lesson I hadn't yet learned.

One time after school, the police were already in wait when we arrived at the mall. We didn't even have the opportunity to set up before they were chasing us down, we on our heels through the shopping levels and parking lot, they calling for backup on their walkie-talkies. I did not have a record and was not about to get one by being at the wrong place at the wrong time, so I hightailed it as fast as I could. As much as I didn't want to go to jail, I wanted to face my mother even less.

CKB was growing quickly, and while some members loved teaching at the studio, others began disconnecting themselves because they felt they were losing their street cred as b-boys—breakers from the streets you did not mess with. Over time, dance clubs or all-night events put on at the roller skating rink replaced the church dances. We all told our parents we were spending the night at someone else's house, but we hung out at the rink instead.

"Hey Ma, can I sleep over Jerry's house on Saturday night?" I might ask. "We're working on some new moves and want to keep practicing. I'll be home on Sunday." Hesitantly, she always let me go, but each time I came home, she asked questions to test whether my story had any merit.

As you can imagine, a bunch of teenagers staying up all night without supervision can lead to some seriously risky behavior. At these all night skates and under-twenty-one dance clubs, I started hanging out with an older crowd of people who lived on the other side of town. They were different from the kids I grew up with from Tatnuck Square—edgier, more independent, and rebellious against society. They seemed to do what they wanted with very little parental permission or oversight. I felt uncomfortable around them because I knew they were up to no good, but the peer influence and their acceptance were more important at the time.

One night, as we sat around a picnic table at the park, one of the older teens who was smoking a cigarette called me out and asked if I wanted a beer. Everyone around the circle had one except me. As I stared at the can, my mind flashed back to both my father and Joe, who sat in the kitchen drinking beer for most of my life. Somehow, I knew this could be a defining moment—I just didn't know in what way. Reluctantly, I popped open the can and took a big swig. As I lowered the can from my mouth, I could see others around the circle with a look in their eyes that said, *Yeah, he is down with us. He is one of us now.* As always, the feeling of acceptance filled me with pleasure, but I also felt something else: fearful of what I could become.

Despite my misgivings, after everyone had a buzz going, we made bets regarding who would be the first to hook up with a girl inside the rink. The only hooking up I had done up to that point was chasing the girls at recess in elementary school and holding hands with them behind the school building. Now the conversations we had were sexual in nature, even X-rated. As inexperienced as I was, I just listened and laughed and hoped it seemed like I knew more than I did.

When we went to the clubs or roller skating rink, we seemed to always meet other guys who felt they were better than our crew. And before I knew it, we started battling other crews in the streets for bragging rights and territorial ownership of different communities. When both crews were about even in the breakoff, the testosterone-fueled spirit of competition meant we had to decide a winner in a different way: by fighting. The crew with the most people still standing after a beat down was the most dominant. All it took was an opposing member to push someone from my crew and it was on. We were all fists and kicks, brutal teenage energy, until someone got hurt or security intervened. I was not one to start a fight, but I didn't back down if someone challenged me. Memories from being bullied remained fresh in my mind, and the comments my mother made about sticking up for myself never left me.

Almost every Friday and Saturday night, I got together with my crew. I was now drinking forty ounces, and we swapped the cigarettes for weed. Again, the peer pressure got the best of me as I took a hit of the bone being passed around the circle, but I did not like the feeling or the experience. Still, that became our routine—some got drunk, others got high, we went to the club or roller skating rink, messed around with girls, and then picked a fight with kids from other parts of the city.

We frequented a club called the Metro every Friday. There were a lot of kids from different communities there, and they were all loaded as well. Once a breakdance song came on, the tension built, and we gathered in the middle of the dance floor. The crew that went out first was the one that got the respect of others. If you wanted trouble, you did not have to go very far to find it.

One night, two other rival crews with big beefs got into a club-clearing brawl, and the dance floor was cleared by the silenced music and the brightened house lights. After the rush of security guards took over the dance floor, one youth lay there motionless in a pool of his own blood. From the looks of it, he did not make it.

The club closed down for some time after that night and installed metal detectors thereafter. Instead of scaring us out of the scene, that fight made all of us carry some type of weapon. I kept a butterfly knife on me just in case I needed to protect myself or one of my crew members. Just like that, what began as a way for some urban kids to express themselves became the makings of a full-blown street gang. More and more, I was drinking, smoking, stealing, fighting, and messing around with older girls that I had no business with. I felt that if I did not change my ways, it would lead me down a path to prison or the grave, but I was afraid to disassociate myself from the group—nor did I know how. My crew was my family, and—at least on the surface—gave me more love than I received at home.

Most kids do negative things because they need and want to be accepted by others. By acting out, they feel they will receive the acceptance or approval they crave from their peers. I have since learned the importance of hanging around people who make you feel good about who you are, people who lift you up instead of bring you down. Hang around people who bring out the best in you and lift up your spirits. Negative friends or toxic people can be like a bucket of crabs—anytime one crab clambers to get out of the bucket, another crab tries to pull it down. There is a saying that *birds of a feather flock together*, and you become like the people you hang around with. If you don't like what you are becoming, the answer lies within the group of people with which you choose to associate. If you don't like the life you are living, change your circle of influence. Most of the members of my crew came from broken-down single-parent households where life was a daily struggle. We started breakdancing to exorcise the frustrations of life, only to create even bigger problems.

Chapter 6

Living Two Lives

Don't try to be someone else to make others like you.
You are an original and not a copy. Do you!

—Chris Corso

After someone my age died right before my eyes, my internal compass went haywire, bouncing in all sorts of opposing directions. The push-pull between wondering if this was the type of life I was meant to live always contradicted the Bible stories my mother taught us about love, patience, and fairness. Deep in my heart, I knew I was meant for more. The outside may not have reflected it, but I knew that just like an oak tree starts as a seed, I wanted to grow into the person my mother believed I was. The problem was that when I looked in the mirror, I did not see that person.

Despite my best intentions, I felt like I held court, every day, with an angel and a devil on each shoulder. I'd take a deep breath and center myself with my new resolve, and I'd turn around and my alter ego would say things like, "Douglas, listen. What you are doing is not so bad! Come on, man up. Enjoy it! This is all you have to look forward to, so get used to it." In those moments, I'd have a clear picture of the two separate directions I was being torn between, but the sad, lonely, and broken-up parts of me believed the darkness more than the light.

During this time, I found myself stuck between two distinct lives: many weeknights, you'd find me sitting on a street corner with the crew smoking weed, drinking forties, and appraising whom to rob next. The next morning I might be playing Tchaikovsky at a nursing home.

As a freshman in high school and at the height of the polar opposite lives, I felt the familiar ocean-rush of blood and nerves vibrating in my ears when I'd go to school, wearing my hand-me-down khakis and second- or third-hand flannel shirts Mom bartered in exchange for cleaning homes. But when I went home, I also felt a similar zing—one that encouraged rebellion. I'd take the day-Doug uniform off and sneak into a different uniform of baggy jeans, hoodies, and hard-toed Adidas. Throughout the halls of my school, I walked around with a chip on my shoulder, an aggravating sense of discontent for a number of reasons—the primary ones being that I was struggling academically and unable to understand who I was or where I fit in the world.

The gangster danger I experienced evolved from the Charlotte Klein Breakers—in the club, at roller rinks, in filthy, dark alleys—and grew the more I dove into that world. I started breakdancing with the Charlotte Klein Breakers, which started as a nice wholesome crew, but from there we created Crazy Action Crew (CAC), which was the dark, gangster side of breaking. Even there, when I was with *that* crew, I never felt like I truly belonged. Every time we'd rally to drum up something fun to do (which was sometimes illegal or unconscionable), I'd get sidelong glances of concern . . . even *they* knew I should have been doing other things. But my butterfly knife and I were intimate, always linked to one another as a perfect match. And despite the angel and devil demands, after a while, I learned how to keep the angel quiet with the right amount of malt liquor.

Forty-ounce beers—the biggest bang for your buck—were our crew's preference. Through the blur and fog of this period, I remember the beginnings of slamming back countless forties. Many of our friends' single-parent households, just like mine, would offer to host us as we drank ourselves into oblivion. Their theory—and this was my mother's as well—was that if we were going to do it, we might as well do it where there was someone around who could keep an eye on us.

One evening, I stayed out long past curfew at a friend's house getting drunk on these infamous beers. Much of that night is completely lost in the black hole of my memory, but having only enough strength to crawl up the stairs to my house is firmly cemented in my mind. It was in early September of the tenth grade, and in the middle of the night. I drooled all over the doormat as I tried to gather the clarity of mind and strength of body to right myself and insert my house key. I sat there, on my hands and knees, moaning and banging my head against the door, which eventually woke my mother.

I heard the deadbolt unlock, then the knob turned, and the door creaked open for her to see who—or *what*—was moaning on the front porch.

"Douglas! Douglas what are you doing? Are you okay?" She rushed to my side in the middle of her sentence, but by the time she fully exhaled, she knew what was wrong—I reeked of stale beer, and I couldn't hold myself up above my elbows. After dragging me inside into the entryway, she rolled me over and stood above me, examining the mess I'd made of myself. I heard her mumble something to Jesus, praying for his mercy, though the only other thing I remember like piercing lead was the phrase: "You're just like your father."

Unfortunately, even though I knew she was right on some level, those words drove a wedge between us that had been growing since I stopped playing baseball. Drinking forties and coming home plastered was the least of my issues—I now had confirmation of my previous anticipation: I was a disappointment to my mother . . . I had let down the only person in the world who really knew my name and truly loved me.

At school, though, my secondhand L.L.Bean getup and decent grades let me inside other social circles that I wouldn't have otherwise known. Ms. G, a fiery Italian, sixty-something, rather petite music teacher always greeted me with a smile that disarmed the worst of my moods, and the songs we sang gave me a momentary reprieve from the uncertain self I lived with day in and day out. I offered to take responsibilities in music class, and fulfilling them gave me a sense of purpose in a world in which I was spiraling downward.

That Halloween, our crew met at the convenience store on a

nearby corner, just after dark. We pooled our money and bought three dozen eggs, and when the clerk rang us up, she eyed us warily but kept her head down. We were already drunk and high and it was Halloween; there was no mistaking what we were up to.

On the way to the wall of bushes near the intersection that we had scoped out, a little old lady came walking down the street towards us. My instinct was nil; I had no impulses toward the grandmother . . . but my friends did. Before I knew it, in the blur of darkness and haze, one of them punched her in the head, knocked her over into the crunching leaves of a stranger's lawn, and the other stole her purse right off her body. Her whimper as we ran away haunted me for another fifty yards—until I was able to chug some more beer down and anesthetize myself.

Once we finished the car-egging spree, which was much shorter than any of us had hoped, Jose, the oldest and most aggressive crew member, turned to us. His hoodie was pulled over his head, and his juvenile eyes flashed with excitement.

"Well, boys!" He rubbed his hands together like he was warming them over a campfire. "I think it's time to bring out the big guns!"

I swallowed hard. Until this point, I had only dealt with hand-to-hand fighting, never with guns. Then Jose clarified.

"Every one of these perfect little houses has a jack-o-lantern on the porch, calling your name. Let's make some pumpkins fly!" He threw his hands in the air, and instantly I knew what he meant by "big guns" . . . We'd switch from egging cars with actual eggs to smashing them with hollowed-out pumpkins. The thrill of terrorizing the neighborhood, of feeling important and involved, boosted me with adrenaline that would last for days.

The shattered glass, dented metal, and slimy pumpkin seeds left a trail that could track us—though no one did. And when we got to the part of town where no one *had* jack-o-lanterns on their porches, our adrenaline, testosterone, and rebellion got the best of us. About every third or fourth car that was parked along the street, we wrapped our determined bodies around and lifted the back ends up and onto the curb. We knew full well we were causing serious damage to the alignment of these cars—and it made us happy.

On regular occasions, we held little get-togethers where the intention was to get girls drunk and have sex with them. None of the guys cared whether the girls were conscious by the time the sex happened or not. As more of an observer than anything else, I'd support the wall, make out with these girls, and get plastered-drunk with them until one of us blacked out. Even though these girls had "consented" to be there, to be drinking and getting loose with the crew, none of them consented to being taken advantage of after they lost consciousness. The shame I carried around this was brought full circle when my wife and I had two daughters. I finally understood the gravity of what we did, and I wept in ways I never had.

At a weekend party one summer up in Hampton Beach, I met a very attractive young woman at an alcohol-free twenty-and-under dance club. She had a dark, short bob, an athletic physique, and some serious swagger. The music thumped and drove our bodies together on the dance floor, and it convinced us to dance for several hours straight. The chemistry between us was palpable, and this young woman knew she had something on me.

"Can you call me sometime?" she asked, handing me a scrap of paper with her name and number, and she turned to talk with her friends. "Really," she added, looking back over her shoulder. "I'd like to see you again." And then she was consumed within her friend-circle. The rest of that night, I couldn't stop eyeing her, catching her watching me, seeing her blush. I had a crush, and I couldn't keep it to myself. I gave her my number before leaving the club.

The next week passed without incident, until I got her call.

"Doug, I'm in town. I'd love to see you. Can you meet me?"

My mouth went dry, but I managed to answer her. "Yeah. Yes, yes, absolutely. Would love to." We arranged to meet at Elm Park just down the street from my high school, on a bench near the centermost oak tree in the middle of the park.

The moment I spotted her across the shady lawn, I felt the same surge of chemistry I'd felt in the club. It was an electric reaction, and the closer I got to her, the more intense it became. The smell of her perfume reminded me of our time together at the club in Hampton Beach slow dancing and grinding on one another. I swept her into a hug and she buried her face in my chest, and I was hooked.

We sat on the bench and talked for an hour when she asked if I'd go home with her and her friends.

"To New Hampshire? Come home *with* you? That's a two-hour drive and I don't have a car . . ." I paused, trying to understand what she meant.

"Well, I'm with my friends here and they drove me down so I could see you. And I want you to come back *home* with me. I want to get to know you better." Her flirtatious tone went further than flushing skin and a wink at the club, and I now knew exactly what she was suggesting. I waited for the joke, for the *just kidding!* to happen, but it never came. Instead, she stared seriously at my face, her brown eyes piercing mine, waiting for me to agree. And as a sixteen-year-old boy who was swallowed in the cave of hormones, the only answer I could muster, *wanted* to muster, was *yes.*

"Ma, I met a girl who lives in New Hampshire, and I'm going to go up there to spend some time with her." I sat down on the weathered plastic kitchen chair and leaned on the scratched table as my mother did her weekend big-batch cooking.

"New Hampshire? Douglas, what in the world are you thinking? What on earth do you need to go to New Hampshire for? There are plenty of pretty girls in Worcester." Mom stuck the wooden spoon in the pot and stirred as steam rose into the air above it.

"I like her, Ma. That's it. She doesn't live in Worcester, and I like her. So I'm going to spend some time with her."

Ma cleared her throat and looked at me with serious eyes. "Douglas, this is a bad idea. I feel it in my bones. You don't need to be running around all over the East Coast for the first girl who rubbed up against you at a club in Hampton Beach."

"It's not just that, Ma. She's special."

"Really? Well, go ahead then. Just know that I am not going to bail you out of this one if things go wrong." Mom returned her focus to seasoning the potatoes she stirred, and waited for me to respond.

I looked up at her, shrugged, and shoved the chair out from underneath me. I was already a head taller than she was, and my body weight shook the floor as I stomped out. Through my huffing and irritation, I could hear her say a "sweet Jesus" prayer just after I left the room.

I met my lady friend at the local library near my house. Her car was what I considered a hoopdie, but it ran, and it was hers. She asked one of her friends to drive and the other rode shotgun, and when we got into the backseat of the car together, I took one look at her and kissed her like I was in a romantic comedy, grabbing the back of her neck and inhaling her into my space. She kissed me back and when the kiss ended, she looked at me, smiled, and shook her head.

"I am so glad you're coming back with me," she said after her friend put the car in drive. The drive was supposed to only last two hours, but we drove slowly and kissed the whole way there, occasionally pulling over to the side of the road for a brief make-out session while her friends got something to eat at a rest stop. When we finally got to her house, around three in the afternoon, she walked me into her bedroom, where she had a stash of alcohol waiting.

I couldn't help but be overcome with the thrill of the situation. A beautiful girl, plenty of liquor to quell the angel on my shoulder, and nothing stopping us from making it all the way to home base . . .

Three drinks into the soiree, we were on the bed kissing. The afternoon light was bright through the windows, but my eyes were screwed tight and I was pretending to be in the full-darkness. Without warning, she pulled away, her face no longer blissed out.

"Did you hear that?"

Ignoring whatever she thought she heard, I shook my head. "Hear what?"

"That!" She pushed back from the bed and went to her closed bedroom door to listen. "Quick! He's here! Hide!"

"What? Who's here? Your dad?" I couldn't think of any situation, other than her parents returning home, that would freak her out like this . . . until I peeked out the window to see who was standing at the front door, rapping his fists against it.

He was about my height—at least six feet tall—and a much darker African-American than me. He had probably one tooth in his mouth, and his Afro was as classic as they come, with a big white plastic pick sticking out one side. And despite the fact that I was here, kissing this lovely girl into my fantasy world, this guy—easily ten years our senior and visibly raging to hurt somebody—was banging the door down.

I could barely make out what he was saying, though I heard things like "my girlfriend" and "I'm going to kill you!"

She looked at me with wide, fearful eyes. "He'll do it. He will!" Tears streamed down her face, and she put forth the plan. "I'm going to go to the front door and let him in, and you escape through the window, okay?"

I couldn't think of anything smart to say. "You have a *boyfriend*?"

She nodded and backed away, wiping the tears from her face and gathering her composure. So, trying to time it as perfectly as possible, as soon as I heard her open the door and let him in, I launched my body out of her open bedroom window and ran.

I felt like there was a pack of trained attack dogs at my heels, because for all I knew, there might've been. But after my heart felt like it was going to explode and destroy my lungs in the process, I slowed down and finally stopped to ask for directions—from a police officer.

"Where are you supposed to be, young man?" The cop eyed me suspiciously, as the area I'd run into was decidedly *not* sprinkled with many African-American youth.

"I'm trying to find the bus station. I need to get back to Worcester, officer. Can you point me in the right direction?"

Doubtful, the officer gave me simple directions, since I wasn't far. The afternoon sun was still hot and the day still bright, and by the time I got to the station, I'd heard my mother's voice echo through my mind ten thousand times: *I will not bail you out.*

I reached into my pocket and pulled out twenty dollars and twenty cents—which was not nearly enough bus fare to get from New Hampshire back to Worcester. I sat on a concrete bench at the station and let my head fall into my hands, reflecting on the last twenty-four hours and on how blind I'd been—and how *right* Ma was. I *had* to call her now. What choice did I have?

"Operator? I'd like to place a collect call, please," I croaked into the phone, dreading the next few minutes.

Once she connected us and I was on the phone with Ma, I had to cop to what happened, though I left most of the scariest parts out. "Ma, I need to get home, but I don't have enough money. Can you Western Union me some? I'm so sorry."

I had never experienced weighted guilt like that before. There I was, asking for money for a bus ride home from a potentially fatal encounter with some girl's boyfriend, and I knew that I'd just taken half of my mother's daily earnings. She agreed to send the money, but the sickening, disgusted feeling that grew inside me was enough to make me consider swearing off girls and partying forever.

I rode that bus, those two quiet hours, with my chin resting in my hand as I stared out at the tree line, thinking about what a mess I'd made of things. When I got to Worcester, I had another ten miles to walk from the bus station to my house—and those ten miles were another element to the thinking time I'd conveniently designed for myself. I felt awful, and selfishly replayed the escape-from-death scene in my mind a million times, trying to pick up the clues I had missed, but I found nothing. By the time I got home, it was full dark, and when I walked through the door, my mom didn't say anything to me. She pointed to the plate of dinner she'd made for me to eat, and after I finished eating, she told me to go to bed.

I never heard from that young woman again, which was for the best. I often wondered if her boyfriend hit her or if he actually tried to hunt me down, but I never heard anything. She was intense with a need for deep affection. After, I laid low and chilled out from the dating scene.

Around a month later, Kaz, Web, Jose, the rest of the crew, and I gathered for a party at Web's cousin's house. It wasn't far from my house, and all of Web's cousins and her girlfriends showed up. We collected into the basement, with a DJ set up on the stairway landing, and all of us kids sitting on the old, worn sofas, smoking joints, drinking forties, pretending we were adults. The mood was perfect—serene and pleasant.

Most of us at this party were people of color: African-American, Colombian, and Puerto Rican, and there were very few white people there. But in the corner was a white guy nobody really knew. He sat alone drinking beer, which made everyone nervous. How I grew up—*where* I grew up—I knew this dude was going to get hurt just because of who he was.

He stood up from the corner, his beer half-full as he staggered toward the ladies, who were sitting and talking on two adjoining chairs. He reached over and put his hand on one of Web's cousin's shoulders. To be fair, she was beautiful and the guy's guard was down since he was drunk, but the second he touched her, she objected.

"Leave me alone!" She flicked his hand off her shoulder in disgust, but he wasn't having any of it. He reached out again, this time pulling and pushing her back and forth in a jerking motion, trying to get her to pay attention to him.

That didn't go well for him.

We didn't waste a moment before jumping on him, kicking him in the stomach and the head, splitting his face open, shouting at him never to come near Web's cousin again. After we figured he'd learned his lesson, we all picked him up, one limb each, and took him up from the basement, throwing him out in the street with one last brutal whaling.

To us, it was business—crew time—as usual. We grabbed a few more forties from the upstairs refrigerator and went back down to the basement, laughing and joking about what an idiot he had been, how much of a good time it was to show him who was boss.

About an hour later, like a scene out of a movie, the DJ scratched his record, the music stopped, and the lighting in the basement went from mood lamps to fluorescent. The kid we'd beat up was back, bloodied and still drunk.

"Who hit me? Who beat me up?" He ran down the stairs, screaming. We all looked around at each other, laughing at the absurdity of his move. Was this guy crazy?

Then another, much larger guy appeared behind him, holding a heavy handgun with the safety off. The big guy's voice boomed an echo throughout the basement. "I want to know right now—who beat up my brother?"

Like a lineup, he walked by each of us, looking to his brother for confirmation, waving the gun around in the air and even holding it up to our faces execution style. The truth was that all of us had beaten him up—all of us were guilty. But none of us were going to rat each other out, especially with a loaded weapon pointed at the middle of our skulls.

"Did you beat up my brother?" He moved on to the next guy, the silence in the room only made louder by the deafening buzz from the overhead lighting. Then he got to me. "Did *you* beat up my brother?" He turned to his brother and asked him the question, this time, pointing the gun at my temple. The metal was cold and hard, and I felt the air being sucked out of the room.

"Was this the guy who did it? Was this is the guy who did it?" he shouted between me and his brother, and even though I was guilty, I lied.

"I didn't touch your brother, man! Your brother is just too drunk . . . he fell and hurt himself." The gun was pressed to my temple, his angry face staring death into me, and without warning, a warm, familiar sensation blossomed on my lap. When I looked down, I saw that I had urinated all over myself.

The room was silent, and the kid was too drunk to either confirm or deny any accusations his brother made. So, seeing that he had made his point, the massive white guy removed the weapon from my head and backed away.

Web spoke next. “Man, just so you know, the cops are coming and they know you have a gun. If you want to get away, now’s the time.”

Backing up, the big guy lifted his shirt and tucked the gun into his pants, letting the handle stick out. “You fools are lucky my brother can’t remember. Otherwise, boom.” He brought his hands to his ears and pulled them away, opening them up like a firework does in the sky. I shuddered, and no one moved until they were long gone.

The rest of the night went back to normal, but I couldn’t stop my crew from making fun of me for being the guy who wet his pants. Even after I went upstairs and rummaged through an old drawer for a pair of shorts, I was still the center of all the laughter. It was fine—I’d put up with the clowning if I got to keep my life—but the burning sensation in my chest, the knowing I was going in the wrong direction . . . *that* feeling ate away at me like a cancer.

Chapter 7

Walking Away

The best teachers teach from the heart, not from the book.

—Anonymous

I simply couldn't stay away from New Hampshire, despite all the previous chaos and lessons learned. Beautiful weather and itchy feet inspired Web and Jerry to come to me with an idea. Web spoke first. "Bro, let's go up to Hampton Beach and go camping. We'll tell our parents we're staying at the other's house, and they'll never know." We crossed the street on the way home from buying snacks and soda at the liquor store, and I looked at them out of the corner of my eye.

"Will there be ladies and booze?" A giant smile landed on my face at the thought of a night in the wilderness with pretty girls, beer, and no adults for *miles*. Web and Jerry low-gangster-fived and shook on it, and they took charge of arranging the details.

The next morning, a gaggle of us met at the park. We piled into separate cars—in ours, which was one of the girls' cars, there were four guys, two girls, and no seat belts—and we headed up to our Hampton Beach getaway. Another carful of girls followed behind, and Web said a bunch of people he knew would meet us at the camping spot. The weekend was planned perfectly.

The car ride, though cramped, sweaty, and without air-conditioning, was a blast. We listened to Michael Jackson's *Thriller* album, sung at the top of our lungs with the windows down, and hid the illegally non-belted girls whenever we approached another car—but on that stretch of highway, there were very few souls within sight.

By the time we got to the campsite, it was only two o'clock in the afternoon, but we were taking hits off a blunt before the car was turned off. Spilling out of the car like clowns at a circus, we assessed the alcohol stores.

"We're going to have to go into town to get more booze." I closed the lid to the ice chest with a thud, and like a stroke of magic, a rusted-out Toyota pulled out from around the corner. Like ours, the vehicle was packed clown-car style, but with an older group of partiers.

Web's face lit up. "Dude! So glad you came! I was wondering if you'd be able to make it!"

The driver was well over twenty-one, tall, white, and painfully thin, but Web seemed cool with him, and anyone who was cool with Web was cool with me. The girls from the car went straight to the picnic table, and one of them called over to us.

"Do any of you have a razor? I have my plate but forgot my razor," one of the brunettes said, laying down a rock of cocaine on top of a reflective three-by-three-inch plate.

Without missing a beat, Web's friend glided over to her and took out his pocket knife, handing it over wordlessly. She accepted it the way you'd accept a dinner roll passed in your direction on Thanksgiving, and she cut the cocaine into a bunch of lines.

It was late afternoon by the time the alcohol ran out, and Web's friend suggested we go into town to buy more beer.

We'd all been drinking and smoking weed, and a few of the ladies were doing cocaine, but to me, everyone was far more sober than I was. Eight of us—Web's older friend, one person in the front passenger seat of his Toyota Corolla, and two layers of three teenagers sitting in the backseat—headed out to go into Hampton Beach's town. It was still daylight, and we figured we would party some more, preferably with more alcohol. That drive, under normal circumstances, is usually benign. It's a two-lane highway each way, flanked by dense forest on either side, and doesn't involve any sharp turns or surprises . . . unless you're drunk or stoned.

A few miles just outside of town, we spotted an ambulance heading the opposite direction on the other side of the road, which was only divided by a faded yellow line. As the ambulance came closer, it flipped its emergency lights on, and our driver's spatial awareness light went out. At fifty miles an hour, I heard and felt a loud and quick snap-crunching as he clipped the side of the ambulance, and my head flung backwards to see the ambulance trying to correct itself. But both vehicles spun out of control, with the ambulance sliding off the road and landing in a ditch, and our unbelted bodies flying in different directions as our car eventually settled into a ditch on the other side of the road.

I could barely tell which way was up as people climbed all over each other to try and right themselves, pull themselves out of the car, check for broken bones, and wipe blood from busted eyebrows. The ambulance driver called the police, and they arrived within minutes.

I had never been in such a sticky situation before, and even though some of my friends had run into the woods to take cover once they knew the police were coming, I opted not to. I knew as an African-American in the wilds of New Hampshire, I'd not get very far running on foot without being noticed as unusual. Two police cars arrived, and by the time our ringleader-friend was cuffed, the girls were all tears and mascara at the mention of calling our parents since none of us were of age.

At the station, the mood was somber. The mascara and tears had dried, the girls' parents were irate but on their way, and Web's mom was coming—in the minivan, no less—to retrieve us guys from the station. I felt like within minutes, we had gone from a thugged-out crew with the world as our oyster to a bunch of reckless kids who simply got caught.

When the parental figures arrived, all around the same time, their stoic silence was worse than yelling would have been, and the knife we'd inserted into our guilty hearts wrenched again and again.

Calmly, Web's mom signed the papers, turned them in, and walked out, with us following behind her like broken, sad little ducklings. And the ride home—all two and a half hours—was only pocked with the occasional loud directional signal of a left or right turn, or a passing eighteen-wheeler. No one spoke, and though it was painfully uncomfortable, we all knew that keeping quiet was the best choice.

Surprisingly, when we got back to Worcester, Web's mom took us straight back to his house. She packed up her purse, grabbed her keys from the ignition, and exited the car, leaving us to wallow in the silent shame we'd brought home. We knew Web was in trouble—but the question of whether or not his mom would call *our* moms hung heavily in the air. I wasn't even sure if they knew one another's phone numbers, but I knew that if she called Mama Luff, all hell would break loose.

It only took me an hour to walk home, but I had prepared myself for the worst: I was convinced that I'd have to struggle through a fight with my mom, and maybe a drunken Joe, about what had happened that day, and I was exhausted and depressed at the thought.

Inside, the apartment quietly buzzed. Joe was passed out in his chair next to the radio, a soccer game still playing and an empty can of Schlitz in his lap. He wore a dingy gray tank top and even dirtier brown pants, was barefoot, and—from the looks of it—was going to be passed out until morning. In the back bedroom, I found Ma lying on her stomach on the bed with Derrick and Darrell on either side of her, and they were flipping through the pages of a book of sheet music. When she saw me, she started.

"Douglas! I thought you were at Web's house for the night! You scared the daylight out of me! Dear God . . ." She prayed a moment and stared at me with her gentle, curious mother's eyes, and though I'm sure she knew there was *something* amiss, she didn't prod further.

I sat on the floor and leaned up against the wall so that I could face them, and she waited for me to speak. "Web got in trouble for something, and his mom kicked us out. So I came home." I straightened out my pant legs and ran my hands over my face and head to try and right my mood.

Darrell looked at me sideways. "You don't look so good." Although I was visibly shaken, I had no other bruises or cuts to show for the drama of the day.

I sighed. What could I tell him? That his older brother had lied to their mother, driven to New Hampshire to get drunk and high, and somewhere in there, sideswiped an ambulance and gone to jail?

"Yeah, long day. Glad to be home, though."

"We were just looking at the next song we wanted to sing. Joe's passed out—hasn't even heard us singing in here!" Derrick pushed himself up on the bed, his bright, happy eyes disconnected from the alcoholic in the other room.

Mom flipped the page back and flattened her hand on one of the pages. Darrell whined. "No, Mom! Please? I hate that Crystal Gayle . . . *especially* that song. Can't we do Jackson Five again?" He sat upright and shot her his best puppy-dog glare.

She sighed in acceptance. "Fine. Douglas, turn the cassette player on. We have it cued up, just in case." She waited for me to acknowledge her and look her in the eye. "Do you want to be Michael again?"

Seeing as how this day had already gotten as bad as it possibly could have, I conceded to the family lip-sync secret. Derrick popped off the bed and grabbed a pencil from his backpack that was leaning against the dresser, giving it to me to use as my microphone.

"Close the door, Douglas. We don't want to wake the sleeping giant," Mom said, and with the click of the latch, she smiled and I pushed the play button on the boom box. When the music started, we fell in line with the famous, choreographed Jackson Five moves. Something about music always elevated my mother. She broke away from us and twirled around the room, playing invisible basketball and dribbling a pretend ball between her legs and around her body to the beat of the song like an old-school Harlem Globetrotter. The four of us eventually exploded in laughter, though I tried to keep my cool. It was hard for me not to be the Doug they'd always known, but on the heels of the day's events, I couldn't figure out on which side of the fence to stand.

We shushed ourselves, knowing that if we were too loud, Joe might come in. The previous weekend, I'd heard Joe wake up from a drunken slumber on a Saturday afternoon and make sexual advances toward my mother—and she had refused, saying she wasn't interested. Luckily, he was so drunk that he could barely stand, let alone get too forceful, but we all knew how mean he could be, so shushing ourselves was a necessary precaution.

At school, I continued struggling academically, though I was motivated to pass my classes since I was on the junior varsity basketball team. I'd played pickup ball in the neighborhood as a younger kid, but my competitive streak added extra stress to my game, since I knew I had to keep my grades up to play, and I had to play to keep myself in school.

Over the next few months, our family sank into a deep financial challenge. Joe stopped going to work as regularly as he had, and Mom worked overtime to make ends meet—though they rarely did. I felt stuck between trying to figure out how my family would make it financially and making sure that I fit in and stayed connected with my breakdancing crew and chasing girls on the weekends. The partying and rebellious side of me raged on alongside my double life as a quiet, polite violinist and basketball player, only I was becoming more and more aware of the painful duality in which I lived.

One day during a heavy rain, I snuck into Ms. G's music classroom during lunch to keep dry. She was perched on a stool in front of a black music stand weighted down with a book of sheet music. She looked up from her work, pulled her glasses down her nose, and welcomed me.

"Nicer to be in here than out there, isn't it, Douglas?"

Ms. G was always so respectful that it was hard to imagine anyone responding to her in a way that was anything but. "Yes, it's nice in here, Ms. G. Is it okay if I sit in here until lunch is over?" I hesitated at the threshold, but she waved me in with a *don't be silly* look on her face.

"Sit, sit. Douglas, my classroom is always open to you."

We made idle chitchat for the next twenty or so minutes until the lunch bell rang, talking about family, the "tough economy" (though I knew only a sliver of what that really meant in the grand scheme), and music, and when I stood up to go to my next class, she passed a kind smile my way.

"It was lovely chatting with you, Douglas. We need more kids like you around, you know. Remind people they can be cool *and* musical at the same time." She slid her pencil behind her ear and folded her hands in her lap. "Have you ever thought about auditioning for choir?"

I made a perplexed, exaggerated frown. Did she not know who I ran with? That I was nothing but trouble, with a capital T?

"Um, no, I've never really thought about it," I answered.

"I imagine with the ear you have for Tchaikovsky that you'd be a wonderful singer. Auditions are next week. I hope to see you there." She took her pencil from her ear and tapped it atop the music stand. Watching her slide off the stool reminded me how little she was.

"Hurry on now, you don't want to be late for your next class."

The rest of the day, I thought hard about what Ms. G said. Could I really do both? Find a way to merge my lives? The answer to that question lurked in the parts of my mind I couldn't reach, so I sloughed off the search and went on with the day. And because I'd forgotten to look for the answer to my other question, I forgot about the choir auditions altogether.

Toward the end of that school year, in late May, our entire crew gathered for one of our infamous kickbacks at one of the guys' girlfriend's houses. We started pounding forties around eleven in the morning, and by one o'clock, I was completely wasted. I staggered into the living room to find enough floor space to flatten out so I could take a nap, and within what felt like seconds, I was fast asleep.

It was the kind of nap where you're only half-asleep, incorporating the noises around you into your dreamtime, somehow making sense of both worlds. I dreamed we were at another party, and we were dancing to classic disco music. I was so excited to be there, to be wearing my disco outfit and showing off my moves while brushing my teeth with the most potent mint toothpaste. The dream-crowd thought it was so wonderful that I was brushing my teeth that I kept brushing and brushing and brushing. In the dream, everything made sense . . . until *everything made sense.* I heard Web's laugh, and as distinct as a thunderbolt siren, I knew the laugh was coming from outside of my dream, and not from within it. When I stretched to wake myself up, I reached up to rub my eyes and heard another cackle from Web, then from Herb, another guy in our crew.

"Oh my God, this is the best!" I heard one of the girls shriek. The laughter roared through the living room, and as I rubbed my eyes, I realized why they were all laughing: while I was asleep, someone had covered my eyes in toothpaste, taking special care to completely coat my eyelids. My rubbing them worked the toothpaste even further in, and a burning fire rippled through my eyes. I screamed, feeling my way around the unfamiliar house, listening to the knee slapping and happy-breath-catching as I staggered in pain. I felt the most vivid rage I had ever felt as I tried, as a newly blinded person would, to feel my way toward the bathroom to find relief.

I splashed cold water over my eyes for twenty minutes, trying to get the burning to subside, and even though I got the toothpaste out, the fire remained. A rush of angry, betrayed tears rushed to my eyes, and I wept into the running water at what had just happened. These guys—especially Web, whom I had grown up with—were *my family.* You don't mess with your crew . . . I was devastated and electrified with venom at the idea that these guys would do this to me. But I knew who had to have initiated the prank: Jose.

Jose was one of the oldest in the crew, and we didn't always see eye to eye. Since disagreeing was unheard of within a crew, Jose and I never had it out, but the looks he shot me and the subtle attitude he sent my way flagged him as the leader of this stunt.

I opened the door to go find him, my vision red from rage and toothpaste, and there he stood at the end of the hallway with a smirk on his face.

"We thought you'd never come out," he said, cracking his knuckles in his opposite hand.

Without answering, I charged forward, tackling him, trying to unleash all the anger I had on this one person. Unfortunately for me, Jose was bigger than me, and he landed one punch to the side of my head that sent my vision into stardust for a full minute. When I came to, I sat on the couch on the opposite side of the room. The rest of the crew had pulled us apart.

"You can't fight, guys. We're on the same crew," Web said, subduing another burst of laughter and avoiding my gaze.

"I am not your *stupid* practical joke, asshole!" I shouted at Jose, who stood with his feet planted firmly and his eyes half-closed in indignant stare.

"Really?" he chuckled. "Sure looks like it to me."

The rest of the crew—even Web and Jerry this time—erupted into laughter again. I knew this was the end—the sinking feeling that I no longer had my friends, my *crew,* at my back or even at all, took over my body from the inside out. Every fiber in my body wanted to rip Jose's head off, tear Web and Jerry and Herb apart for laughing at my misfortune, but I knew that if I did anything, I'd end up dead. Their alliance was no longer with me . . . it was with Jose, with the crew. And I was no longer part of that circle.

With my best double-middle-finger salute, I turned on my heels and left the party. It was now mid-afternoon, early summer, and my eyes watered painfully with the remnants of the toothpaste incident. When I remembered where I was—another twenty miles from home—the sadness came again . . . this time bringing with it the weight of all my poor choices, my stupid alliances, and how heavy I felt it would be to try and pick up the pieces. I was done with them, with those people and that lifestyle, but the void it left inside was big and empty, so I had to fill it with something.

After the toothpaste episode, I wandered the halls of my high school like a zombie, shuffling my feet and staring at only the ground in front of me when I walked. When I returned home from school, I'd look at my neatly folded and creased breakdancing gear, my hard-toed Adidas, and want to kick something. I was no longer a part of that life, that crew, and yet, I also wasn't just the buttoned-up, secondhand-store wearing, L.L.Bean dude either. I felt like I was spiraling into a losing battle.

Every time I had music class, though, my mood lifted, and I felt like I was closer to who I wanted to be. Other than Coach Miller, Ms. G was the only other adult whose opinion mattered to me—besides my mom, of course, and even then, things were sometimes strained. When I walked into Ms. G's class, the reminders of the street life, of breakdancing and robbing people, taking advantage of girls and having a gun put to my head, all of that fell away.

One morning Ms. G read a special announcement.

"Listen up, kids. 'This Friday, between nutrition and sixth period, we will have college counselors in the multipurpose room to answer any of your questions. All juniors are encouraged to attend.'"

A lump grew in my throat and chest. I used to dream about going to college, finding a way to escape the hard knocks into which I'd been born. But despite the closely examined Northeastern University TV commercials and regular assurance from my mother, there was nothing else in my life that reflected to me that college was a good idea. I slumped down in my seat and pulled my hood up over my head.

"Douglas, see me after class?"

I looked up at Ms. G with a painful recognition of "the talk" she was about to have with me, and still, a part of my spirit soared in that moment. *She sees me. She knows what I'm capable of.*

After class, I gathered my backpack and zipped it up slowly, just as Ms. G moseyed over to me.

"You *are* planning on going to college, right, Douglas?" She looked at me with those grandma eyes—the ones that will spoil you but never let you get away with anything.

"Yeah, my grades aren't so great. Probably not." I stood, fixing my sweatshirt and tossing my backpack over my shoulder.

"Child, you can play Tchaikovsky on that violin. There's no reason that should go anywhere but college first." She squared her shoulders at me, all four feet and eleven inches of her, and looked up at my face, into my eyes. "Do you hear me? You're going to college, and I don't care who says opposite."

"Ms. G, I'm barely passing my classes, and I haven't played violin very much in the last few years. I think I missed my shot." I shifted my weight from foot to foot and stuck both hands in my pockets, trying to shove out the thoughts of worthlessness, of past violence and trauma.

"Douglas, you come to choir. I'll find a place for you. I'm not hearing any more of this waffling. Say you'll go to college."

I stared down at her petite face and frame, and for the first time since I could remember, happiness, *recognition*, rose in my chest without the aid of drugs or alcohol.

The next afternoon, I attended Ms. G's after-school choir. All the kids were theater kids, and I didn't feel like I fit in at first. But once I opened my mouth to sing, once we *all* opened our mouths to sing, the music brought us together, and I found my new place. It didn't take long for me to consciously put down my violin and bow and put that energy toward my vocal cords in the school choir.

I found out quickly that I enjoyed singing even more than I enjoyed playing the violin; it came more naturally to me. Music always had its way of speaking to my soul without saying a word, and when I'd hear people sing from the bottom of their hearts, it always sent chills down my spine. When I listened to them sing, the heavens seemed to open up over my life, and my perspective became one of endless possibilities. In those moments, I forgot about feeling trapped by used clothing and fearing going hungry. From the bottom of my toes, I felt that through music, I could find joy and happiness.

Ms. G taught us to sing from our hearts and not from our heads, to be one with the music. It was a way that we could express our feelings and develop our God-given potential, so I sang, and sang, and sang. I, like Mama Luff, enjoyed listening to the radio and creating the harmony to almost every song I heard. This preference sometimes got me in trouble in music class or choir practice with Ms. G. From time to time, instead of singing the notes on the page, I would listen to the song with my soul and instinctively add as many harmonies as I could find. In a way, I felt like each of these moments was a combination of Mama Luff's and Ms. G's influences: Mama Luff raised me up singing, and Ms. G showed me how, and that was a powerful combination!

One example of this was at Christmas as we practiced for our upcoming performance. We got to the end of the song, and before I even realized it, the music took control of my senses. I swayed back and forth like Ray Charles, my eyes rolled back into my head, and I ad-libbed the missing bars to the song in perfect-pitch harmony. Then, as was par for the course, the entire piece came to a complete halt.

I slowly put my head forward, opening one eye at a time, and I saw a few students shaking their heads at me, while others laughed. Despite us all being from different corners of the universe, we all loved to sing and found empathy for each other when the time was right.

"Douglas, I need you to stop singing what *sounds* nice to you and just sing the notes *in front* of you." Ms. G always spoke to me in a serious-but-I'm-teasing way, but, at the end of the day, we all knew that Ms. G allowed it to happen because it was a part of growing our self-esteem and self-confidence . . . and we were grateful for it.

Ms. G's love for music and service extended outside of school. That same holiday season where I got busted for singing my own version of "O Holy Night," we went to a nursing home during the holidays to perform Christmas carols.

When the double doors opened up to the main entrance to the home, the smell of antiseptic and old people overwhelmed me. Even the white walls lacked vibrancy, as there didn't seem to be much of any life happening in there. As we made our way to the community room where the residents ate meals and often socialized and played bingo games, a group of seniors sat talking with one another in the corner. I imagined for a moment that they were telling old war or drinking stories, much like I imagined I might if I were to get that old one day. But aside from this little bunch of men, the majority of the residents were nestled in their wheelchairs or hanging onto their walkers with their heads down.

Our youthfulness and boisterous voices were foreign sounds in this otherwise transitory place, and we drew more and more attention with each passing minute from other corners of the facility. Ms. G gathered us to run through the song order once more, and I caught myself in a daydream. *What did these folks do in their heydays? What colleges did they go to, did they have children and grandchildren, and how many of them can sing?*

The moment we hit our first unified chord, the faces of all the residents watching lit up like daylight, and seeing the looks on their faces when we started singing brought so much joy to me that I couldn't wipe the smile off my face the entire performance. I even had to stifle a chuckle or two when the oldest, most tone-deaf resident got so into the carols that he sang them at the top of his lungs, off-tempo, from the back of the room. It was all in good will, and for me, it was magical to see how the whole environment and mood in the room changed because we were singing together.

Music was my lifeblood, and it became the thread that pulled me out of the muck and through the toughest points in high school. I'll never forget Ms. G telling me to go to college; her voice, her reason, became the guiding reminder to me that anything *really is* possible.

Chapter 8

Family Meeting

Nothing will work unless you do.

—Maya Angelou

By the end of my sophomore year, I had completely dissociated myself from the breakdancing world. I had been conditioned to people walking in and out of my life, so it was *nothing* to walk away from people who did not mean me well.

Thankfully, Ms. G encouraged me to put both my time and efforts into my schooling. Along with my mother, she felt that I had the competence to do well in college. "Your junior year is the most important year in high school," Ms. G said, "because this is the year that colleges look at you the most to determine if you are college material."

I took her words seriously, knowing in the back of my mind that I wanted to go to college. Throughout my life, my mother had said firmly, "You just need to go to college, Douglas. Your life will be ten times better than it is now if you become a college graduate."

I did not fully understand what that would look like, but most of the people I admired at that time, like classmates' parents and school administrators, were college graduates. Most of the kids in my school came from affluent homes: parents with college degrees who did not struggle for basic needs such as food, clothing, or shelter. (If Maslow was correct, I had no chance of achieving a sense of safety, love or belonging, esteem, or self-actualization as long as I was still wondering whether there would be toilet paper with which to wipe myself.) The kids that joined the breakdance community, though, were all like me: poor, troubled, from unstable home environments, and just trying to meet basic needs. Each day, we woke up and did not know what challenges we would face. I hated that feeling and decided to direct my focus toward something that could help me stay out of that perpetual lifestyle: education.

So, as my junior year approached, I decided to concentrate on three things: doing well in school in hopes of going to college, finding a job so that I could help out more at home, and getting more involved with after-school events to occupy my time away from home and keep me out of trouble. I had been primarily a B and C student during my freshman and sophomore years, so my goal was to go from that to As and Bs in my junior and senior years. I enrolled in more honors and college-level classes so that I could challenge myself and prove to myself that I was, in fact, college material. I was not the brightest student, but I did work hard and gave it my all to learn as much as I could. After school, I made it a point to do homework as much as possible so that I did not fall behind in my studies. Whether it was staying after school for additional help from my teachers or getting peer-to-peer tutoring from other students, I made academics my top priority since grammar school. I found that I enjoyed learning and was a well-behaved student.

In addition to investing time in my education, I desperately wanted to find another job besides teaching breakdancing, where I could make more money, get more hours, associate with a new group of people, and stay away from the house as much as possible. One day after school, I was in the main office and saw a flyer for a ten-hour part-time position at the Worcester Public Library. The job only paid minimum wage, but the work hours were right after school and some Saturdays. I filled out all the paperwork that night.

The main library in Worcester was downtown and a popular place both for families and those who fit into both the intellectual and homeless communities. In other words, smart, "eccentric" people lingered there for hours, reading things like the *Iliad* and the *Odyssey*, and carrying on conversations with one another in such a serious way that I used to stop what I was doing just to watch them. I was captivated by the big words they used and the debates they carried on with all the seriousness of attorneys, even though they were dressed in tattered clothes and probably did not take regular showers. I did not grow up going to the library and only went during the summer to fulfill the summer reading program that our school implemented, so the whole scene fascinated me.

I pressed my shoulder into the large wooden door to open it and walked toward the center of the library. Under a rotunda stood a plain, somewhat homely librarian with her hair in a bun and sterile black cat-eye glasses with a silver chain dangling from the ends.

"Good afternoon!" I said brightly. "How are you doing today?"

The librarian stared at me as if I was confused or had walked into the wrong place. "How can I help you?" She had the personality of a snail.

"I'm here to apply for this position," I said, unfolding the flyer I took from school. The librarian had me fill out an application and then collected my information and told me someone would give me a call if they wanted an interview.

Each day when I came home from school, I asked my mom whether anyone had called, but it seemed the phone had gone dead the day I applied for the job. Then, about two weeks later, the phone rang after dinner. Joe answered, and instead of immediately and loudly speaking Ga, he said in quiet, broken English, "Please hold on, and I will get Douglas." My ears pricked up as he shouted, "Douglas!" in his typical Schlitz-slurred fashion. "Someone from the library would like to speak with you!"

I was embarrassed that Joe answered, but my heart surged with the same sense of excitement I'd felt when my mother called me to the phone to speak with Coach Miller about playing in Little League. This would finally be a way for me to help my family through our hardships. Pushing past my sense of shame about Joe, I picked up the phone and said enthusiastically, "Hello, this is Doug."

On the other end of the phone, a soft-spoken, elderly sounding woman explained that she was scheduling interviews for part-time positions within the periodicals department and needed to know a forty-five-minute slot that I was available for the following week. *Yes!* I thought and quickly rattled off a time that worked best with my school schedule. When I told my mom that I secured the interview, she was elated.

"Yes!" she exclaimed, echoing my own thoughts. "I knew you could do it, Douglas. Thank you, Jesus!"

The next day, my mom came home from her housekeeping job with a pair of khaki pants and a dressy plaid L.L.Bean oxford shirt for me to wear for my interview. The clothes did not match the b-boy baggy pants, T-shirt wearing persona that I'd acquired through breakdancing. I held them in front of me, making a face. Clearly, they were hand-me-downs from some middle-aged white guy giving his old clothes away to the poor to make room for something more modern. But the way my mother saw it, those clothes would help me fit in with a culture not accepting of young, black, urban, menace-to-society, ear-pierced, shag-wearing, pro–Afrika Bambaataa brothers like me who tested societal norms and values by breaking laws with a who-gives-a-rip spirit. My mom acknowledged my individuality by letting me wear what I wanted to wear when I was actively working at the dance studio, but she said, "Son, in order to get where you want to go, you have to fake it until you make it. Look at what other successful people are doing in life, and emulate them so that you can be successful!"

I immediately fired back with, "That's being phony, Ma. I need to be me—straight up." She put her head down, shaking it from side to side and laughing like I was some type of comedian. "Then you are going to be one straight-up broke Negro!"

For a moment, I just stared at her, taken aback.

"When you are making some real money, you can say whatever you want," she said. "But until then, your broke ass better try on this shirt and pair of pants that I got you for your interview, you hear me?"

Affirming that my mom was dropping some real truth, I put my head down and responded with a "Yes, ma'am" as I made my way to my room to try on my semi-new clothes.

The day of my interview, I woke up early to find that my mother had already ironed my clothes. I'd been ironing my own clothes since middle school, but today, she beat me to it. I took a shower, took out my earring, combed my hair, and got dressed, and I felt like a totally different person when I looked in the mirror. The breakdancer with the butterfly knife had finally disappeared. Instead, the guy in the mirror looked like a productive member of society who was doing something with his life instead of just wreaking havoc. I kind of liked the clean-cut preppy look.

As I finished buttoning my shirt, my mom started in on me again. "See?" she said, grinning. "You look like someone of substance instead of some ragamuffin, no home-training, breakdancing fool without a dime in your pocket type-of-a-brother."

I sighed and smiled weakly.

"If you look like a corporate executive, people will treat you like a corporate executive; if you look like a gang-banger, society will treat you like a gang-banger! Because you are black and poor, you have to try harder to fit in with others. You may not have the newest or nicest clothes, but you have no excuse not to be clean and always iron your clothes, even your handkerchief, you hear me? Look at me when I'm talking to you."

She ranted until, worn out, I just gave in. "Yes, ma'am."

Once I arrived at school that day, it did not take long for other students to comment on my new look. Some encouraged me, but one African-American student came up to me with a serious up-and-down appraisal.

"Dude, what's up with you?" he asked. "You look like a wigger!"

"What's a wigger?" I asked, already dreading his response.

In total disgust, he said, "A wigger is a white nigger, a black dude trying to act white!"

My heart sank and my head lowered, and everything my mother had said to me earlier that morning shattered. Angry and wanting to fight back, I told the kid unapologetically, "Dude, I'm trying to get a job. I'm not playing around with getting money in my pocket, and if I have to, I will fake it until I make it, fool! Save your wigger comments for someone who cares."

And I walked away as quickly as possible from the conversation.

I tried to not let those comments consume me, but I was deeply self-conscious. I even thought about going back home to change my clothes and then re-donning my preppy attire for my interview, but I didn't want to face my mom. I also couldn't ignore how I'd felt when I looked in the mirror that morning: as if I mattered.

Right after the last bell rang, I hurried to take the bus downtown for my interview. As I made my way upstairs to the periodicals department, I saw a big open area bustling with patrons reading newspapers and magazines on the cluttered tables. It smelled like used newspaper, and dust drifted above the carpet through the rays of sunlight from the bay windows overlooking City Hall. It was a surprise to me that I was so happy to be there, though I definitely stood out. I was the only sprinkle of color on the entire floor. My clothes were the only thing that made me fit in, and I said a silent thank you to my mom.

I checked in at the reception desk, and they told me to wait at one of the open tables on the second floor. Just before the interview started, I prayed that God would open this door if it was His will. Then, out of nowhere appeared a white woman with straight black hair pulled into a bun. She wore a black, gray, and white argyle cardigan, a black skirt that made its way to the floor, and 1950s-looking reading glasses perched on the tip of her nose. Her name was Virginia Quinn, but she preferred to be called Mrs. Quinn.

"Thank you for coming in to interview with me," Mrs. Quinn said. "Tell me a little something about yourself."

I thought about what my mother had told me about emulating successful people and remained as positive as I could. "Well I'm currently in high school and looking for part-time work after school to help out my family," I responded.

"Are you punctual?" Mrs. Quinn asked, looking at me sternly.

"Absolutely," I said. "I was taught that if I arrive fifteen minutes early, I'm on time, and if I'm on time, I'm late, and if I'm late, I'm fired! My baseball coach taught me that!"

Mrs. Quinn laughed. "Well, it sounds like your baseball coach and I are cut from the same cloth."

"He also taught me how to follow instructions," I added, "and I work well with others, too. When they succeed, I succeed—that is the attitude I would bring to the position if you choose me."

At the conclusion of the interview, Mrs. Quinn thanked me for coming in and told me that she had two other interviews to conduct that week but would give me a call by the end of the week if they decided to give me the job.

When I got home, my mother was waiting for me at the door.

"Well, son?" she asked eagerly. "How did it go?"

After I shared the details with her, she gave me a thank-you card to send to Mrs. Quinn. "Tell her you appreciated her time," Mama advised, and I wrote the note as carefully and neatly as I could.

As Friday approached, I felt a tremendous amount of anxiety. The first thing I did when I got home from school was ask if anyone from the library had called. With a tone of defeat in her voice, my mother said, "No, not yet, baby."

Feeling that no call meant no job, I retreated to my room and crawled into bed. The beginnings of a thick depression settled on me as I tried to sleep off the pain of failing, again. Why hadn't I gotten the job? What had I done wrong?

Then, right around five o'clock, the phone rang. I could hear my mother talking in a polite and excited voice. A minute later, she walked into the room with a smile on her face: "Douglas, Mrs. Quinn is on the phone and would like to speak with you."

Not wanting to get my hopes up, I took the phone hesitantly. "Hello, this is Doug."

With a smile in her matter-of-fact voice, Mrs. Quinn said, "Doug, this is Mrs. Quinn, and I just wanted to call and invite you to be a part of our team in the periodicals department. If you accept our offer, we need you to start working right away."

I felt a sense of numbness, as if I was dreaming the whole scenario. Overwhelmed with shock, it took me a few moments to respond. I finally managed, "Wow, I would love to get started right away, too."

"Great," Mrs. Quinn replied. "Then it looks like I will see you Monday after school, and we will just go from there."

"Okay, thank you so much!"

I was overwhelmed with joy, and so was my mother. As I went back into my room to lie down and imagine what was to come,

I could hear her talking to Jesus again. "Thank you, Lord!" she cried. "Thank you, Jesus, for opening an opportunity for my son. Thank you."

Two weeks into the job, Mrs. Quinn called me into her office. With a smile on her face, she said, "Doug, you've done a great job the past two weeks, and it gives me great pleasure to give you your first paycheck!"

She handed the check to me across the desk, and I almost swooned when I saw my name after "Payable To." During my break, I went to the bank and cashed my check. I had a great lunch that day at the nearby mall and could not wait to get home and give some of my money to my mom. But first, I would stop by the store to pick up some household items—soap, toilet paper, milk, a bag of chips, and a two-liter of Coke. I did not get a lot of money that day, but the sense of accomplishment in being able to contribute financially to my household was astonishing. For the first time in my life, instead of feeling like a taker, I felt like a giver. I liked the feeling of rolling up my sleeves and earning compensation for a hard day's work.

Days turned into weeks and weeks into months, and I became a real part of the periodicals department at the Worcester Public Library. Mrs. Quinn taught me the importance of a professional work ethic and doing my best every time I pushed through the library doors. She was a stickler for punctuality, which was not an issue with me considering my tenure with Coach Miller, and she made it a point to teach me something about life during every shift, much like my mom. One time, I recall being a part of a staff meeting where Mrs. Quinn talked with all of us about the importance of customer service.

"People do not come to our department just to read newspapers; they come here because they love the environment we provide for them in which to read the newspaper. We need to make sure that we always treat our customers with kindness and give them a 'Neiman Marcus' experience. They need to feel like they are the only ones we are waiting on and that nothing else matters!" She spoke matter-of-factly, and peered out into the general area. Towards the end of our staff meeting, she said with a firm voice: "And remember—the customer is always right!"

Perhaps one of the greatest things she emphasized was to have a spirit of excellence. She would tell me and others she supervised, "If you are going to do something, do it to the best of your ability!" These words would later become my mantra, my daily goal: living my life with a spirit of excellence.

The right people come into your life at the right time—especially if you are looking for them. After my breakdancing days, I needed someone to bring me back to the type of life I needed to be living, and in her soft-spoken yet firm way, Mrs. Quinn was that person. Today, in my cupboard, sits a coffee cup that Mrs. Quinn gave me when I was sixteen years old. More than twenty-seven years later, its inscription still inspires me: "You're an exceptional man . . . There's never been anyone with your personality, ability, and unique way of seeing things. There's never been a man like you before, and there won't be again . . . so go ahead! Take the world by storm! You've got what it takes!"

As I write these very words, I'm drinking coffee from that cup. It will stay with me for the rest of my life as a reminder that there are caring adults out there who want to see people like me win in life. During this time in my life, Mrs. Quinn was the only consistent and stable individual I had to look up to. That was probably why I gravitated to her so much and listened more than spoke when we were together. She was solid all around—I knew she would never walk out on me. She provided me with the backbone I needed to get my life straight. She had such a positive influence on my life that it gives me great joy to share her with the world.

The notion of working hard and working often seemed to be rubbing off on other members of my household: Joe took on more hours throughout the week and even on a few Saturdays for overtime pay, and my mother got a full-time job as a housekeeper for the Crowne Plaza Hotel in Shrewsbury, in addition to her regular house-cleaning hours. While I was excited to see more money come into the house, what little family unity we had was giving way to longer hours at work or late-night social events with coworkers. Coming home on a Friday night to an empty house made it tempting to return to my old ways of drinking and partying, but in my heart, I was done with all that. I was used to having a lot of unsupervised time as a child, but this was different because I could see that Joe and my mother's relationship had drifted apart.

In fact, my mother had already divorced Joe when I started high school, but since she had three boys and nowhere to go, they agreed that we would stay in the house. Darrell and I still had our own rooms, but my mother and younger brother Derrick slept on the living room couch, an embarrassing reality that I hid by rarely inviting friends over. And even though they were divorced, my mother sometimes spent time in the back room with Joe. I suppose she had to pay a price for keeping some type of roof over our heads. Back then, though, I wondered why she did not muster up the courage to try to make it on her own since her boys were growing up, but as an adult now—a father—I look back and understand that she was trying to hold a semblance of family together for our sake.

Naturally, working multiple jobs and multiple shifts took its toll on my mother. Because Joe was a horrible example, we grew up letting my mother do all the cleaning and cooking around the house. If she asked for help, we helped, but we did not take the initiative to do it unrequested. One day, my mom came home from work and found my brothers and me sitting in the living room—her bedroom—watching TV. As soon as she came through the door, her housekeeper uniform still on, I asked her if she could clean the bathroom because it was filthy. She looked at me as if I were Joe. "Get your ass up and clean it yourself!" she responded.

"But I don't know how!" I protested.

She lost it. She screamed and cursed at me and grabbed whatever was closest—her purse, her shoe—and let me have it. That was when I knew she was pushed to the edge. Upset with myself for being such a bonehead, I ran to the bathroom and frantically grabbed a towel and the bar of soap on the sink, but the emotional damage to her was done.

"Ma, I finished cleaning the bathroom," I ventured when I finished cleaning as well as a novice could. "I'm sorry for saying that."

She walked away from me. "Good," she said, bone-tired and angry. "It's about time you learn how to do things around this house."

So I did what I always did when things did not go well in my life: I left the house and got drunk. I had someone buy me a forty-ounce and went to the park alone, letting myself sink into buzzed relaxation with each sip.

When I came home, I had to weave through the living room to get to my room, so I knew I would encounter my mother, but I didn't care anymore, either. I opened the door, and our eyes met in silence as I made my way to my room.

During that season in my life, there were many mornings when I woke up to find that both Joe and my mother had left for work, leaving me with the responsibility of making sure my brothers got up, got dressed, got something to eat, and made it to school, especially Derrick, who was still in elementary school. The additional money coming into our home mattered less to me as whatever family unit we previously had vaporized before my eyes.

One night, the phone rang, and it was my mother. She had missed the last city bus for the night and was not able to get home. "Douglas, please go ask Joe if he can come pick me up so I can get home."

Now, it being late in the evening, Joe had already downed a couple of beers and probably should not have been driving in the first place, but I did not want my mother to be stranded alone in the streets of Shrewsbury for the night. As I made my way to Joe's bedroom door, I thought twice about knocking. I even thought about just taking his car, even though I did not have a driver's license, but I realized that might have done more harm than good. So I knocked hesitantly on his door.

"Joe, Ma's on the phone and needs to speak with you. It's important."

On the other side of the door, I could hear him whispering under his breath, put off by having to talk to my mother. In one surprisingly fluid motion, he opened the door, took the phone from my hand, and slammed the door back in my face. Hoping that he would man up and just go get her, I put my ear to the door. At first, all I heard was silence. Then he said, "What do you mean you missed the last bus? Well, you better start walking because I'm not picking you up." When he flung the door open, I fell into the room. He threw the phone at my chest. "Here, take it," he said, grabbing his silver can from the nightstand. "I don't have anything else to say to your mother tonight."

"Joe, why can't you just pick her up so she is not stranded in Shrewsbury?" I asked, scrambling up from the floor. "What the hell is wrong with you?"

Agitated, Joe told me to shut up and closed the door in my face for the second time that night. In desperation, I told my mother I would just take Joe's car and come get her.

"No, Douglas," she said firmly. "You don't have a license, and that will just make matters worse. You just go to bed, and I will figure something out. Don't worry about me. I will just see you sometime tomorrow. Take care of Darrell and Derrick for me."

Before I could get in a last word, my mother hung up the phone. I stood in our kitchen, staring at the phone in dismay as my chest filled with rage toward Joe. I was getting old enough to no longer be afraid of his drunken escapades and thought that I could actually take him. I harbored a lot of resentment and anger toward him, and I knew that one day I would not be able to hold it in any longer.

I gathered my brothers from their respective beds (or, in Derrick's case, the couch) and shared the news with them, adding that it would be best if we all stayed in the same room that night. Without my mom, there was a big void in the house, and I wanted us to feel like we at least had each other. But I could not sleep at all. I kept thinking that somehow, some way, my mother would walk through the door, and for some reason, I felt it was important—necessary, even—that I listen for the moment her key turned in the lock. But as the minutes turned into hours, it became obvious that she was not coming home. My mind filled with fear for her. Would she have to sleep outside? It was bitter cold, twenty or thirty degrees with wind that cut to the bone, and her jacket was as thin and patchy as any of ours. What if she didn't make it through the night? The uncertainty nearly killed me, but there was nothing I could do.

The next morning, I woke up and said nothing to Joe. I just did what my mother had instructed me to do: get Darrell and Derrick up and ready for school. I spent the entire school day not knowing what had happened to my mother. I did not know if she was alive or where she was, but I prayed throughout each class that she would be home when I got there.

I ran full speed toward home as soon as the school bus dropped me off. As I made my way up the stairs, the aroma of my mother's fried chicken got stronger and stronger. Before I reached the door, my mother opened it with a smile. As if she had been home the entire time and there was nothing to worry about, she said, "I've been expecting you. Take off your shoes and wash your hands because I made you and your brothers something to eat." I had never been happier to see her except the time she came back for us when we stayed with our grandparents in Norfolk.

As we ate, I asked for details on where she'd spent the night, but she did not want to talk about it. She just shared that she had friends from Crowne Plaza that lived in Shrewsbury and was able to crash with them. And that was it. She did not want me to bring it up again.

After that encounter, Ma and Joe acted like two rival boxers getting ready for their final fight. On a daily basis, our house was either a silent universe where everyone kept to themselves or a war zone where profanity, yelling, and sometimes fists ruled the night. The financial pressures, lack of family intimacy, and long hours at work were taking their toll on all of us. Over the next several months, my mother worked late-night shifts and stayed in Shrewsbury with a friend from her work—or at least that was what she told us.

One night when she was home, she gathered us in my room for a Bible study. She carried in a kitchen chair to sit on, and we gathered around her on the ground. Because of after-school commitments, our Bible studies became few and far between when I entered high school, but that night, we all found comfort in the old routine. That Bible study was on how God will never leave you, nor forsake you—that no matter what you do, God is with you and loves you unconditionally. Speaking with compassion, Mom said, "God loves you with a love that is unconditional as long as you ask him for forgiveness for what you have done!" And just after finishing that statement toward the end of our Bible study, my mother broke down in tears.

Not knowing what was happening, we all jumped to our feet. My first thought was that Joe had hurt her again and that I was going to kill the son of a bitch.

"No, no," she said, waving us back into our seats. "He has nothing to do with it." Fighting more tears, she blurted it out with urgency. "I need forgiveness! I want you all to know that Joe and I have been divorced for some time now, and even though we have been staying here, I met someone else from work, and now I am three months pregnant, and it's not Joe's baby."

You could hear a pin drop. I did not know what to do or think; I was dumbfounded by the whole situation. Of course, we knew about their divorce, but part of me still thought, *Ma how could you do that?* and the other side of me said, *Good for you. You deserve a decent man and to be treated well.* I wondered if this would have happened if Joe had just picked her up from work the first time she missed the bus. I blamed him entirely for her finding someone else. After all, he'd never treated her, or us, for that matter, as if he loved us. But reality quickly set in: when Joe found out about this, he was going to hit the roof. I can only imagine what was going through my mother's head at that time.

"Ma," I managed after a while, "what are you going to do?"

She sighed. "I'm going to tell Joe. Eventually. Not a word from you all until I do, you understand me?"

She looked the three of us in the eyes, and we would have done anything for her. We all nodded and agreed to keep quiet. But I knew the outcome was not going to be good . . . at all.

Chapter 9

Homeless

There's no place like home,
there's no place like home!

—Dorothy, *The Wizard of Oz*

Two months passed, and we found out that my mother's next child would be her first girl. You could cut the tension in our home with a butter knife as we all waited for the day my mother would drop the baby-carried-by-a-white-stork bomb on Joe. I wasn't sure how she'd managed to keep her secret for so long, but now she was heading into her third trimester and there was no way she could continue to hide her bulging belly.

Then came the Friday night we all feared. In typical fashion, Joe burst through the door with a case of Schlitz and a carton of Marlboros for the weekend. I was in my room settling in for bed when I heard Joe yell, "Are you pregnant? Have you been sleeping around with other men? You bitch!" I could feel the rumble of bodies being thrown around, and like a track star, I sprinted to the kitchen. When I got there, I saw Joe screaming and hitting my mother. He pushed her up against the stove, slapped her in the face, and with just inches in between them, yelled into her face. "I know I'm not the father, who did this, tell me now!"

With tears streaming down her face, the only thing I heard her say was "Get off me, just let me be!"

I lost it. Eighteen years of anger and resentment raged from me like a tsunami. At the commotion, my brother Darrell rushed from his bedroom and joined the fray in the kitchen. Darrell grabbed Joe from behind, restraining his hands, and we wrestled him down to the ground and both started kicking him in the back, chest, and head.

"Douglas! Darrell! Stop it! Stop it right now!" Ma yelled, but she couldn't get ahold of either of us enough to pull us off Joe. I was numb. My subconscious self had taken over, and I completely lost control over my behavior. It felt like the time I fought the kid in third grade who called me the N-word. I hated Joe. I hated everything he stood for and everything he'd put my mother through. I hated him for everything he'd put my brothers and me through. I wanted him to feel the pain and anguish that had stored up in my soul for over a decade. The only way I was going to stop fighting him was if I killed him, and I set my sights on doing just that. Then, to my surprise, my mother picked up the phone and called the police.

"Ma, what in the world are you doing?" I shouted, continuing to throw kicks and punches. I could not understand why, after taking years of verbal and physical abuse from this man, she would defend him. I will never understand that. It was the same behavior she exhibited when my father and her brother grappled when I was a kid, each determined to tear the other down.

In less than fifteen minutes, the front door flew open. "Police! I need everybody on the ground now! Now, I said! Get your hands up and drop to the floor."

The police had arrived to a home at a breaking point. The house was thick with raw emotion: hatred, hurt, frustration, heartbreak. How we really felt about our lives came out that night, and the police could not tell the aggressor from the victim. I was in such a rage that I blacked out, not remembering later what I said or did but recognizing that if I did not get a handle on myself, I would go to jail. I thought jail might be the best place for me right then because I was so filled with hatred that I wanted to take out my rage on the next person to cross me, even if it was an innocent bystander. Hurt people, almost without exception, hurt people. They don't need cause or provocation. They think that by hurting others, they will be able to beat out their own pain, and in those moments when my fists made contact with Joe's skin, I felt the great release of years of pent-up aggression. I didn't see yet that when the adrenaline wore off, I would feel more depressed than I ever had.

My mother, whose belly was round and full, lowered to her knees while another officer pressed her to get down. "Ma'am, I need you to get on the ground."

I leaped to my feet and directed my fury at the officer. "For the love of God, can't you see that my mother is pregnant? Take your hands off of her."

Almost immediately, I felt the crushing blow of cold steel against the back of my leg; the officer's baton knocked my entire body to the ground. With a knee to the middle of my back, a third officer was able to calm everybody down so that even heads would prevail.

Drunk and with a cigarette still dangling from his upper lip, Joe yelled, "Pack your shit up and get the hell out of here—I'm done with all of you. Get out of my house, now!" At his words, we all froze. The only income my mother received as a housekeeper was under the table. Therefore, and as the police would later confirm, all the bills and the rent were under Joe's name; if Joe wanted us out, we had to get out.

Desperately, my mother begged Joe to reconsider, but the deep sense of betrayal he felt was too much for him. "Just get out," he repeated, wiping his forehead of blood and spitting into a trashcan.

Just get out. The words rang through my entire body as, in complete shock, I hurried back to my room to pack a couple days' worth of clothes and my books for school. I flashed back to the early morning sounds of an annoying vacuum cleaner buzzing and my mother talking to Jesus, and for the first time in my life, I wondered if Jesus was really there and why he would allow our family to be broken apart like this.

As I crammed T-shirts into a bag, I mumbled, "Jesus, if you are there, please rescue me and my family. Please, Jesus, help us now!" I neither heard nor felt anything back and retreated into a cocoon of depression that would manifest itself in destructive ways in the days, weeks, months, and years to come.

My mother, Darrell, and Derrick took a little longer to gather their things, partly because my mother was the only one who knew where everything was. They also may have been procrastinating; hoping that Joe or the police officers would feel a shoestring of pity and not force us out into the blistering New England winter-night streets. In the shadows of crushed beer cans and an overflowing ashtray of cigarette butts, Joe sat quietly at the kitchen table, not uttering one word in our defense.

Once we were outside, the reality that we were on our own settled in. Dazed and bruised, both physically and emotionally, my brothers and I followed behind our mother with our coats half on, each of us weeping for our own reasons. One police officer had stayed in the house to get a statement from Joe, and two others escorted us down the street. When we got to the bus stop at the end of the road, the officers hung back. We sat down on the steps leading to a big white Protestant church, and I hoped someone would open the doors and help us find a place to stay.

"Where are we going, Ma?" Derrick asked in a small voice. He was ten or eleven, dark-skinned like Joe, with ivory teeth and a sweet, soft-spoken disposition. "Where are we going to stay the night?"

"Just shut up and be quiet, Derrick," Darrell said. Like me, he was still emanating rage, clenching his jaw and fists. Darrell was a loose cannon and didn't seem to notice the cuts and bruises marring his face and knuckles.

Rubbing her pregnant stomach as if looking for an answer, my mother did not respond. She just peered further down the road to see if a bus was anywhere in sight. The police car still idled between our house and the bus stop, but otherwise, the street was quiet and empty.

Ten minutes turned into twenty and then forty-five minutes, and as an hour approached, I realized that we'd been so in shock when we left the house, we had not realized it was close to ten o'clock at night, and the city bus had stopped running hours ago. Numb and cold, my mother alternated covering our hands and ears with her hands to keep the blood circulating and help us avoid frostbite. Then the police car came to life as the officer inside drove forward to check on us.

As he rolled down the passenger window, steam flew from the combustion of the cold outside air with the heated car air. "No more buses tonight, huh?" the officer asked.

My mother shook her head without a word, her shoulders held back proudly.

The officer sighed, and I saw compassion on his face. "Listen," he said, "I know of a shelter on the other side of town that might take you guys in for a couple of nights. Why don't you get in?" He gestured toward the backseat of his cruiser.

My mother looked into our eyes, seeing how hard we shivered, and decided to take him up on his offer. We loaded into the police car fast in search of relief from the frigid, black night. Ma sat in front with the officer, while Darrell, Derrick, and I piled into the back. I was eighteen, and although I had already done much that could have landed me in the back of a police car, I'd never had this experience. I hid my head on the way to the shelter, embarrassed that someone from the neighborhood might see us. I made up my mind that I would never experience this again: this confinement to the back of a police car, feeling the absolute absence of freedom. As we drove down Main Street toward the downtown area, the silhouettes of sterile housing projects overwhelmed me. Life as I knew it was changing.

When we arrived at the shelter, called the Abbey House, we were greeted by a young white woman in her twenties who had a warm smile and a spirit of caring about her. My brothers and I stayed in the car as the police officer and our mother inquired about emergency shelter for the night. At eighteen, I knew that I would not be able to go into the shelter with my family. I feared the worst, thinking that I would be dropped off at the men's shelter. I knew what that meant, what some of the men in there might do; I did not want to be another man's girlfriend for the night, or ever, for that matter. The thought of defending myself as fresh meat terrified me. It was true that I grew up fighting and had just finished fighting Joe, but fighting grown, strong homeless men with nothing to lose was a different story. I just could not go there—I would rather sleep out in the bitter cold and die on the streets than emotionally and mentally die in the arms of a sick, twisted, homeless man.

In just a few minutes, my mom and the officer returned to the police cruiser with puzzled looks on their faces. My fears had been so vivid, so forceful, that I was certain bad news would follow. But when they entered the cruiser, no one said a word, and our heads lowered in the backseat as we drove off. Before we turned a corner, I glanced back at the Abbey House and saw the young white lady standing on the snowy front yard, a look of disappointment and apology on her face. I sensed that if it was up to her and she had the power, she would have let us all in the shelter that night, but the rules and regulations would not permit her to do so. I would find out later that the Abbey House was a short-term emergency shelter for women and children only, so my brother Darrell and I would be off on our own to face exactly what I feared most. Thank God, though, my mother wanted all of us to stay together, so we had to find a different solution.

Still in the police cruiser, we headed northeast on Route 9 toward Boston. We made our way through Shrewsbury, stopping at a dilapidated motel that had daily, weekly, and monthly rates posted outside the front door. The motel sign was dangling by one or two stubborn bolts, and some of the light bulbs were out on the sign. The police officer dropped us off, and we collected our belongings and went to the office.

It was now around eleven, and the office looked unchanged from the 1970s. A picture of John Travolta from *Grease* barely clung to the wall, and James Taylor played on a small transmitter radio with a long antenna. The office was empty, but my mother didn't hesitate. She strode to the countertop and banged on the bell, signifying the need for service. A middle-aged man emerged from behind a door toward the back of the office. He was overweight and disheveled, with long hair and an overgrown mustache, and he looked my mother and all of us up and down before asking, "So what brings you here tonight?"

My mother replied, "How much does it cost to stay here for a week? We need a place to stay for a little while."

The man seemed to soften. "Well, if you need a place to stay and can pay me by the end of the week, you can stay here."

We walked, single file, through the narrow hallway to a room on the second floor. We all stayed close to the building because the railing was unstable and rattled back and forth with each step.

Mom opened the room door with the key, and an immediate reek of smoke made us cough and cover our noses with our shirts. The room was illuminated by a yellow-white light in the middle of two twin beds. My mom asked me to take off the top blankets on the beds because, as a housekeeper who also worked in a hotel, she knew the common practice was to wash only the bed sheets. As we got settled in and took off our shoes, we found that the carpet was sticky, trash from former guests was left behind in the trashcan, and the bathroom was filthy. It was clear that the room had not been cleaned that morning. My mother launched into housekeeper mode, actually going to the office for cleaning supplies, and the room felt more comfortable and livable in no time. I welcomed the strong smell of bleach, especially in the bathroom.

After she finished cleaning, I could see the depression in her eyes, and she said nothing to us as we watched television. Making herself small in bed, she turned to face the wall and just went to sleep. Traumatized by this entire experience, I told my brothers to get some rest because we had school the next day.

The lights from the motel shone through the translucent curtains, and tears ran down my cheeks as I wondered why God was making us go through this. I had never experienced such internal pain, fear, and anger before, and I did not know how to process what was happening to us. I started to feel that it was my fault. If I'd just let Joe do what he wanted to do and hadn't threatened him, perhaps we would still be in the apartment and not in this run-down motel off a two-lane highway.

Throughout the night, I was woken up by the moaning, weeping, and sobbing of the others, but no one said anything because the cries represented what we all were feeling. Hopelessness deposited itself into my spirit that night. I wanted to close my eyes and sleep forever.

My mother woke us at the crack of dawn and told us to get dressed quickly so we could take the public bus to school and not be late. Without a shower and wearing the same clothes we had on from the night before, Darrell and I made our way to the nearest bus stop. It was just down the street from the motel, and we did not say a word to one another on either the walk or the long ride to school. The shock and reality of being homeless had hit, and the last place I wanted to be was school.

In high school, your social status defines you. There were the jocks, the nerds, the preps, the druggies, and the poor kids; until then, I had identified myself as a prep and a jock at school, even when I was a gang member outside of school. We looked down on the druggies and the poor kids, and now I was officially one of those poor kids. My brother and I now had to take two different public transportation buses to school, where before we'd only had to catch one school bus at the corner of our block.

Since this was our first time taking the bus to Doherty High School from a motel in Shrewsbury, the trip took several hours. I trudged in twenty minutes after my homeroom period began, and the teacher wasted no time before asking why I was late. I froze in front of the whole class. Had someone told her I was homeless? My legs and arms were numb with fear and embarrassment, and because I could think of nothing to say, I just forced myself forward to my seat. Of all the uncertainties in my life, I knew this: I did not want anyone to know I was homeless. I did not want them to know that my family was now living in a motel in Shrewsbury off Route 9. I did not want them to know that Joe had kicked us out of our home because my mother—even though she had been divorced from Joe for a while—was pregnant by another man who was no longer in our lives. The thought of anyone finding out my family's secrets filled me with shame.

But my teacher didn't see any of that. "Mr. Luffborough, if you think you can just walk into my classroom and not explain to me and your peers why you were late, perhaps you can come after school for detention with me."

I stared at the teacher the way I used to stare at rival gang members before fighting—a mad dog look of unmistakable threat. I stood to my feet. "Yes," I said. "I will see you after school."

Fear came over the teacher's face; she knew I lived a different life outside of school. Quickly, she moved on to talking with another student. No one else in class acknowledged the encounter. Many of them had put their heads down or turned the other way in order to disconnect from the conversation. But I was pissed and ready to fight anyone who challenged me. Of course, what the teacher didn't realize was that my getting called to detention was a blessing; I did not want to begin my depressing journey back to the motel.

From one class to another, I had a hard time seeing eye-to-eye with both teachers and students. I kept remembering the night before, my mother and two brothers sleeping in a motel. I did not know how to process what was happening or whom to talk to about it, so the anxiety bubbled. I felt like I was about to explode.

During lunch, students segregated themselves from one another as usual. The jocks sat together, the preppies sat together, the gang members and breakdancers sat together, the druggies sat together, and the poor kids sat together. I felt myself slow down as I passed the poor kids' table, looking into their eyes and feeling in my heart that this was my group now. I was one of them, just pretending to be someone I wasn't. I wanted to be accepted by a group that looked down on the poor and made fun of their circumstances. I had grown up poor but always wanted to break free from a life of insufficiency—a life where the basic life necessities like food, clothing, and shelter were a daily struggle. A life marked by not knowing where my next meal would come from. A life of not knowing if we would have enough heat not to freeze to death during the wintertime, or enough toilet paper so I wouldn't need to use newspaper as a substitute. I had gotten a job to help pull us away from this life, and now we were more entrenched in it than ever.

Finally, I ended up where I set out to go and ate lunch at the preppie table as I had for most of my time in high school. Today, though, I was more mindful of the conversations regarding the students who sat at other tables. It amazed me that these same conversations did not mean much to me before being homeless, but as my peers at the preppie table joked about the poor kids, I wondered what they would have to say about me.

"Look at the way they're dressed. Where do they buy their clothes, from a secondhand store?" one of my friends snickered.

"They're so lazy they didn't even bother to take a shower," another student remarked.

As everyone talked and laughed around me, I became hyper-aware that I was wearing the same clothes I had on the day before. What if someone noticed? It was only a matter of time before I was called out. The conversations at the table became more and more judgmental until I could not handle it anymore. "I've got to get some fresh air," I said with frustration and finished my lunch in the courtyard by myself. What was I going to do? I knew I wouldn't be able to keep this a secret forever, and when people at school found out, there was no doubt in my mind that they'd make fun of me as easily as they did the other poor kids.

For most of the day, my mind was consumed with how much my life had changed in less than twenty-four hours. I just wanted this bad dream to end, but I knew normal would not come anytime soon. I don't think I learned anything that day, and when the teachers assigned homework, I brushed it off because I was not sure what our situation would be like when I got back to the motel.

After the final bell rang, I ran into Darrell, who was standing with a group of friends. They were shaking their heads, saying things like, "Man, that shit ain't right" and "You can crash at my house if you want." I didn't waste a second before pulling Darrell away.

"I can't believe you told them!" I hissed. "What the hell is wrong with you, Darrell? It's nobody's business but ours."

Darrell looked surprised by my outburst, but I didn't give him the chance to respond.

"I got in trouble and have to stay after school for detention, so tell Ma, and I will just see you guys later," I said.

In my homeroom, where I would serve detention, I found myself among the troublemakers and renegades. These kids chronically caused problems, came from dysfunctional families, and struggled academically. Most were students of color and accepted detention as just one extra class, one more excuse to stay in school and not have to face their dismal living situations at home. Most of them actually enjoyed detention because they could come together and commiserate about the challenges they faced at home. This resonated with me, and I quickly immersed myself in their conversations. Then out of nowhere, one of the students said, "Hey, Doug, why are you here, anyway? We've never seen you in detention."

Put off that I was now the center of the conversation, I shot back, "What's it to you, dude? Do you have a problem, bro?" I stood to my feet as if ready to throw down.

The student held out his hands. "Take it easy, dude, I just was curious how you got here." He shook his head as he walked away from the table where I was sitting.

I spent the rest of detention watching time slowly and agonizingly pass by. I put my head down on the desk and daydreamed that we were not homeless and that I would arrive home that day to the sweet smell of my mother's cooking. Just as I was getting ready to take a bite of her homemade potato salad, my dream was abruptly interrupted by the ringing of the last period bell. It was time to start the long, cold, and arduous journey back to the motel in Shrewsbury.

I hung around school for a while, because I didn't want other students to see me heading in the opposite direction from where I used to live. Finally, on my way down the hill from the school, I ran into a couple of homeboys who were a part of a rival break-dance crew that I had battled against at the Metro several years earlier. We'd made peace since then, but one of them walked up to me and, to my surprise, said, "Yo, homeboy, what are you doing in this neighborhood?"

The guy knew that I lived on the other side of town, so I quickly responded with, "Chill out, bro, I don't want a beef with you. I just want to pass through the neighborhood."

"Wait a minute, bro," the other one said, his chin up and a palm out to halt me. "You can't walk through our 'hood just because you want to—that's disrespectful, bro, and you will have to go through me first."

Without thinking, I took out the six-inch butterfly knife I always carried tucked in the back of my pants. "I thought our beef was over, but if you want to throw down, let's do it homeboy," I said.

I had fire in my eyes and the image of his blood on my hands.

"Hey, chill out, bro," said the second guy, backing up.

Then the one who originally challenged me took off in a dead sprint. "I'm going to get my gun so we can take care of this fool!" he yelled over his shoulder.

My butterfly knife was no match for a gun, so I hauled it through Elm Park and up the street towards Elm Park Elementary, where I was bullied in kindergarten, and then past the Worcester Auditorium, and then into a new community past Memorial Hospital. I ran several miles without stopping and didn't look back until I got to a bus stop off Route 9 that would take me back to the motel. *Can my life get any worse?* I wondered as I boarded, breathing hard. I stared out the windows. Now I'd have to find a new route "home."

When I got back to the motel, I was struck by the quickness with which my family seemed to acclimate and settle in to our humble one-bedroom home. Our bags were unpacked, and my mom had covered the cheap TV console with a tablecloth and a few of her favorite scented candles. As soon as I settled in, she called a family meeting.

"Turn off the TV so we can talk about what's going to happen for the next couple of weeks . . . or even months," my mother said.

We sat on the beds, and she stood between them. Her voice was matter-of-fact, and we listened with the desperation of those who need a leader.

"First, I need you guys to continue going to school. Use your education as the key to get you out of this kind of life. Second, I need you older two, Douglas and Darrell, to find better jobs quickly to help make the money we may need for food and to contribute to where we are staying."

Darrell and I nodded seriously. We agreed that this was what we needed to do; it felt like we were all coming together to rally behind my mother and fight for our survival. My whole life, I watched my mother fight to keep our family together, fight to establish ourselves and become self-sufficient, and even though this was one of the toughest times we had experienced, my mother always maintained a sense of resiliency.

"This, too, shall pass," she said firmly. "You understand? We'll continue doing what we are doing and believe in a better tomorrow."

My mother's strength and spirit of survival were a source of inspiration and hope. She was like a lighthouse, its radiant beams leading wayward ships in the night. Before returning to the motel, I had been very pessimistic about our future, but after our family meeting, I felt encouraged to fight through this circumstance by not giving up.

After our meeting, my mother decided to hold a bible study for us the way she did at home. She sat down on one of the beds and opened the Bible to Romans 8:37–39 "In everything we have won more than a victory because of Christ who loves us," she read. "I am sure that nothing can separate us from God's love—not life or death, not angels or spirits, not the present or the future, and not powers above or power below. Nothing in all creation can separate us from God's love for us in Christ Jesus our Lord!"

She went on to tell us that God's plan for our success was built on the premise that we had already won through our struggle . . . we were all together, out from beneath Joe's reign, and now we were free to write a new script—to live a new life. That night, she wanted us to understand that God still loved us and always would.

Afterwards, my mother wanted us to finish our homework and go to bed so that we could leave for school earlier the next morning. Like the night before, everyone slipped into sleep with moans and weeping, and no one said anything to acknowledge the pain we all felt. I wept silently, feeling the harsh reality: we would live in this sleazy motel for a week with no plans after that. That night, I dreamed that I was back in Norfolk, and my mother and father were still married. We lived in our own home and ate dinner together. My parents loved each other, and that night, in my dream, we all lived together as one big harmonious family.

Chapter 10

Crossroads at the Overpass

Like a bridge over troubled water, I will ease your mind.

—Simon and Garfunkel

It was still dark when I felt my mother tugging on my shoulder. "Douglas, it's time to get up and get ready for the day," she said with a warm smile on her face.

I groaned, pulling myself from the hard motel bed, and noticed that my mother was already dressed and ready to go. She was always the first to wake up in the morning and the last to go to bed at night. My mother was a worker-bee. She always said that laziness is a poor man's playground and that if you wanted to get anywhere in this world, you have to get up off your rusty dusty and work for it.

Before we left the room, my mother prayed. "Lord, I ask that as we leave today, you bless our words, bless our steps, and bless our minds to stay focused on you, Lord Jesus. Your will be done today and every day, in Jesus' name, Amen."

No matter how bad our situation, my mother was steadfast in her belief that God would get us out of it. Her faith inspired me and motivated me as well. I was not as strong a believer as she was, but I felt and knew there was a God. At the same time, I struggled to imagine how any God would let my mom and my family endure all of the hardships we encountered for most of my life. I started to use prayer as my time alone with God but always wondered if my prayers reached him. I watched and listened to my mom as she talked to Jesus and often imitated her in practice, even though I did not fully understand. I felt like I had nothing to lose, so why not try to become a God-fearing man.

Brisk wind chapped our faces as we tucked our heads down and walked to catch the first of two buses. As we neared the bus stop, my mother told us that she was going to school with us to meet with the principal and other key administrators and teachers. She intended to let them know about our temporary housing situation and seek advice from them, if they had any.

As we hit the front steps of the school, other students stared at my visibly pregnant mother, who walked with us towards the principal's office. I validated their perceptions by putting my head down, concentrating on the ground, and wishing I could disappear.

At the time, the principal was one of only a few African-American women in the district who were administrators, so we thought she might be able to empathize with our situation. Her office door was open, and when we walked in, she stood up to greet us from behind the enormous mahogany desk that nearly filled the entire room.

"Hello, Mrs. Luffborough, Douglas, and Darrell. What brings you all here today?" Behind her silhouette was a wall filled with framed degrees and accolades displaying her credentials to be the leader of the school.

"Thank you for meeting with us," Mom immediately said. "Me and the kids are going through a hard time right now and are temporarily homeless, and I personally wanted you to know in case you hear anything. I am working on applying for section 8, but if you can let their teachers know, I would appreciate it."

"Oh wow. I understand, Mrs. Luffborough, and I will share this information so they are aware of your situation. I can only imagine how you all are keeping it together. Has this happened before?"

Put off by the principal's inquiry, Mom fired back, "No, this is something that just happened and is only temporary." The conversation was brief and cordial, but the principal's tone appeared condescending. My mother wanted her to know that if I was late to school it was because I was coming all the way from Shrewsbury and needed to take one bus and then transfer to another. The principal said that she understood and would talk to my teachers, particularly my homeroom teacher.

"But," she said, "my best advice would be to start your mornings earlier."

My mother, seeming somewhat intimidated by the principal, said, "Why, that is great advice, and, yes, we will do that. I also would like to keep this matter as private as possible for the sake of the boys, who have many friends here. Sometimes young people can be not as accepting as adults, if you know what I mean."

The principal nodded. "Yes, I know what you mean, Mrs. Luffborough. I will let you know if any resources become available for you and your family and will speak to the boys' teachers and guidance counselors about your current situation."

When we left the principal's office, my mother told me she was going down to the welfare office to see what housing assistance they might be able to provide. As she walked away, I could hear her talking to Jesus again. *Wow*, I thought. *She never goes anywhere without her friend Jesus by her side!*

The day started like most days, and I tried as much as possible to take my mind off being homeless by plugging into my schoolwork. One teacher that I felt comfortable opening up to was Ms. G. She had been with me since day one in high school, and our relationship had blossomed tremendously since then.

"Ms. G," I told her, "my mom and stepfather got into it, and now my mother, my brothers, and I are homeless," I said with my eyes watering. Saying the words out loud was jarring but also gave me some form of release. I hadn't realized how badly I needed to talk about it. "I can't help feeling like just giving up or maybe dropping out of school so I can make more money to get us out of this motel we're staying in."

The small, nimble, grandmotherly Italian woman walked over and hugged me until I broke down in tears. She didn't say a word. She just let me rest my head on her shoulder as she swept a maternal palm up and down my back. Her presence was all I needed at the time—I needed to know that someone cared about me and that my life mattered, and in the long, somber moments during which she comforted me in silence, that was what I felt. Even though we did not exchange words, I felt as though I did not have to suffer in silence.

Some of the students in my music class overheard our conversation, and they comforted me as well by doing what we did best in

Ms. G's class: sing. "Hey, Doug, remember that song with three-part harmony by the Gatlin Brothers? Let's sing it to take your mind off things!" "Yeah!" another student interjected. And then, without missing another beat, other students started singing:

"All the gold in California is in a bank in the middle of Beverly Hills in somebody else's name . . ."

When our voices came together, I forgot about my struggles and about being homeless. We stood in the middle of the room as a small impromptu quartet singing our hearts out, casting out our fears and frustrations through our vocal cords. Music was the best way for me to feel better, and that's why music was one of my favorite classes throughout my four years in high school.

Then it was time for lunch. After our talk with the principal that morning, we now qualified for free-and-reduced lunch and needed to select food from that menu. My stomach turned inside out as I followed the surging crowd of students to the lunchroom. I thought, *The minute I get in line with my free-and-reduced lunch card, everyone is going to know that my so-called preppy status is being revoked, and my poverty status is being activated.* The question most in my mind was which table I should sit at now—the preppy table, as I had done for most of high school, or at the poor kids' table. The decision was killing me, and I thought about just skipping lunch and eating when I got back to the motel, but I pushed myself to deal with the inevitable.

I hid my card until the very last minute in line and then quickly handed it over to the lunch lady, only to have her broadcast my new status: "Oh, Mr. Luffborough, so you are now on the free-and-reduced lunch plan," she said. If looks could kill, the lunch lady would have dropped dead right then and there.

I snatched the card out of her hand. "You don't have to broadcast it to the world, lady—give me a break!"

Of course, the very folks from whom I wanted to keep this information were the first to hear our conversation. My secret was out.

"Sorry, bro, this seat is taken," said one "friend" as I approached the preppy table. Another and another rejection followed as I stood holding my plastic tray, breaking out into an embarrassing sweat. Finally, I shuffled to an empty table, hoping that someone from my circle of friends would join me. Nobody did. Even my old breakdance buddies stayed away. *Some friends*, I thought bitterly. I learned then that you find out who your real friends are in moments of tribulation. In moments of glory, friends are easy to find, but when times get tough, they scatter like a room filled with cockroaches when a light is turned on. I was done with those kinds of "friends." I'd rather be alone.

It took me hours to fall asleep that night, tossing and turning in anxiety of what the next day would bring. When sleep finally came, I slipped into a vivid, lifelike dream. I saw myself in the middle of a quad of buildings, using my backpack as a pillow as I lay on a well-manicured lawn. The clean smell of grass lingering in the air was a reminder that the lawns had been mowed that morning. I watched people walk by, catching snippets of conversation from other students and professors leaving one class and heading into another. I remember telling myself that if I stayed there too long, I would most likely miss my own class. Then a male figure approached me and asked how I got to college. I remember telling him about being homeless and sometimes looking for places to sleep and meals to eat but that the road to college was for me. Suddenly, I saw myself in a cap and gown and realized that I was at my college graduation. My heart soared with emotion as I stood on the stage, and then, when I least expected it, I heard over the PA system: "And our next graduate is Douglas Edward Luffborough III." As I made what appeared to be a fifty-foot walk from the side of the stage to the center, all I could think about was holding the diploma in my hand and saying to myself, "I knew I could do it. Look at me now . . . a college graduate." As I walked off the stage, gripping my diploma, my ticket to a better future, I felt someone tugging on my arm. I turned to see who it was, but the dream came to an end when I realized it was my brother. "Douglas, hurry up! Wake up. We need to get ready for school."

The dream was so real that I had to look in the hotel closet to see if there was any trace of the black cap and gown I had worn so proudly just moments earlier. I was disappointed to see myself in the motel and still in high school but felt encouraged by my dream to one day go to college. The entire way to school, I could not get over how real the dream appeared to be. It was so real—as if I could actually feel and touch the words engraved on the diploma. I'd never had a dream like that before and had a strong feeling that my dream was a foreshadowing of what was to come, if I didn't give up and did my best in school.

We approached school at the same time the school bus from our old route arrived. Almost immediately, I began to receive questions about my personal situation.

"Hey Doug, how come you don't take the bus with us any longer?" one kid asked.

"Hey, I heard that you guys don't live on Copperfield Road anymore. Is that true?" someone else chimed in.

"Listen," I said, thinking fast, "my family is going through some challenges right now, and I need to take care of a family member on the other side of town. Actually, I am living there, so you won't see me on the west side of town anymore. I commute from the east side now. The principal already knows everything. Any more questions?" I asked curtly, stopping the bombardment of unsolicited inquiries.

For the life of me, I could not get my college dream out of my head. Even though I was living the life of a homeless teen, my dream of all dreams was to go to college. Deep inside, I felt that the doors of higher education would be the only way for me to leave the life of poverty and uncertainty behind. Educational research studies had shown that a college degree gave greater earning potential and power than if you just remained a high school graduate. My mother always told me that my life would be ten times better with a college degree than without one. I made up my mind: whatever it took, I was going to college.

That day, I went to go speak to my guidance counselor about college, as all seniors doing that were college-bound. As I approached his office, I was overwhelmed with the various college pennants that proudly covered the landscape of the walls, from Harvard to UMASS to Worcester State College. I felt like I was standing at the doors of a college admissions office, and on the other side was my dream becoming reality. I teared up with inspiration and was grateful that I would be able to go through the process.

"Thank you so much for meeting with me," I enthusiastically said. "I had a dream about going to college, and I wanted to talk with you about how you can help me apply and get accepted."

My guidance counselor looked across the desk at me and told me words that even to this day send shivers down my spine. "I hate to tell you this, Douglas, but I don't think college is for you. You are just not college material." For a moment, I thought I was dreaming again, but I wasn't.

"Excuse me? I don't understand. Don't you advise and help all students who want to get into college or just those who fit a certain profile?" I was clearly defensive.

"Listen, Douglas," he said, "your family is facing extraordinary challenges right now. I heard that you are working and that is what you need to do. You need to support them by keeping that job, by making money so you can help your family get off the streets. Your mom is also pregnant, right? Wouldn't you agree that you have other emerging things in your life to work on first that are more important than going to college?"

I nodded mutely.

"You need to be the man of the house. College is for other kids. You are doing what you need to do right now—working!"

I was devastated. On one hand, I knew my guidance counselor was right: staying home and finding a job nearby was a viable option. But I was dying for someone to recognize that I was college material and just needed a chance. Academically, I felt that my grades and extracurricular activities were strong enough to gain college admittance, but I did not know anything about the process or where to begin. And all I heard that day was "Don't even try."

Depressed and hopeless, I decided to stop off at a church that was on the same bus route as the motel. I was hoping to find someone to talk to, anyone who might contradict my guidance counselor's advice and assure me that I *was* college material. As I reached the intimidating twelve-foot-tall doors of the church, I knocked, praying that someone would respond. To my surprise, a blue-eyed, red-cheeked, Irish-looking man dressed in a classic black pastoral robe opened the door. When he saw me, his open expression changed to one of mistrust, perhaps even instinctive dislike.

"What do you want and who told you to come here?" he demanded.

My first thought was to tell him that Jesus sent me, but then I said, "Excuse me, sir, but I just need someone to talk to. I am currently homeless and staying with my family in a motel. My dream is to go to college, but my guidance counselor just told me that I wasn't college material."

The pastor blinked once. "If it is God's will for you to go to college, then He will make it so." As he finished his last words, he slammed the big door right in my face.

That's it? That's all he has to say to me? God's will? Angry and confused, I walked back to the motel with my head down. Was it God's will for my family to be homeless? Was it God's will for us to be sleeping in a run-down room, sharing beds with one another? Why did I have to go through this? First, my friends in school turned their backs on me, then my guidance counselor told me I wasn't college material, and now even the church closed its doors on me. Nothing good would ever come from this, I thought. What was the point in trying? I retreated inward like never before, hating myself, hating my family, hating my guidance counselor, and hating school.

I decided not to go back to the motel but instead, I would spend the night at Elm Park down the street from my high school. It was not a very big park; you could see from one side to the next. It was centered in a residential community, so many families spent time there after work playing with their children. When I was little, we played there as well. I sat on one of the benches, almost in a trance over the events of the day, replaying the conversations I had earlier with my guidance counselor. As the sun went down, the wind chill of a New England night came upon me; I needed to find a place to sleep that would protect me from the elements. I made my way over one of the bridges in the park and decided to sleep under the bridge. I did not sleep at all that night, between the stray dogs barking and the police sirens blaring through the park. The hard dirt and smell of urine under the bridge made me feel like I was sleeping in a cesspool, but it didn't matter; at that point, my life had become a cesspool.

The next day, I wandered through the park, unable to take the chaos of my own thoughts anymore. I crossed over a freeway overpass that I frequently used during my daily walks to the bus stop, and had the thought that jumping into ongoing traffic would be a quick and easy way of ending my suffering. The next thing I knew, I was standing on the overpass, and what seemed like a dream was actually reality: I was climbing over the barrier and getting ready to drop into the cars rushing past below. The only thing I could hear was the racing of my heart, just as loud and fast as the cars passing by underneath me. Images of growing up passed by: my mom getting beaten up by my father, me being bullied, staying back in school, being told that I had delusions of grandeur, watching Joe make an ass of himself, and being told I was not college material. *Just jump,* my thoughts whispered, *and then you will no longer feel any pain. Just jump. You have come too far to turn back now.* I closed my eyes, feeling a swoon of vertigo as a gust of wind rocked me. And then I heard a voice. Someone called out to me.

My eyes flew open. Standing just ten feet away from me was a raggedly dressed white homeless man with a bottle of Jack Daniels in one hand and what looked like a weathered Bible in the other. I snapped out of my trance, curious as to what he was saying to me and why he was talking to me in the first place. I will never forget what I heard next.

"Hey, man," he called out. "Jesus loves you. He told me that He has a plan for you, brother. He has hope and a future for you! Let me show you what I'm talking about," he said, pointing to his Bible with the pages almost falling to the ground.

I wasn't sure if the guy was drunk or just plain crazy, but what he said was exactly what I needed to hear. *Plan, hope, future . . .* words I had sought from school and from church and which had seemed absent in my life just moments before. I was hungry for them. I couldn't jump when someone was ready to offer me some hope.

I climbed over the barrier and walked over to the homeless man.

Without acknowledging what we both knew I was about to do, he turned his Bible to Jeremiah 29:11. "For I know the plans I have for you," declares the Lord, "plans to prosper you and not to harm you, plans to give you hope and a future." Out of all the scriptures in the Bible, that one was written especially for me.

All my life, I grew up witnessing my mother talking to Jesus and not understanding the difference it was making in her heart and in our lives. However, at this moment, it was clear to me that Jesus was now talking with me. I felt so comfortable talking with this homeless guy that I shared with him my story and my situation. We both shared something in common—we both were living on the streets, but, unlike me, he was filled with joy and peace and was content with where he was in his life.

"Man, I have been on the streets for years, and what I learned is that life is what you make it, young man. God did not get you this far to let you down." Together, we sat on the side of the street, looking up at the overpass, reading the Bible, and finishing off his bottle of Jack Daniels.

Chapter 11

Purpose

Do not wait; the time will never be "just right." Start where you stand, and work with whatever tools you may have at your command, and better tools will be found as you go along.

—Napoleon Hill

When I got back to our motel room, I found my mother cleaning and my other siblings watching TV. My head buzzed pleasantly, and words tumbled out of my mouth without thought.

My mother looked at me the way she had the night I got drunk and came home with just enough energy to crawl up the front stairs and use my head to knock on the door. Sharply, she said, "Have you been drinking? You reek of alcohol."

"Yes," I said, scratching my head. "And if I told you the complete story, you wouldn't even believe me, so let's just leave it at that."

Knowing that I was at least home and safe, she continued doing what she did best: she took a nearby cloth rag and wiped the surface of the nightstand in between the two beds, saying nothing else about the issue.

That night, all I could think about was standing on the overpass, anticipating my jump into oncoming freeway traffic. How had I gotten to that point? Even more, who was the homeless man, and where had he come from? As I thought about it in bed, eyes open and staring at the dark ceiling, it was clear to me: the homeless man was an angel sent from God to remind me that He had a plan for my life and a promise for my future. Though I was still sleeping in a motel off Route 9, I had a new assurance that our situation was only temporary, and I felt more encouraged and motivated than I ever had. I was determined to not let this situation define me, but *refine* me.

As I thought about the homeless guy, I smiled, recalling his positive outlook on life. Despite his situation, his attitude was contagious and made me want to listen to him more and more. It is true that your attitude determines your altitude, and I felt a deep sense of gratitude for the life I did have. I was glad I hadn't jumped, glad I was alive, and I decided at that moment that I would start speaking the power of positivity and life over myself and my situation.

On my way to school the next morning, I sat on the public bus and visualized myself graduating from high school and going on to college. I could see myself reading my acceptance letter and showing it to my mother, the smile on her face filling the room. I imagined her talking to Jesus as she always did in times of trouble or complete joy. At my high school graduation, after calling my name, they would share the college that I would be attending. I would pack for college and hug my mother, and clear as day, I could see myself looking into her eyes and saying, "I'm going to be okay, Ma. I am a college student on my way into a new season of my life."

If I wanted to see this become a reality, I knew I had to start carrying myself as if I were already there. *Fake it until you make it*, Ma used to tell me.

When I got to school, I had a new, laser-like focus on my academics and extracurricular activities, like music—my constant—and student council, the Latin club, and my church basketball team, which I had joined that year. I filled my days and weekends with work, school, and extracurricular events so that there was no room for me to get sidetracked or in trouble. My mother, my teachers, and other students could see the new vision in my heart. My mother no longer needed to wake me up in the morning. Some days, I even rose from bed before she did, getting my clothes ready for the day. Teachers remarked on how I was taking on extra assignments and how they could see my commitment to doing my best. Even my peers talked about the difference in me. "Doug," they would say, "something is different about you. It seemed like you just tolerated school before, but now it's like you've found your purpose in it. Now you talk about going to college—more about your future than your past."

My guidance counselor saw things differently. I hung around his office regularly, but he was always too busy to talk me; there was always another student for him to meet with or give advice to. One day, I intercepted him just as he was leaving his office.

"Mr. Kent," I said breathlessly, "I really want to sit down and talk with you about my chances of getting into college."

Without hesitation, he responded, "Considering your situation, you should get a job to help support your family." His voice was sure and steady, as if he had no doubt that working was the right thing for me to do. The words came as a punch to the gut. It was the emotional equivalent of all the times I had been bullied or overlooked and undervalued, the way I had been in the third grade, or when my minor league coach had told me that I was not good enough to play. Mr. Kent's reaction was yet another blow to my self-esteem, another mental setback to keep me off track.

He was right in one way: I needed to find a higher-paying job with longer hours to help my family, because the library, with its funding challenges, was cutting back on my hours. But, I did not—*could* not—give up on my dream of going to college. And if my guidance counselor wouldn't help me, who would? With renewed hope and faith, I knew that at the right time this question would be answered. *For now*, I thought, *I must continue to press forward without his support.*

After school, I went to the library and asked Mrs. Quinn if there was an opportunity to work more hours. She confirmed that due to budget cuts, the library would be giving out fewer hours, not more. Still grateful to have a job, I thanked her, though I knew I needed more.

I asked my friends at school if they knew of anything, and one told me that the factory where he worked was hiring. They wanted hardworking students to work after school and some Saturdays for eight dollars per hour. That was three dollars more per hour than I was making at the library. With a skip in my heart, I asked him what I needed to do to work there, and he told me he would speak to the owner and see if they would grant me an interview.

The next day at school, my friend told me that the owner was interested in interviewing me. So, just as I had for my interview with the library, I ironed a pair of khaki pants and my best-looking long-sleeved L.L.Bean plaid dress shirt. My mother gave me another pep talk before I left the motel.

"Remember to use your home-training and be polite, thoughtful, and thankful, and the Lord will do the rest," she said.

After school, I went to the interview with my friend. I was nervous and did not share a word in the car, but I knew that I could get this job. Things just seemed to be turning in my favor.

The company was called L & J of New England. It was a small, family-owned business that ran an assembly line of various metal parts, like nuts and bolts, used on large machinery. Back in those days, several well-known factories in Worcester employed blue-collar workers. L & J was similar in function, but on a much smaller scale.

When we arrived at the factory, I asked God to be with me and just went for it. I entered through the back, where the assembly line workers eyed me with resentment and suspicion, no doubt thinking that I was coming to take their jobs. The smell of burning oil and metal filled the entire open area. As I wound my way through the building, the factory slowly transformed into an office-like environment, with oversized desk lamps that brightened up shabby cubicles. We stopped at the only reception desk and told the lady I was there to apply for the open assembly line position advertised in the paper. She told us to wait in the executive conference room for someone to come see us.

There, I sat in a big fat leather spiral chair that made it almost impossible to get back up. A mahogany conference table filled the space, leaving little room to pass behind someone who might sit at it. After a few minutes, two middle-aged white men walked in. One was casually dressed with his oxford shirt hanging outside his pants and his hair disheveled on one side of his head; the other looked more conservative. Before they could say anything, I stumbled to my feet and thrust out my hand.

"Hi, my name is Doug Luffborough, and I would first like to thank you for granting me this interview," I said with confidence.

The men looked at each other and exchanged a small smile. "So why do you want to work here?" asked Don, the conservative one. He was an overweight mustached man with a Clark Kent haircut and a white shirt tucked into black slacks. His red tie was the only pop of color.

Without missing a beat, I replied, "Well, sir, I am currently working at the Worcester Public Library but looking for a different opportunity to work hard and make more money with more hours, and that is why I am here."

Surprised by my confidence, the other man, Duncan, said, "You seem like you're someone who is determined to make something of himself."

I looked both of them in the eye, feeling my own well with tears. "You have no idea, sir. I would be honored to work here and would be a great employee—someone you can count on to get the job done."

They looked at each other and then at me, and the other said, "Well, congratulations, young man. You got the job!"

Overwhelmed with joy, I stood up and threw my arms around each of them. "Thank you, sir! Thank you, sir! When would you like me to start?"

"Two weeks," they replied.

The next day, my stomach was all in knots. I did not want to tell Mrs. Quinn that I needed to leave. I had planned to tell her after my shift so I could say what I needed to say and then leave, but as soon as I saw her, I had to tell her right then and there.

"Mrs. Quinn," I said in a rush, "I really enjoyed working with you, but I have to give you my two weeks' notice. Unfortunately, I have to get a higher-paying job that will give me more hours to help my family, and considering the looming cutback, I have decided to resign from my position at the library."

Mrs. Quinn removed her glasses. "I understand, Douglas." She sounded like a mother talking to a son who was moving on to a new venture in his life. "It was great having you around and teaching you how to act in the library," she added with a smile. "Two weeks works fine. I will talk with the rest of the team about your departure, but we are cheering for you."

Unexpectedly, a lump rose to my throat. Like Coach Miller and Ms. G, Mrs. Quinn had been a great role model to me. These were people giving of themselves and genuinely considerate of others. *When I grow up and make something of myself,* I thought, *I'm going to reach back and help others like they did for me.* I wanted to mentor those who wanted mentorship, teaching them life lessons through my setbacks and failures.

Two weeks sped by, and I found myself walking out of the library for the last time as an employee. I knew it was time to go, but it was hard to leave a place and people that had been good to me. Because of Mrs. Quinn's leadership, everyone had welcomed me with open arms, taught me about the work, and made me feel as if I was a part of the family unit I did not have. At my going-away party, each staff member in our six-person group shared one thing they learned from me or would remember most about having me on the team. "I will always appreciate your willingness to go the extra mile and help out others," one uttered, and another added, "Yeah, even if the help you were giving them was not what they asked for!" We all laughed. But what moved me the most was a book that Mrs. Quinn gave me. A page was bookmarked, and when I turned to it, I found an inspirational message by Kenneth McFarland:

You are a wonderful and worthy person, appreciate that about yourself. No one has ever been, or ever will be, quite like you. You are an individual, an original, and all those things that make you uniquely you are deserving of love and praise.

It was just what I needed to hear, and almost thirty years later, I share the same message at every motivational speech I make as a way of giving back what was given to me and to remind others just how special they really are.

My first week at L & J of New England was an eye-opener. Besides my two other buddies from high school, everyone who worked with us was either a high school dropout or high school graduate but nearly twice our age. Our job was simple: work on the assembly line, taking various random pieces of scrap metal, putting them on a pallet, stacking them, and then wrapping them up to be shipped. It was a monotonous job that was easy once you got the hang of it, but you had to stay focused, because if you fell behind, production would stop, losing the company time and money. I quickly learned that you didn't want the machine to stop, because if it did, it meant that somebody had just lost their job. I fell in love with the job because I liked manual labor—I liked feeling like a man, which, to me, meant getting up early in the morning and taking responsibility by getting my hands dirty to make a living.

Becoming the overachiever I always wanted to be, I figured out how to remove items from the conveyor belt in a way that allowed the company to get two full pallets completed in the time that it used to take to get one done. It made the job more exciting, and I thought if I could figure out a way for the company to make more money, I could be first in line for a promotion. Unfortunately, most of the old-timers who worked there lived by the rule that "if it ain't broke, you don't have to fix it." Since I was innovating, they were not happy with me. And I did not understand why they wanted to do things in a mediocre fashion. Finally, a man in his forties approached me.

"Great," he said, waving a printout at me. "Thanks a lot, pal. You just made my workload double what it needs to be. Are you working for them or for us, dude?"

I gaped at him. The printout was confirmation to the management team that we could do more, do *better.* This man had been working for twenty years in the same position I was in. Why *wouldn't* he want to learn a more efficient way of doing things? But the anger in his eyes told me everything I needed to know: I was working with a group of people twice my age that had barely finished high school and had no drive, no motivation, and no interest in moving up or moving forward in life. I had seen this job as an opportunity to make more money and learn new skills, but I understood now that I would only be there for a season. I wanted to challenge myself to do new things with a spirit of excellence, and I decided (again) that college had to be my next step. I couldn't work in a factory all of my life. More importantly, I couldn't maintain a factory *mentality* about life. Education was the key.

I had been applying myself in school and doing great work in my classes. Teachers commented on how much more engaged I was in class or how they liked my initiative to take on new leadership roles. Their acknowledgment fueled me. I liked school now, because I could see myself growing academically and contributing more to classroom conversations. I knew where I wanted to be in the future. However, even as a high school senior, I still struggled to read aloud in class.

One time in English, everyone took a turn reading a full page of Shakespeare. As the first row took their turns, I read along silently to build up my confidence. But as they moved to my row, I started biting my nails, bouncing one leg up and down under my desk, and sweating as if I had just worked out. That self-doubting voice in my head said to me, *You are going to mess up, and the other students are going to laugh at you.*

I took out a handkerchief and wiped my forehead. The negative voice was getting louder. *The teacher is going to embarrass you like in third grade. You don't want them to hear you stutter, do you?*

Wanting the negative voice to go away, I threw my hand up as if it were an emergency. "May I please go to the bathroom?" I gasped. "It's important!"

Seeing the sweat now dripping from my face and my leg shaking uncontrollably, my teacher let me leave the class. The minute I was outside, my anxiety left. I decided the longer I was out of the classroom, the safer I would be, so I went to the bathroom on the other side of the school. Along the way, I silently berated myself. *What's wrong with you? Why, after ten years, is that experience of being called in front of the class to read out loud still so fresh in your mind? Why can't you just get over it?*

I locked myself in a bathroom stall and sat on the toilet with my pants on and my hands on both sides of my head, trying to collect my thoughts. Two minutes turned to twenty. I knew that I needed to face my fear of reading in public. I could not continue to run from this phobia.

As I walked back to the classroom, my anxiety mounted again. I peered through the window to see if my row had completed reading, and to my relief, students were reading in the next row. "Thank God," I said out loud before opening the door and returning to my seat. Then, over the intercom, the principal interrupted the class and asked if I could be excused to come down to the office. My mind raced, anxiety at an all-time high, and I thought I was going to pass out. *What did I do now?* I thought. *Did someone see me wandering the halls when I should have been in class? Does the school now have a problem with me living outside its boundary area, homeless and in a motel? Whatever the case,* I thought, *this is not going to be good.*

In the office, the secretary took one look at me and said, "Just go on back. The principal would like to speak with you."

I felt as though I was walking in to a firing squad. But when I opened the door, the principal stood up with a big smile. "Congratulations, young man. Your mother just had her baby! She wants you and your brother to go see her right after school."

I dropped onto one of the chairs across her desk. I was happy for my mom, but as I looked out the window, I wondered, *What's going to happen now? How are we going to make it on the streets, in a motel, or staying with friends now that we have a newborn in the family?*

When school ended, my brother and I walked together to the hospital, which was on the same road as the motel. By then, I was just eager to make sure my mother and the baby were okay.

"Come on, Darrell, hurry up," I said, pulling on his arm.

"I still can't believe Ma had another baby!" Darrell replied as he picked up his pace. The excitement in his voice matched my own, even if mine was tempered by fear.

At the hospital, we rushed upstairs to the maternity ward to find our mother's room. I got more nervous the closer we got. What if something had gone wrong and no one had told us? As I opened the door, I saw my mother sleeping. Right next to her, in a portable hospital crib, a tiny little baby also slept, tightly swaddled. Since we had little family, the room was sterile and dressed with just standard hospital fixings. Darrell and I did not have money to brighten the space with flowers, plants, or balloons, but we lit it up as much as we could with our presence.

I walked up to the bed, putting my hand on my mother's shoulder. "Hey, Ma, it's me, Douglas. How are you feeling?"

Her eyelids lifted heavily before lowering again. "Tired," she managed. "Just tired."

"Well, Darrell, and I are here, and we want you to get some rest," I said.

As my mother slept, Darrell and I peered into the crib with big eyes and curious spirits. Our little sister was wrapped up in a pink blanket that my mother had purchased just before giving birth. The words my mother had spoken—"Tired, just tired"—resonated with me. They seemed to describe more than just her experience giving birth. The way she had to live her life, working hard day after day and struggling to make ends meet . . . I thought if she was tired before, the demands of a newborn just might send her overboard. I realized that I needed to help her out more, not just with my new sister, Danielle, but also with all my siblings. I needed to be more of a father figure to them, even though I lacked a fatherly example in my own life.

With a sigh, my mother turned over and seemed to come around. She smiled warmly. "It is so great to see both of you," she said. "Now, I lost a lot of blood during my delivery and will need to stay in the hospital for the next couple of days. I need you both to take the money in my pocketbook and pay off the bill for the motel room. Pack our things, and then I will need you guys to stay with one of your friends for a while until I figure out what we are going to do next."

With her words, the roller coaster ride I had been on crested at its peak. On our creaky seat, we were just moments away from taking off faster than ever before.

"What about Derrick?" I asked. "Where will he stay once we check out of the motel?"

Reluctantly, Mom said, "When I knew I was getting close to having Danielle, I called Joe. I asked him to take care of Derrick until I could get out of the hospital. I need you to stay at the motel tonight—Joe will come by with Derrick to pick up our belongings and take them to his new place. I need you to hurry before it gets too late so you can also call one of your friends and see if you can stay with them for a while after school tomorrow."

I was embarrassed to have to call one of my friends, but what other choice did I have? I just needed to follow Mom's instructions. My brother and I kissed and hugged her and our new sister and headed to the motel.

When we got there, I went to the main office to pay and let them know that it would be our last night. Soon after we returned to the room, there was a knock on the door. I looked out the peephole to see Joe, with Derrick beside him. This was the first time I had seen Joe since the fight that had led us to the streets and the motel we'd called home for several weeks. Warily, I pulled the door open.

"Your mother asked me to take some of your belongings and Derrick's stuff," Joe declared. "I can't stay long, so get the stuff together so we can go."

I wondered why he needed to take more than Derrick's things, but I wanted to have as little conversation with him as possible. Joe seemed to feel the same. He stood on the balcony, smoking a cigarette and watching cars drive by on the two-lane highway while my brothers and I packed up as much as we could. There was little conversation between the three of us as we shoved our belongings into trash bags and the few suitcases we had. It was ironic that the last time we had done this was under the pressure of the police at Joe's demand that we "get out," and now we were doing it to return his biological son, Derrick, to his house.

We finished packing and helped load Joe's car while he sat there without helping us. I did not want Derrick to go with Joe. I felt I could do a better job fathering him than Joe. If he'd never stepped up to the role of father in the entire time I had known him, why would he be motivated to do it now? As Derrick got into the car, I looked into his eyes and wanted to grab him in a tight hug. He was just going into middle school and seemed caught in the middle of wanting to be with his father while also wondering whether the life we were living was normal or not. It was so frustrating to me that there was very little I could do to help. I needed to believe, as the homeless man by the overpass shared with me, that I might not have a place to call home, but I still had hope. And it was that hope that kept me going.

That night, when Darrell and I were the only ones left in the motel, I called one of my friends. My palms were sweaty. "Hey, man, what you doing?" I asked. "This is Doug, and I wanted to ask you something. I'm not sure if you know, but my family has been having some tough times . . . Can I stay with you and your family for a couple of weeks?"

"Why?" John laughed. "What did you do this time?"

"Nothing!" I said. "Look, I have been staying in a motel or on the streets because my family is homeless right now. My mom just had a new baby, will be in the hospital a while longer, and needs me to stay somewhere else for the time being. Can I crash at your house?"

The long silence that followed told me my friend was hesitant to have me, but I had no one else to ask.

"Let me ask my parents," he said finally. "I'll let you know tomorrow at school."

"Thanks, man," I said, my shoulders slumping with relief that he was at least going to ask. "I really do appreciate it."

As I put my head on the motel pillow for the last time, I was thankful that at least we were in a room and not on the streets.

In the morning, Darrell and I awoke, grabbed our backpacks, and left the motel for the last time. Neither of us knew for sure where we would sleep that night, but I was relieved that we were leaving that place—a place that shouted that my family lived in shambles, we were homeless, and we had no father figure to guide us.

Once we got to school, I searched for my friend to ask him what his parents had said.

"Yeah," he said, "if you need a place to stay, you can crash in our basement for a while, but eventually they will need to charge you rent."

I was still working at the factory and knew that I could contribute something, so I was excited. Even though it was not my home, it was *a* home, at least.

Days turned to weeks and weeks to months, and one night I overheard my friend's mother talking to him about me. "I feel bad for Douglas! Look at him sleeping downstairs in our basement. That boy really has no one in his corner. I want you to watch him, because since he does not have a lot, I don't want him stealing from this house, you hear me?"

Stealing! I thought. *I may be poor, but I'm not a thief.* That night, I packed up my belongings and left.

I stayed out on the streets for a couple of nights, sleeping at the park and beneath freeway underpasses. In the mornings, I showered at school. Other folks let me stay on their couch for a night or two at a time over the next few weeks. Darrell was doing the same. Rarely did we sleep in the same place. My mom knew little about what was happening and just wanted desperately for all of us to be together again.

One day, she met Darrell and me after school. She held Danielle, and her eyes were tired but determined. "Douglas, Darrell," she said, "we have been staying with Joe since I got out of the hospital."

She went on to explain that Joe had moved out of the old three-bedroom apartment and downsized to a one-bedroom on the south side of Worcester. I was speechless. How could she? How could he? How could they live together after everything that had gone down over my mother's unexpected pregnancy?

"Listen, Douglas," my mother said, "now that Danielle is born, I can apply for section 8, and we can get our own place away from Joe. But right now he is the only help I have, so I need you and Darrell to come with us."

Like a defeated warrior, my head sank and my body slumped as I raised my white flag of surrender and returned to Joe's world.

Chapter 12

Dreams Do Come True

All our dreams can come true, if we have the courage to pursue them.

—Walt Disney

Joe's one-bedroom was in the Washington Heights complex off Mill Street, and Mom narrated the route so we would know what buses to take after school. The smoke from the bus exhaust burned our faces as we stepped off, and we covered our eyes and coughed. When the smoke disappeared, my mother—cradling my newborn sister—and my brother Darrell and I stood at the bottom of the hill preparing to climb back into Joe's crazy world that just several months earlier we had been forced to leave. As we hiked uphill, I couldn't help thinking that this was just what my life had always been like: an uphill battle of survival. I followed behind my mother, dreading each step and painfully reliving the last physical altercation I had with Joe, as well as his manipulative and abusive behavior. I wondered if I would be safe moving back in with him. I was both resentful of him and afraid of his unpredictable, violent streak. I felt like it would have been better to stay on the streets, far away from him.

To add insult to injury, Joe's apartment was located on the second floor. Worn apartment doors lined both sides of the hallway, resembling a cheap motel. Unattended babies in diapers crawled across the dirty floors, and the thin walls would make it almost impossible not to hear the personal and often graphic conversations happening all around us. I thought, *We were better off in the motel with the peace and quiet. At least there, we wouldn't have to see Joe.* I felt that I had been there and done that, and I was sick and tired of feeling so much uncertainty and fear that he would hurt my mother or us again.

As we opened the door, the smell of Joe's food cooking on the stove curdled my stomach, and I decided I couldn't eat that night. Joe did not say a single word to me. The look on his face said, *See? You need me. You can't do anything without me.*

That night, we slept on the living room carpet without blankets while Joe rested by himself in his own room in his queen-sized bed. All night, I thought about where I could go or what other friends might let me stay with them until something else opened up, but I felt myself again losing hope and faith that living a normal life was possible.

After that, I again put my focus on school, work, and extracurricular activities, spending very little time at Joe's place. I would wake up, dress quickly for school, and stay there all day. Afterwards, I would play a sport or hang out with friends and study. I returned to Joe's only to wash up and go to sleep, and my conversations with him were limited to only yes/no responses.

A month or two went by, and then the news we had all been waiting for arrived. The letter was addressed to my mother.

Dear Mrs. Luffborough-Mensah, your application to receive section 8 housing has been approved.

There was more to the letter, but the first line was the important part. It was the beginning of regaining my life and keeping our family together under one roof, in our own place, with my own room. It was all I wanted.

I remember taking what little we had out of Joe's apartment. He was cooking in the kitchen, ignoring the fact that we were in the living room packing our belongings. When we were finished, no one said anything. A horn beeped outside: the cab my mother had called to take us to our new home. There were no goodbyes to Joe, and he didn't even turn his head away from the stove to see us off. But for a moment, as I made my way to the front door, our eyes locked. The look on his face when I was leaving was exactly the same as when we arrived: *You know you need me. You can't do anything without me.* I shook my head, saying to myself as I walked out the door, *I'm done with you. I hope I never ever see you again. Lord knows, if I become a father, I will never follow your example.*

No one should ever do what you did to me and my siblings.

When we walked into our own apartment, the first thing I did was go into my room and scream internally, *YES!* My room was an offshoot from the living room and was medium-sized with neutral wallpaper covering every wall. The smell of clean carpets thrilled me; there was no trace of the footprints of past residents. The room was mine, all mine, and I knew that my life would begin to turn around. We had a stable place to live now—one with no violence within its walls. A place of peace, a place of healing, and a place of reconciliation—that's what our new apartment represented to me. We had very little furniture, but I had a roof over my head, our family intact and back together, and one last shot to get into college.

Throughout my junior and senior years of high school, I was heavily involved in extracurricular activities, including being a peer educator/mentor to middle school students, serving as the president of the school choir, and working with and for Ms. G. I was on the student council with my brother Darrell, I played church basketball and won the state championship, I maintained my part-time job at the factory, and I was voted Best Personality in my graduating class. My grades improved from Cs to Bs to As, and my growth accelerated once we had more stable housing. The only thing missing was support and an endorsement from my guidance counselor to help me apply to college. I was determined to be accepted, and I wrote down all the reasons I felt he should work with me: academic standing, extracurricular activities, work, my struggles at home, and how all of this prepared me for any college campus. Through adversity, I had proven my own resiliency. Nothing could be as bad as living on the streets. Nothing could be worse than growing up in a home filled with numbing, angered silence, isolation, resentment, rage, and violence.

College acceptance was the one mission that I had not yet accomplished. All I needed was my guidance counselor to believe in me like he believed in all the other students who, like me, desired to leave Worcester and go to college. He had already discouraged me from applying to college once. "Not college material," he said. I wanted to go back to him again, but this time with my list of reasons why I *was* college material. I felt that once he knew I was no longer homeless, that I was still working, getting mostly As and Bs, and that I was involved with many extracurricular activities, he would reconsider his point of view.

The day came when I had to petition his approval. When I arrived at school, I went into the office to see if I could meet with him. He told me that he was busy most of the day but that he could meet with me after school for fifteen or twenty minutes. Eager to know sooner than later if he would support me, I confirmed the time he gave me and contacted work to let them know that I would be half an hour late.

As the last bell of the day rang, I was anxious to talk to Mr. Kent. My hands were clammy in anticipation of my meeting with the person I thought was the gatekeeper to my college future. In my mind, he was the only one shutting the cast-iron doors on my college aspirations.

In the past, every time I made my way to his office, he was meeting with other students. The same was true this time. Despite my having an appointment, he still put me off. However, I put caution to the wind and pushed my way into his office at the first opportunity.

"Mr. Kent, I know that you are really busy," I started, "but I have been working on bringing up my grades, I'm involved with many extracurricular activities both in school and outside of school, and I'm still working. The next step for me is college, and I really need your support to help me through the process." I said my piece in a clear and succinct manner.

I will never forget the words that followed.

"Doug," Mr. Kent said, "you are a good kid. But some kids are just not cut out for college, and you're one of them. Stop talking to me about college, and just be happy where you are. You really have come a long way, but I don't think you're college material."

College material? Really, what does college material look like? I wondered, standing in front of him holding the work I had prepared. I was speechless as I ruminated on his words. How could he make such a judgment without even reviewing the material I had brought? Without even hearing me out? A swell of frustration and devastation tightened my chest. I was crushed and did not know where to turn. Defeated again, I put my head down and walked out of his office, not wanting to try anymore.

When I went home that night, I shared the story with my mother; she said she would call the school and talk with somebody about it. The next day, true to her word, she came to school to meet with another guidance counselor. After hearing what had transpired, he gave my mother a business card and said, "It is clear to me that the other counselor will not help you, but I have an external resource that could. Her name is Pam Boisvert, and she runs an Educational Opportunity Center (EOC) Trio program for low-income, first-generation college students. Perhaps she can help your son out." He said this to her with uncertainty, but it was another option for me to try.

My mother called the number on the card that same day to schedule an appointment for us. Our meeting was at the end of the week, and I took everything I had prepared for my guidance counselor with me. I was so concerned and worried that she would say the same thing my guidance counselor had said to me, that I was not college material, and I vowed to do everything I could to prove my case. I was the only advocate I had, and I was desperate for a *yes*.

When we arrived at Pam's office off Main Street in the clean business district of downtown Worcester, I was struck by the college pennants hanging on the walls. They were visual confirmation that this center could help kids like me get into college. My mom asked for Pam, and out walked a well-dressed, conservative-looking middle-aged white woman. We went into her office, where she shared what she did as an EOC counselor and reviewed the information that my mother had filled out. She was friendly yet professional, and wanted to know more about my family, my story, and me. After the interview, she told us that we qualified for the program.

"So what does that mean?" I asked eagerly.

"It means that I will help you get into college!" She beamed, sensing the mounting nerves between my mother and me. I nearly fainted when I heard those words. I hadn't even applied to college yet, and the joy I felt in that moment was unmatched by anything in my life. I felt as if the proverbial eight-hundred-pound gorilla had finally jumped off my back.

"I want you to know that I am committed to doing whatever I have to do to make sure I get admitted to college," I said, an ear-splitting smile painted on my face. With great enthusiasm, I ran through my litany of accomplishments, both inside and outside of school, to add to the college application process. I was talking faster than I ever had, and was intent on covering it all.

Pam held her hands up in mock-defense. "Hold on, we're just getting started. You will have plenty of time to make your case. First, let's put together a plan for what we need to get accomplished over the next several months."

I laughed, and my mother calmed me down by saying, "Douglas, Pam is going to help us. She believes in us, so trust the process and let her do her job."

I nodded in agreement, saying to myself, *Yes, Pam . . . do your job, do your job, do your job, and help me get into college!* My excitement was uncontainable. As we wrapped up our first meeting, Pam gave me a homework assignment, which was to create a list of colleges that I wanted to attend. I was encouraged to put them into three categories: safety schools, good schools, and dream schools. We would discuss each of them the next time we met.

That night, I went home to start my research. For the next couple of days, I was obsessed with my search and talked incessantly to other students about it, asking adults if they were college graduates and where they went to college, and I watched several television shows about university life. The week before our next meeting passed quickly, and by then, I had neatly written out the list of schools I wanted to focus on. My safety school was University of Bridgeport, which is no longer in existence; my good schools were Fairfield University and University of Hartford; and my dream schools were UMASS Amherst and Northeastern University. Even the safety school seemed like a dream school considering everything I had been through. Regardless of where I attended, I wanted to leave Worcester and one day come back as a contributing member of society, giving back to other youth and families that were going through some of the same life challenges I had experienced.

I went by myself to my next meeting with Pam, because I felt that my mother had taken me as far as she could and that I needed to take control of my own future. It was time for me to break new ground as the first member of my family to attend college.

The meetings with Pam were all very productive, and we treated the application process as though it was a second job, working on deliverables on a daily basis with laser-like focus. Pam helped me fill out each college application, helped me craft my personal statement of purpose, helped me fill out my financial aid application, and helped me research and apply for scholarships that I was eligible to receive.

Each time I met with her, I could not get over how willing and open she was to helping me. The support Pam gave me was the fuel that got my ignition going and was such a contrast to the guidance counselor who tried to ice me out of a college future. It was clear to me as I worked with Pam that my guidance counselor had no interest in helping me, and I was glad that I did not let his advice become the final authority over my situation. My heart went out to other high school students who, one way or another, were told not to apply to college because they were not college material. Each day I went to school, I passed the main office and glanced into the guidance office. *Never again will I allow the voice of someone else to dictate what I will become in life,* I thought. *Never again!*

With Pam's help, I did everything I needed to do and completed the entire college application process. The EOC paid the application fees. Now it was out of my hands and up to the colleges. And God. I knew that whatever happened, I did what I needed to do. Just one month after getting off the streets as a homeless teen, I had applied to college. Something I thought was merely a dream was starting to come true.

Several months went by, and even though the process of applying to college was over, I continued my relationship with Pam because I had very few adults in my life who genuinely helped me and wanted me to succeed. I decided that I would try, come what may, to keep her in my life as a source of inspiration and motivation to continue to do my best in life.

During the spring of my senior year, students started getting letters from colleges regarding their acceptance or denial. The news came in one of two forms: regular-sized, light envelopes meant that you did not get in, while thick, heavy 8½ × 11 envelopes meant official college acceptance . . . You were a college student in the making. When I sent in my last application, I prayed every day for God to make a way for me to receive at least one of those giant, heavy envelopes.

Sometime toward the end of the month of March, I received my first large envelope from the University of Bridgeport. My mother put my mail on my bed, and when I saw the University of Bridgeport as the return address, I ripped open the letter and read:

Congratulations on your admittance to the University of Bridgeport.

I did not need to read the rest of the letter. I dropped the paper and fell to my knees. "Thank you, God," I shrieked out loud and buried my head in my pillow, crying tears of joy that all my hard work had paid off. I sat in my room for close to an hour, reading the letter over and over again. Eventually, I made my way back to my feet and out of my room to share the news with my family.

"Ma, I got into college. I can't believe it, but they want me, I *am* college material!"

My mother, beaming with joy, cheered and jumped up and down, putting her fists in the air. "Yes, God is so good!" she shouted.

Later that week, the next acceptance letter came from Fairfield University, then the University of Hartford, and then the University of Massachusetts Amherst. My last acceptance letter was from Northeastern University. I had gotten into all five schools I applied to. Not bad for being told that I was not college material. By the time I read the Northeastern letter, I was face down on the ground, thanking God for making possible what had seemed to me to be the impossible. Pam Boisvert was an angel sent down from heaven specifically to be my bridge from homelessness to college in less than six months.

Over the next few months, I did my research and tried to figure out the best college for me, considering all the factors: financial aid, scholarship awards, location, and the culture of each college campus. Because of a lack of finances and because my mother did not have a car, going to visit all of the colleges was out of the question, but I was able to visit the University of Bridgeport, my safety school. My mother asked her good friend, Mrs. Humphrey, to lend me her car so that I could drive down to Connecticut—just for the day—to visit the school. She said yes, and before I knew it, mom and I were on our way for my first college visit.

The entire ride down, my mom beamed with joy. "My boy's going to college! Douglas, I am so proud of you. You stayed focused on school, and now you are on your way to a better life by getting into college. Boy, God is so good!" After she said some iteration of this a number of times, she got so wrapped up in what she was saying, it was as though she were motivating herself as well as me. She'd alternate her excitement with verbal talks with Jesus and start laughing and crying, and sometimes at the same time. But I knew. I knew Ma was grateful for the journey, and that somehow, some way, we made it. I even held on to the steering wheel harder, as if I were pinching myself, wondering if everything we were experiencing was merely a dream. But it was reality . . . I was going to college.

The trip to Bridgeport was unscheduled, and we did not have any formal meetings with folks at the university. We walked around and observed other students, professors, and college administrators. We touched the brick and mortar, sat in the cafeteria, and strolled through the quad. By the end of the day, we were able to say we had *been there and done that.*

After we returned home that evening, I wanted so badly to visit other schools, but logistically it was not an option because of a lack of transportation. My top schools were UMASS Amherst and Northeastern University. UMASS seemed like a great school, but many of my classmates felt that it was a party school, and that factor alone might make it difficult for me to focus on my studies.

Northeastern, on the other hand, was known for its Cooperative Education Program, or Co-op, which allows students to work in a career within their major field of study for a three- or six-month interval, and then return to the classroom setting for three or six months, a process that continues for their entire five years at the school. I knew that gaining work experience within my major before I graduated was a plus, and not many colleges had this type of program. I did not want to be added to the list of college graduates who were part of the growing unemployment line in this country. The Co-op program gave me a foot in the door, an edge over other college students who had no work experience. Of the five colleges, Northeastern was the only university that ran commercials on television, and they were done professionally. I used to sit at the television and say, "One day that will be me!"

Given that I seldom left Worcester and the school was located one hour east in Boston, it seemed like a world away. But it was close enough not to matter, and it felt like the right choice.

A few months before high school graduation, I received several scholarships and qualified for a full financial aid award because of my living situation. I had enough money between scholarships, financial aid, and loans to go to my first college of choice—Northeastern University. One of the proudest moments in my life was putting on my cap and gown as I got ready for my high school graduation that hot June day. I reflected that just months before, I was on the streets without a place to stay, I was told that I was not college material, but I was now graduating from high school with a guaranteed spot as a freshman at Northeastern University, *and* with full financial aid. I was so relieved. All my life, financial barriers kept me from doing what I always wanted to do, but now they were no longer going to hold me back.

The student commencement speaker for my high school graduating class delivered a very moving and powerful speech about Michael Jackson's "Man in the Mirror" song, and spoke of how the lyrics reflected our journey towards graduating from high school. As my name was called, the announcer said, "Next we have Douglas Edward Luffborough III, who will be attending Northeastern

University in the fall." Once he said those words, chills went down my spine. I walked to center stage, looked into that mirror, and saw a young man who did not let his setbacks in life paralyze his aspiration to one day go to college—and not just any college, but his dream school. It was the school I had dreamed about while in the motel, the dream so real to me that I could taste it.

Chapter 13

Northeastern—My Dream School

A college degree means something.
It means more than the piece of paper you receive
at graduation. It represents accomplishment,
knowledge, and the pursuit of lifelong learning.

—Doug Luffborough

During the summer after graduation, I spent a lot of time in my room, daydreaming and trying to visualize what my college experience would be like, preparing for my departure from the familiar into the unknown. I was always paranoid that I forgot a step in the process or that I missed my financial aid deadline and would not be able to go to college. I spent countless hours listening to Tracy Chapman, Billy Joel, James Taylor, and Elton John, trying to build a new persona as an incoming college freshman. I no longer wanted to be the gang-banging, homeless teen that was my identity for most of high school. I remember sitting down to eat with the family one time. My mother had come home from the store with a flannel, checkered, collared Dickies shirt.

"Ma, I'm in college now, and I can't be seen in that. I need to dress like a college student. I need more polo shirts and oxfords so I look the part!" I even started wearing school boys, which are big, plain, non-prescription glasses that I felt made me look smarter and more sophisticated. I had 20/20 vision, but I had a strong desire to see myself both literally and metaphorically through a new set of lenses. I was dedicated to representing myself as having grown beyond the choices in my past, both internally and externally, and I wanted others to see that, too.

In order to have money for my transition into college and be able to pay for my books, I decided I needed a summer job. I had received financial aid and loans, and with the exception of meals and books, my tuition and boarding was paid for my entire freshman year. Through a friend of a friend, I found the best summer job an eighteen-year-old could have: working for Frito-Lay as a delivery driver. I was by far the youngest employee they had on staff. I received $19 per hour, which was more than two times what I was used to making, and I worked anywhere from twenty to thirty hours per week. I even had my own truck and route to service. However, I did have one little problem: the truck was a stick shift, and I had never learned how to drive one.

I was given the keys from my manager, and when I opened the truck, the large stick shift stood vertically as if to say: "Do you think you can handle this? You got to get past me first before you'll be successful with this job."

My jaw dropped to the ground. I told my manager that I had never driven a stick shift before but that I would be willing to learn. He laughed and took me out back to practice. I appreciated the fact that he gave me a chance, and boy, was I a fast learner . . . I had no other alternative if I wanted money for school. When people have no other option, they find a way to make things work.

For almost an hour, I started and stalled a twenty-two-foot Frito-Lay white delivery truck until I started to get the hang of it. Then the facility was closing, so they wanted me to take it home for the night because we started our shifts at six every morning. Just before leaving, I called everyone I could think of who knew how to drive a stick shift and asked them if they would drive the truck home for me the first night and help me practice some more in a nearby parking lot. A buddy of mine, Bob, was happy to help, and met me in front of the Frito-Lay facility. Within a few minutes, we found a parking lot with a flat surface. Right away, Bob put the truck in neutral.

"Okay, Doug, the truck is in neutral. Put your left foot on the clutch and your right foot on the break. Now, put the truck in first gear. Now, slowly take your right foot off the break and over to the gas while at the same time taking your left foot off the clutch."

As I took my foot off the clutch, the car started to roll backwards and I panicked, taking my foot off the clutch too fast and stalling the truck. "Wow. I need to get this!" I laughed nervously as I started again. This process continued for close to thirty minutes, and by the end of the half hour, I started to get the hang of it.

When the session was over and I was satisfied with my progress, Bob said, "Hey, why don't you just drive home from here."

Still feeling the stage fright, I said, "No that's good for tonight. How about you drive it home?" I totally wimped out and was still too intimidated to try it myself, but I knew in the morning I would be all on my own. Right when I got home, I stood at the foot of the stairs and called up to my mother to have her come out back and see the truck. The vehicle was twenty-two feet long. It was painted white, and had a picture of a Lay's potato chip bag on both sides. I even thought if times got tough again, I could actually live inside it.

My mother walked outside. "Lord, have mercy! How in the world did you drive this thing, Douglas?"

"I know, right!" I responded. "But I think I got the hang of it, Ma. Let me give you a ride around the corner." With a stunned look still plastered on her face, she assumed the co-pilot position, and we were off around the block.

"I'm really proud of you, Douglas. You have come so far and are truly working your way to college," Mom said, in between her frequent calls out to Jesus as she gripped the dashboard when I accidentally lurched the truck forward.

"I need to be at work early, Ma, and need to leave the house around five o'clock every morning, so, do you think you can wake me up around four thirty so I can be on time?"

"I can wake you up at four if you like, because you will not be late for this job," she said with confidence. And, like the sound of a rooster at the crack of dawn, my mother woke me up the next morning at the time I had requested, and to help set me up for the day, she cooked me breakfast and ironed my clothes for my first day of work. The dress code—a collared shirt with khaki pants—was the same attire she had me wear for my interviews at the library and the factory. I felt more than ready.

My first day went very well; I made it safely to and from work, driving that stick shift like a man on a mission. We worked hard and I loved it. From one store to the next, we made sure that our customers were happy and satisfied. In the quiet space of the driver's cab, while buckling my seat belt, or pulling out the map to orient myself to the route, I realized that most of the other drivers were twice my age, and none of them had college degrees. Even so, they put the H in hustle. Each morning when I got to the warehouse, the guys were already busy loading their trucks. They had their processes down: check in with the manager on shift, print orders, and run back and forth from the warehouse to the truck, loading boxes as fast as possible to beat the morning traffic. Toward the end of the summer, all I did was eat, drink, and sleep Frito-Lay. Besides taking off the side-view mirror, backing into a parked truck while unloading, and one or two small fender benders, the truck and I were both still intact at the end of August. I left the job with several thousand dollars that would help me throughout the school year; but more importantly, that summer, I learned the value of a hard day's work for a good day's pay . . . and it felt right.

On Monday, September 26, 1988, I woke up extra early because the day had finally come: I was officially moving out of my home and into my college residence hall. My mother prearranged for me to drive her friend's car up to Northeastern with all of my belongings, since we did not have our own car. I was eager to pack and get on the road because I did not want to be the last student checking in after everyone else had settled in. The drive from Worcester up the Mass Pike was surreal. Mom and I went back and forth, sharing stories and the excitement that I was going to college. Due to overcrowding, I was assigned to a residence hall on the campus of Wentworth University, just up the street from Northeastern. As we drove up to the building, I was overwhelmed by the chaos of U-Haul trucks and parents getting their kids situated.

"Hi, my name is Doug Luffborough and I'm here to check in," I said to the resident director, who wore a bright red Northeastern University logo shirt.

"Yes, here you are," he said with a smile as he handed me a packet full of papers and some miscellaneous other items. "This is your ID, and the keys to the front door and to your room. Folks are getting settled right now, and then we have a meeting this evening around six as your official welcome."

I smiled at my mom and held my new college ID to my face as if to say, "I know this guy!" My mother laughed in relief that I had made it, that *we* had made it.

"I'm so proud of you, Douglas. Wait until your brothers and sister see that . . . so impressive," Mom said as she looked into my eyes. The other students were excited and were showing off their IDs, as well. I put the keys on the Northeastern key chain I had purchased at the bookstore. But no key could lock away the new feeling I had that, both literally and figuratively, I was holding the keys to my own place.

As Ma and I made our way to my new room, I was in awe. This was it. I was now a college student. A few months prior, I had been homeless . . . but not anymore. I opened the door to my room. One side of it had already been prepared, so I went to the side that was still bare. Mom started doing what she did best: cleaning my room as if it was a house on her regular route.

"Ma, stop! You don't have to clean the room." I cleared my throat. "It's already clean."

Ignoring my request, she started making my bed and putting my clothes in the dresser and closet. While Ma was still hanging things in my closet, a punk-rocker guy, about my age, with blonde hair, a medium build, and black gloves on, walked into the room. Both Ma and I looked at each other as if to say *this is not going to be good*. However, his demeanor was friendly and inviting as he threw his bags on his side of the room, put out his hand and said, "What's up, dude. My name is Tom, and it looks like I'm going to be your new roommate." His carefree and open approach to being my roommate surprised me, but I accepted him as he was and went back to unpacking.

"Where are you from?" I asked Tom.

"Plymouth . . . you know? Plymouth Rock!"

Shaking my head, I said, "Cool . . . I'm from Worcester. You know, Woosta." We both burst into laughter, which broke the ice. Once Ma and I finished, we left right away. We had to drive back to Worcester to return the borrowed car, and I still had to take a bus back to school in time for my six o'clock orientation meeting.

The drive back home to Worcester was quiet. "Your roommate seems okay," Ma said.

"Yep, he seems cool." I replied. As we drove on the freeway, I thought about the months and weeks leading up to this day. My mother seemed to be doing the same thing, just staring out the window, admiring the vibrant New England fall foliage.

"You okay, Ma?" I asked to break the silence.

"Yes baby, just taking it all in, just taking it all in. I'm just so proud of you, Douglas."

As if on cue, after that, songs that we both liked to sing came on the radio, and we sang and harmonized the rest of the way back to Worcester. My heart swelled in moments of bittersweetness. We both worked so hard to get here, and this was a time of transition, joy, and growth. We shared only one or two sentences the rest of the way back, but we didn't need to exchange much more than song. Once we returned to Worcester, I picked up Mrs. Humphrey and thanked her for letting me use her car. She drove me immediately back to the bus station.

Outside the terminal, I hugged my mom and swallowed back the feelings as I told her I would see her during the Thanksgiving break, and I would call her when I made it back to campus. On the bus, I wept both tears of joy and tears of sorrow for the journey I had taken to get to this point in my life. It was a surreal experience to know that I was heading back to my room on a college campus and that, despite the obstacles before me, I had made it this far.

When I got back to the residence hall, I had less than two hours to rest before the orientation meeting. Tom stood on the opposite wall, at the open window.

"What are you doing?" I asked.

"I'm smoking some bud out of this soda can. Do you want some?"

"What . . . *what* are you smoking?" I fired back.

"Weed, my man, I'm smoking some good weed," he said, with his head tilted back in bliss.

I jumped to my feet and had to fight from raising my voice. "Dude, you must be crazy. This is our first night, and already you are breaking the rules and smoking pot. You have no idea what it took for me to get here, and I will be damned if I get kicked out because of your sorry, drug-addicted ass. Put that shit away now, or I will put it away for you."

Tom held his hands up in defense, a look of confusion on his face. "Chill out, dude. I got you. I won't smoke with you in the room . . . I just like it, you know. It helps me relax," he persisted. Even as he stood there, trying to put me at ease, I was angry. I left the room to hang out in the common area with other students until our meeting.

In the common area, many of the other guys on my floor were casually meeting each other, and I easily slipped into several conversations about where folks where from and why they chose Northeastern. At six o'clock sharp, the orientation meeting started. Dave, the resident advisor, had a larger-than-average build and an obviously kind and gentle spirit.

"Well, hello guys! My name is Dave Peters, and I want to welcome you to your first college experience at Northeastern University—home of the Huskies!" In unison, everyone cheered and high-fived one another, and as chills went down my spine, it settled in that I was accepted here and more so, that I *deserved* to be here. I had earned it.

Dave continued. "I want to make sure that you have a great experience here, but first, I have to go over some important rules that you all need to be mindful of." His voice was serious and steady. "I want to make it clear that you are here to get a college education and one non-negotiable is that this is a drug-free residence hall. If you get caught with alcohol and/or drugs in your room, your college experience, as you know it, will be over."

As I heard the word *over,* in my mind's eye, I heard the loud bang of prison doors closing behind me. I lifted my head and saw Tom across the room, red faced and half-baked. The look on his face conveyed confidence that masked his guilt, and I looked around the room and saw other similar expressions of guilt on people's faces. I suddenly felt as if all these incoming freshmen thought going to college was going to be a big pot-fest and that not many planned on taking it as seriously as I did. I felt my blood heating up with flashbacks of homelessness and hearing that I was not college material. I thought to myself, *I'm not covering for Tom, some guy I met less than ten hours ago, at the expense of getting kicked out of college. This dude must be crazy. My mother would kill me . . . and* I *would kill* myself, *for that matter.*

The rest of the meeting was a blur to me, and I was hell-bent that I needed to talk with Dave as soon as possible. I had to explain my situation to him . . . the only ass I was covering at this point was my own.

When the meeting ended, I could see Tom looking at me, wondering what I was going to do, but I decided to hang out with some of the other guys and get to know them to avoid Tom altogether. Around ten o'clock, I went back to my room. After I closed the door, Tom looked at me sternly. "Hey dude, you didn't say anything, did you?"

"No," I responded. "But, if you do it again, I'm out of here and will ask to be switched to a different room." He nodded his head in understanding, and we both went on with our business for the night. The next morning was the freshmen orientation with the president of the university, Mr. John Curry. I tried to wake Tom up, but he decided that it wasn't very important, so he slept in. As I strode down the hallway to make it to the meeting on time, I thought to myself, "This guy is a bad example for me, and he will be lucky to make it through his first year if he keeps it up."

Dave told all of us that he would take us down to the auditorium if we wanted to go with him. I walked right next to him, taking it all in like a little boy getting his first bike for Christmas from Santa Claus.

What seemed like thousands of bouncing and eager college freshmen filled the traditional auditorium with excitement as if we were attending a concert. The buzz of a new dawn filled the room, and President Curry came to the podium to make his opening remarks.

"Let me be the first to welcome you to Northeastern University!" The auditorium, full of freshmen, erupted in hoots and applause. When the excitement waned, he continued. "I want each of you to look to the person to your left and the person on your right. One of you will not make it through the next five years—and right here, right now, I want you to be one of the two that does make it!"

I sat there, feeling triumphant, thinking of my mother, Coach Miller, Ms. G, Mrs. Quinn, and Pam Boisvert. I looked into the eyes of the students flanked to my sides as if to say, "Sorry that you are not going to make it." President Curry's message was inspiring but also scared me because I knew he was speaking the truth. If I was going to make it, I had to treat going to college with the same discipline with which I treated my jobs at Frito-Lay, the factory, and the library.

After President Curry spoke, he introduced the next speaker as Maya Angelou. I thought, *Maya Angelou, wow, she's big-time. I wonder what she's going to say.* Exhibiting a stoic demeanor and confident gait, she took the stage, grabbed the microphone, looked out among the crowd, and opened her speech by singing. I don't remember the name of the song, but she sang a song that rocked the foundation of my core because the place from which she sang was all too familiar to me. It was a place of moving from despair to hope, from anxiety to peace, from hurting to healing, from fighting through barriers to overcoming obstacles, and from meaning-making to becoming. I tried my best to stop the tears from streaming down my face, but it was useless. The tone of her voice and the expressions on her face resonated so deeply within me in the same way I sang away my homelessness with my classmates in Ms. G's class. A student sitting next to me patted me on the back, and another leaned in and asked, "You okay, brother?" I nodded my head, because I knew I was going to be okay. I thoughtfully repeated my statement of purpose to myself. *I'm not going to be the one that doesn't make it. I have come too far to turn back now. I'm graduating from this school. This is where I belong. I am Northeastern University!*

After Ms. Angelou's speech, I was overflowing with enthusiasm for and commitment to my success than ever before; it was just what I needed to hear.

Later in the first week, I sat down with Dave and shared that I wanted to switch rooms. I told him that I suspected my roommate was using drugs, and I did not want to get in trouble for his drug use. I asked him in confidence to not say anything directly but to do a room inspection and see for himself. Dave understood, and had me talk to Jeff, another guy on the floor who happened to need a roommate. Jeff was a rich kid from Jersey who was born with a silver spoon in his mouth. At first, we got along well, but he, too, had a friendship with weed. He partied a lot and was a bad influence on me. Over time, I lowered my standards and started drinking in the residence halls—something that I was sure I had left behind.

As the quality of my schoolwork declined, I took refuge in joining the Northeastern chorus. I did not take it as a formal class and only received one semester credit; I took it because music was a love that I'd wanted to continue pursuing. Choir practice was once a week and was a great place to meet all kinds of eclectic people—nerds, alternatives, conservatives—it was a melting pot of unique personalities brought together by their love of classical music. All the years of playing the violin and singing in high school felt natural in college. I got along well with all the guys in the bass and tenor sections and found out that one of them was looking for a roommate at a different hall in the center of campus, and I knew it would be a better choice for me.

Again, I went to Dave. "I really love being here, but I think I need to find another roommate. I just don't have much in common with Jeff. I know of another student who lives in Speare Hall who sings in the chorus with me, and he needs a new roommate. Would you help me transfer to that residence hall to live with someone else?"

Dave looked at me with a kind smile and a face full of optimism. "Doug, you're a good kid, and all of my rooms are full . . . but I will call the resident director over there to see if we can make the change."

"Thank you! You know, ever since I met you, I've been impressed with your outlook on life and how you treat people," I added.

"No problem! That's what I'm here for!" he fired back. That would be my third roommate in four months, but I felt that I was finally getting to the place I needed to be.

I moved again, and Frank, a fair skinned, blue-eyed, blonde-haired guy who looked like he could have been in an L.L.Bean commercial was my next roommate. He was from a small town in Maine and was an all-around good guy who also loved singing. We had no problems rooming together, except that Frank liked to drink beer as well. We drank every weekend and sometimes on weekdays.

One evening, there was a knock on the door.

"Hi, my name is Chris Corso . . . but you can call me Corso." I recognized him as someone who lived a few rooms down the hall. "I am having a few guys over to my room later tonight and wanted to extend the invite to you guys." Corso was short and Italian, with a big spirit. He seemed like a little Napoleon who rose as a leader on my floor, only he was kind and friendly to everyone. He was in most of my classes, and we instantly connected with one another. I would later find out that he was from Attleboro, went to private school, listened to AC/DC, and was the captain of his high school cross-country team. We couldn't be more different, but we developed a very strong brotherly bond with one another that still exists to this day. I went to the majority of my classes, but they were all lecture-style, some with more than one hundred students in them, so it was hard for me to focus. I lacked the discipline necessary to study and complete the course readings. Corso and I partied every weekend, but he also was a great study partner. We definitely worked hard and played hard.

When the semester came to a close, I received a D+ in my Introduction to Business class. And as a business major, I was demoralized. My total GPA in my freshman year was a 2.0, and I was put on academic probation. Simply put, I got too comfortable with my social life and neglected my studies. That was the wake-up call I needed to get back on track, and I set a goal to raise my GPA each semester after that to a 4.0.

For the first year at Northeastern, all of the freshmen had to live on campus. But when I received my letter indicating that as an upperclassman, I would not get housing support, it was a gut-punch. I was sitting on a grassy slope outside of the library when I opened my mail, and even though the sun was shining and the sky was blue, I felt a dark cloud hovering too near. The letter also indicated that I wouldn't get the same type of financial aid package for my second year.

I went straight home and pulled out my address book to start making calls. I called three friends—two of them didn't answer, and the third said he wasn't coming back the following year. My anxiety level rose as I flipped through my contacts, trying to find someone, *anyone,* who could give me a place to stay. Then it dawned on me that I could ask Keith. We had gone to high school together, and he was also attending Northeastern. Keith and I were in the same homeroom class for four years during high school, and my mother was a housekeeper for his family.

Keith's off-campus apartment was small; he shared a two-bedroom unit with three other guys. He asked his roommates if I could crash on the floor in the bigger room. They agreed, so with a mattress on the floor, wedged between a bed and a study desk, I spent the start of my sophomore year grateful to have a roof—any roof—over my head. But the apartment was small, and even though I had a campus work-study job and the guys were nice, I knew the situation was only temporary.

One Saturday night, we all decided we were going to go out but that we'd start drinking at the house first. Drunk before the party left the house, I decided to go to sleep, but folks were coming in and out of our apartment as the party continued. As I lay there in bed with my face toward the wall, I heard my roommate say, "Doug, are you awake?" I didn't answer him, but I shut my eyes tight and willed myself to fall asleep in that moment. I couldn't. He whispered to someone again. "See, he's asleep. He won't hear us."

Knowing that my roommate had someone with him and not wanting to blow his chances of hooking up, I breathed quiet, shallow breaths and said nothing. For the next twenty minutes, I lay motionless with my eyes squeezed closed, listening to the moans and groans of my roommate and his date having sex. The sound of the headboard banging against the wall was enough to wake the neighbors next door. I had all sorts of thoughts running through my head, and I laughed at myself for being stuck in that situation, less than ten feet away from them. The incident was a glaring wake-up call that I needed to get my own place, where everyone's privacy would be respected and appreciated.

After that, I was on a mission to find alternative housing options. One day when I was in the student center, I found a posting on a corkboard that caught my eye. It was an invitation to apply for a resident assistant (RA) position through Residential Life. It was extremely difficult for sophomores to get RA positions, and the openings were rare. With the cards stacked against me, I filled out the application anyway, making my case as a sophomore worthy of the honor. I spoke openly and honestly on my application, telling them about how what I had been through set me up as the perfect student leader. I knew I was able to help other students through challenging situations that might arise during their college experience, and I went to great lengths to relay this to the committee.

Once my application was in, I prayed daily that God would open the right door. Later that same week, I received word that my application was accepted, and I moved on to the second and final round of in-person, group interviews. My joy overwhelmed me; I tried my best to prepare for the interview but didn't know how. Full of anxiety, I called my mother to get her solid advice.

"Ma, I need to find a different housing situation because we have too many guys living in this place, and I can't afford it. I found an application to be an RA, which offers free room and board to up-and-coming student leaders, so I filled out an application and have my final in-person, group interview, and don't know how to prepare for it." The words spilled out of my mouth like confetti at a parade.

Without a pause, my mother said, "Douglas, God would not open this door for you if you weren't supposed to walk through it. You already have all the preparation you need within you. Just remember to mind your manners, be yourself, and convince them that you're the right choice—because you are."

A big smile spread across my face in relief. "Thanks, Ma! That's exactly what I needed to hear. I really appreciate you. This has to work out for me. I do not have another option."

My interview was on a Saturday morning, so unlike my roommates, I decided to stay in the night before to get ready for the next day. While everyone was out partying, I pulled out the ironing board and ironed my shirt, pants, underwear, and even my handkerchief as I had done in high school when applying for the job at the library. As I was ironing, I prayed to God. "Lord, I know you opened this door for me; now prepare my heart and mind to say the right things and be exactly who they are looking for. You know where I am, and you know what I need, and I ask you now to open this door for me so that I can stay and finish college." I continued praying in this fashion for over an hour, ironing my clothes to be as crisp as if I had taken them to the dry cleaners. That night, I knew somehow that the next day would be a big one for me, and when I finally laid my head down on the pillow, I knew I was ready.

The next morning, I woke up earlier than I had expected because I was anxious to get to the interview. I wanted to get there early, just like on the days when I played Little League with Coach Miller and would stand on the sidelines, sizing up my competition. Fortunately for me, I arrived an hour before my interview, while the staff from Residential Life was still setting up in the student-center building. My blood pressure rose as I got closer.

"Excuse me, my name is Doug Luffborough, and I'm interviewing for an RA position, but I'm here early. Can I help you set up anything?"

"Oh, hello, my name is Rosie Colucci, and I'm an area coordinator. I feel embarrassed asking—but yes, I could use the extra help setting up. My staff is not here yet." Rosie was slim and athletic, with features like Italian women had in renaissance paintings. She was in her early forties, but she looked like a college student. It was just me and the area coordinator setting up for what would soon be my interview.

Thank you, God, I thought, and I recalled what Coach Miller said to me when I was just ten years old: *If you are fifteen minutes early, you are on time. If you are on time, you are late, and if you come late without calling me, you run.* On this day, coming early just may have gotten me the job; I could feel it. Rosie and I set up for thirty minutes until her staff started to arrive.

"So why do you want to be an RA?" she asked as we were setting up alone.

I thought this was a perfect opportunity to make my case. "Well, when I saw the application and read the description, I thought I was a perfect fit. You see, I was homeless in high school but did not let that circumstance stop me from being the first person in my family to go to college." I felt more confident and relaxed as I spoke, and all of it was the raw truth. "Now I want to serve as a student leader and role model for other students here at Northeastern that may find themselves in a challenging life situation and need help and support getting through it. I think with what I've been through, I could be the right person to help them out."

"That's great. That's exactly what we are looking for, and I hope you do well today on your group interview." A big, genuine smile lit up her face.

The time for my interview arrived and what looked like stiff competition filled the room. I had seen some of the other students in my class involved in other leadership opportunities on campus. I was focused, but by this time, I could not stop the sweat dripping from my brow, as one by one our names were called for a panel interview. When I walked out of the interview, most of what was said was a blur, but I felt that I had done my best, and that would have to be good enough.

Two weeks passed, and the anxiety from not knowing if I got the job finally slipped away. On the last day of the second week, I received a call from Rosie.

"Hello, can I please speak to Doug Luffborough?"

"Speaking!" I blurted out. I could barely contain my nerves.

"This is Rosie Colucci from the Department of Residential Life, and I'm calling to let you know that we have never offered an RA position to a sophomore before, but you were one of our top applicants during the group interview process. I wanted to see if you were still interested in becoming an RA for Northeastern University. A position just opened up in one of our upperclassmen apartments, and I would need you to start in a few weeks."

Without thinking—because I already knew this was the right choice—I spoke right on the heels of her last word. "Yes, I would be honored. Rosie, thank you so much for this opportunity! I won't let you down!" I hung up the phone in shock, and ripples of excitement shot through me as the good news settled in.

I immediately called my mother to tell her. "Ma, I walked through that door and got the job! I'm going to be an RA at Northeastern with free room and board and the opportunity to help other students on campus." I spoke faster than I thought I could.

"Well, praise the Lord! Thank you, Jesus, thank you, Jesus!" My mother mumbled as if she was talking to me *and* someone else in the background.

The biggest reason I chose Northeastern was because of their Cooperative Education program, or Co-op program. During high school, I watched the Northeastern commercials about spending half of your college experience in the classroom and the other half working in your field of study. Even though I had some work experience, I knew the opportunity I would receive during Co-op would be in line with my major and profession.

My first Co-op position was with Northeastern University's Fenway Project, a nonprofit social services organization that provided support to low-income children, families, and the elderly living in the residential areas around the Northeastern campus. My first job with them was to develop an after-school component working with elementary age children and seniors from a nearby senior citizen home. Less than one hundred yards from the walls of the university stood the drug-infested, broken-down, government-subsidized Roxbury apartments. After dark, the neighborhood was not a safe place to travel through, even for an African-American male within attending college in an African-American community.

One night, after finishing a tutoring session with a young man inside his apartment, I realized that the sun had gone down while we were working, and the only thing illuminating the streets were the flickering streetlamps. As I left his house, I felt a familiar chill run up my body that always came when something bad was going to happen. I thought back to the memory of when I learned about the white student that was jumped by a group of black teenagers on his way back to his residence hall. He'd been walking home from a party when he was beaten and stabbed repeatedly and left to die on the streets of Roxbury. My heart pounded in my chest as I left my tutee's house, and I was determined to avoid the danger.

As soon as I hit the main street, I secured my book bag to my back and broke out into a jog toward campus, making sure to stay close to the streetlights so others could see me. As I passed several alleyways, I sprinted to avoid the pimps and prostitutes that lingered in the shadows. As I ran, I noticed a group of around ten African-American teens walking towards me in a straight line, spreading out enough to block the sidewalk and make me slow down so that I did not bump into one of them. When I was a few yards in front of them, I slowed to a walk and had to turn sideways to get through.

"Excuse me, brother!" I said to one teen as I walked past him, our backs rubbing.

"Brother?" the boy said. "I'm not your brother, homey! You see these guys here, *they* are my brothers! What are you doing in our neighborhood anyway? Where you from?" They started walking toward me and I walked backwards, facing them, terrified and unsure of what would happen next.

"I go to school at Northeastern and was just helping a young boy that lived in the Roxbury projects with his homework. I am trying to get back to campus. That's all."

"Well, tonight is not your lucky night," another teen responded. "How about this—give us all your money and we will let you walk."

"Come on, guys," I pled. My voice was full of fear, mingled with sadness that they wanted to rob me and take the little money I had. I knew that ultimately, them taking my money was better than them taking my life, so I reached in my pocket and pulled out twenty dollars and whatever change jingled loose. I handed over the cash and added, "I don't want any trouble, guys . . . I just want to get back to campus."

After the leader took my money, he laughed out loud. "Is this all you have, man? These college brothers are just as broke as we are." This caused an explosion of laughter from everyone there, including me, though mine was all nerves. "Alright man, you get back to your college campus so you can get that college diploma and start making some real paper."

"Thanks, guys," I said, and nodded my head out of respect. I continued jogging down the street all the way until I made it back safely to my room. Even though I grew up in similar circumstances, those were not the streets that I grew up on. Therefore, for my next Co-op, I decided to work in another area: a for-profit corporation specifically dealing with my business major with a concentration in human resource management.

I worked hard with my Co-op advisor after that experience to find a corporate placement working in human resources. When an opportunity came up for me to work as a Co-op student at John Hancock Insurance Company in its human resources training department, I was beside myself with excitement. My role and responsibilities were to assist the other trainers with their training needs and to make sure that all of the training rooms were organized, cleaned, and presentable. My manager was an African-American man named Steven Bell who looked like the adult version of Steve Urkel. He always wore a tie and suit when he came to work. Steven was like an uncle to me and helped me navigate my way through a corporate environment that was predominantly white. He was a strong advocate that encouraged me to get involved in the company choir, follow through with daily workouts at the company gym, and join the company basketball and softball leagues. I carried myself like I was a full-time employee instead of a three- or six-month Co-op student. I built relationships with my coworkers throughout John Hancock because I wanted to be hired after my graduation from college.

As I was moving into my senior year in college and preparing for my next Co-op assignment, Steven recommended that I work in another department to get a wider variety of experiences for my resume and to broaden my network to include other John Hancock managers looking for young, talented, and eager college students. It seemed that moving to a different department was a good move for my next Co-op assignment, so I heeded his advice.

Chapter 14

Day-O, Day-O

You only get one shot, do not miss your chance to blow,
this opportunity comes once in a lifetime, yo!

—Eminem

After two successful Co-ops working with Steven in the training department, I chose to do my last Co-op with the long-term-care insurance division, which was a growing department led by a young, up-and-coming manager named Seth Kilgore. Seth was an assertive, clean-cut, confident, make-the-big-decision-on-the-spot type of leader. Working with him was quite different from working with the other long-term, career-minded professionals at John Hancock, who seemed to manage by status quo decision making. His office was clean and modern and always neat, as if he was rarely in there.

My interview with Seth lasted less than thirty minutes, and although he was laser-focused, he had a way of disarming whomever he was with. At first, I tensed at how direct he was, but he had a calm way of expressing himself that made me feel at ease in his presence within minutes.

"Hello," he greeted me, smiling. "Thanks for coming in. I understand that you are a Co-op student and already did your other Co-ops inside the company. You may not know this, but you come highly recommended. Tell me why you want to work in our department." Seth's voice and face were relaxed. He spoke as simply to me as if he were remarking about the weather.

"Well, I have done all of my Co-ops in the human resources training department, and for my last Co-op assignment, I wanted to diversify my experience by trying something new. I heard that you give Co-op students a challenge as well as an opportunity to grow their leadership skills, and that's what I'm looking for." I looked him squarely in the face. "I'm a senior now and want the chance to work in a different department, because I would like to work at John Hancock as a full-time employee upon graduation—"

Before I could finish my sentence, Seth interrupted me by laying out the mission and vision of the department and explaining where he thought I could fit working with two other Co-op students from Northeastern. I was pleasantly surprised at the interjection and felt more at ease with each passing moment. I thought that working with two other Co-op students would not only be fun, but also a way to prove to Seth and the company that I was the right person to hire after graduation.

For the remainder of my "interview," we shared small talk about the company, my experience at Northeastern, and coffee. Then Seth said, "Well, Doug, I'm not here to waste your time or mine. I like having Co-op students in my department and think you will do great here if you want the job."

"Absolutely!" I replied as he stood to his feet and moved towards me. I stood up with my hand outstretched to shake his. "Thank you, Seth, for giving me this opportunity."

After we made plans for my start date, Seth walked me to the door. I sighed with relief and gratitude. I could not help but think that my earlier work-readiness training at the library under Mrs. Quinn and at the factory was paying off.

I enjoyed my new Co-op assignment and quickly made friends with other employees. I already knew many of them from the other, non-work-related activities I participated in after work, such as playing on the softball and basketball teams, working out at the company fitness center, and singing with the company chorus during the holidays. Meeting new people and making new friendships came naturally to me, and by the end of my first week, I felt as if I had been working in the department for months.

Two other Co-op students had been hired at the same time I was, and while the three of us were friendly, we also shared a competitive spirit. Each time Seth proposed a new initiative, the three of us vied for a stake in the game. Whenever the opportunity came up to serve on a committee, each of us tried to jockey a position for the top pick. As time went on, I noticed that if one Co-op student did something questionable, another one would tell Seth in hopes that the other student would get reprimanded. This dog-eat-dog competitive atmosphere started to bother me because, in my mind, the competition was to spark more initiative between us, not to tear each other down. I approached the experience as though I was cheering on good friends, but instead, I found myself in a ruthless race for a full-time position with the company.

One morning, I went to the lobby to get my standard breakfast—coffee, a banana, and a plain bagel with cream cheese. Both of my hands were full as I approached the elevator, and one of the other Co-op students pushed the button to call it to our floor. After a minute, more employees gathered around us in wait.

When the doors opened, I slid back to the far corner to make room for others to enter. I started small talk with my Co-op counterpart, and he looked at me with a straight face.

"Hey, I like the suit you have on today," he said. "Where did you get it, the Salvation Army?"

Embarrassment filled every part of my body as other business professionals in the elevator turned and looked me up and down. Some laughed. I was mortified, feeling as exposed as if I had wet my pants. It felt as if no elevator had ever moved slower than that one did for me.

Filled with rushing anger, I looked the other Co-op student straight in the eye. "My mother gave this suit to me, man, and what you said is not cool."

Hearing the hurt in my voice, the student replied, "Sorry, man, the suit looks nice, really!"

When the elevator doors opened, I hurried out on my floor and ran directly to my cubicle, trying not to draw more attention to myself. As I bit into my bagel, I decided two things: one, I would never talk to that guy again, even though I would see him on campus and had to work with him for the duration of my Co-op assignment; and, two, that was the last time I would ever wear that suit. The next day before work, I donated it to the Salvation Army.

Truth be told, I was not sure where my mother had gotten the suit. Most of the clothes I wore growing up—especially on Co-op assignments—were clothes my mom received as gifts or hand-me-downs from her housekeeping clients. I didn't mind wearing them, but to be called out the way I was within a professional setting like that crushed my spirit and my sense of belonging to the corporate culture. I wanted so desperately to become a part of that culture that I was determined to straighten out whatever bends there were in my professional image—and fast.

Back on campus, I moved into the West Apartments as one of the veteran RAs. I was in heaven and felt like the BMOC (Big Man On Campus). At the time, West was considered the Trump Towers of residential life; the who's who of upperclassmen who lived on campus wanted to be there. As the most experienced RA, I got first pick of my room. I chose a nice, spacious, fully furnished apartment that included a full kitchen, walk-in bathroom, living room, and large bedroom on the top floor, or what I called the penthouse floor. That apartment was better than the motel we'd stayed in when I was homeless and was also bigger than the one-bedroom apartment we stayed in with Joe after we got off the streets. The first couple of days, I just wandered around the space, thanking God as I had observed my mother doing over the years. "Thank you, Lord! Thank you, God! Thank you, Jesus!" I said it over and over again, touching the walls and obsessively opening the empty refrigerator. *How can this be?* I thought. It felt amazing to call the apartment my own. All my senses were heightened, and I had to see it, touch it, smell it, and feel it to know that this *was* it. My rituals and conversations with Jesus lasted for weeks.

Because the apartment came furnished, I did not have to spend any money on a kitchen table, chairs, couches, desk, or bed—it had it all. I did buy a few things, though, like a microwave, coffee maker, toaster oven, and television, and I even went shopping for pictures to put up on the walls to make the apartment look and feel like my own—something I never felt like I had growing up. When I received one of my Co-op checks, I spent close to $500 to get my pictures professionally framed. One was a picture of a violin with sheet music in the background. Music played such a powerful role in my life, and by this time, I realized why my mother made me play the violin and just how much it had helped me express myself. Through studying violin, I also learned the discipline and focus I would need to be successful in college.

The next picture was a Looney Tunes poster with Bugs Bunny and Michael Jordan from the movie *Space Jam*. The movie was popular at the time, and I decided to put it up in the living room for what Michael Jordan represented to me: determination, pursuit of excellence, and laser-like focus on goals, all qualities I felt helped me get to college and that served as a reminder of how I wanted to live my life.

Then I found a cute painting of a three- or four-year-old African-American boy sitting in the bathroom sink as he brushed his teeth. The first reason I loved this picture was because the boy was African-American, and I could relate to him. The other reason was that the little boy represented independence and the self-assurance that he could take care of himself, which was what I had been searching for and felt as soon as I boarded the Greyhound bus heading to college.

Over the foot of my bed hung a picture of a boardwalk with a pier that stopped in the middle of a lake. On the horizon beyond the pier was a range of ancient mountains, with the sun's rising rays touching the shadowed ridge. Every morning when I woke up, I stared at the picture and imagined myself standing at the tip of the pier, breathing in the crisp air, feeling the warmth of the sun on my face. I thought, *It took me this long to get here in my life, and there is no turning back now. I just have to figure out a way to build the bridge to the other side of the mountain where the sun is coming up—where my breakthrough is.* To me, the picture represented my journey in life; I had much to be proud of and had built my bridge to success this far, but my journey was not yet complete. The picture was a source of inspiration and motivation for me—if I wanted to sleep in or skip class, one look at the picture propelled me to shower and get dressed for the day. Today, that same picture hangs inside my home office as not only a reminder of my past, but also of the continued pursuit toward new dreams and new visions.

My first homemade meal in my new place was dinner: steamed broccoli with stuffed tortellini, smothered in alfredo sauce, with a plate-sized piece of garlic bread to pick up every ounce of extra sauce left on my plate. I had Basia, Yanni, Enya, Jim Brickman, and John Tesh, to mention a few, on my New Age music playlist, and it became the soundtrack for my life that year. To this day, I feel relaxed and peaceful every time I turn that playlist on.

During this time, I also started listening to nature music as I studied, though this did not last long. One too many times, I found myself waking up in the middle of the night, my face flattened on the same spot where I had started reading, with saliva covering most of the unread pages. I found other ways to study more effectively, and though I was in study groups with friends, I did not have many people over. I wanted to keep the place to myself as my own safe haven from the rest of the world. I was also mindful that it was my senior year, and I wanted to finish college strong without doing something that would jeopardize all my hard work.

As RAs, my peers and I were ambassadors to other students in our residential halls, and many times, RAs were the first to receive information from the university to distribute to other students throughout the residence hall. The day I received the notice that carved a new path in my life is one I will never forget. The notice was on yellow paper and had big black letters typed in caps across the top: FOR SENIORS ONLY. The notice contained information and applications to complete in order to be considered for the student commencement speaker at graduation. Before distributing the packets to the seniors on my floor, curiosity got the best of me, and I reviewed the qualifications, keeping one application for myself.

After I reviewed the entire application from cover to cover, I tried to find a reason that would disqualify me from applying. On the contrary, I felt a deep knowing that I was born for this. To go from a stuttering speech impediment in the third grade and a phobia of public speaking, to applying to become the student commencement speaker at Northeastern seemed like a huge leap of faith for me. My time in college as RA of the Year, my membership in the choral society, and my distinguished Co-op student award with an eligible GPA reinforced for me that I qualified for such an incredible honor. I started working on the application right away, even before I distributed the rest to the seniors on my floor.

As I left for class that afternoon, I ran into other students and told them about the speaking opportunity, but none of them shared my excitement or enthusiasm. In fact, I bumped into a guy I grew up with in Worcester—we both went to the same grammar school, middle school, high school, and now college—and as a response to my happiness, he sighed heavily. Irritated, he said, "Doug, why do you always have to try to be better than you are? Why can't you be satisfied with where you are? You've already accomplished so much, overcoming homelessness and the way you grew up to get to college. What more do you have to prove?"

I was shocked. I had known this guy since I was eight years old, and now as a senior in college, he endeavored to keep me small. His response was the perfect example of someone who did not celebrate my success the way I did for my peers. In fact, over time, I started to feel that my success bothered him. But his voice was familiar to me. I had heard it from my third-grade teacher, I heard it from my minor league coach, I heard it from Joe, I heard it from the college student who was my assistant coach in Little League, and I heard it from my high school guidance counselor. And now I heard it from someone I had considered a friend for many years. I adamantly rejected that thought, feeling just as passionate about applying for student commencement speaker as I had about applying to Northeastern. I decided that I would put everything I had into this, disregarding his recommendation and, eventually, his friendship.

From that moment on, I decided to surround myself with people who would lift me up in life instead of tear me down. I wanted people in my life who filled my cup instead of emptying it, and living by myself gave me the confidence and freedom to limit the negative influences of others. Through that interaction and subsequent lesson, I learned that sometimes the people closest to you are the ones trying to stop you from pursuing your dreams. They are the dream stealers, the *yeah, but*-ers around you. By this time, I could stand on my own two feet and was not moved by what others thought I should do. I was moved only by what I felt was best for me in that situation.

When my classes ended that day, I retreated to the serenity of my apartment to reflect on the conversations I'd had with others throughout the day regarding the student commencement speaker application. I was surprised that none of my friends had any interest in applying for the opportunity and was even more surprised at the revelation that most of the naysayers in my life were people who were close to me—people I had known for a long time. With this thought as the backdrop in my mind, I started working on the application. In just two nights of purposeful intensity, I finished a first draft of the speech, which was the major component of the application; however, I decided that I would not share my progress with anyone until my application was submitted—I was finished letting negative people sprinkle their opinions in my life. Every day for a week, I worked on the application, refining sentences, phrases, and whole paragraphs. I wanted each statement, each word, to reflect a universal message of hope, accomplishment, and inspiration, not just to my fellow classmates, but also to all who would hear it.

By the end of the week, and several days before the deadline, I submitted my application with all the required documents. I felt very strongly that the speech represented me, the student body, and the university well. The process beyond that point was out of my hands.

There were three rounds to the application process: the first was passing all the application requirements; the next was having the speech reviewed, evaluated, and scored by a mixed group of student leaders and faculty members; and the final part was auditioning in front of a panel comprising the dean of students and other faculty members and student leaders.

After I submitted my application, I went back to my life and did not think about the application any further. My goal was just to apply and see what happened. Two weeks later, I received a letter in the mail informing me that I met the requirements and that my speech was moving to round two. It would be reviewed and scored by the graduation commencement review board. Less than one week after *that*, I was in my room when I received a phone call.

"Mr. Luffborough," said a man with a baritone voice, "I am with this year's graduation commencement review board, and I'm calling to congratulate you for passing the second round and to schedule your final oral audition with our review board next week!"

I was beside myself with surprise and excitement. I immediately took out my planner to reserve one of the available slots. I was ecstatic. I had made it to the finals, and now it was on! I decided that I needed to take it up another level, but how? I only had one week to prepare.

I took out the speech and read it from beginning to end, pausing and taking notes where I thought I could improve it. When I finished, I still felt like something was missing . . . but I could not figure out what it was.

Deciding I needed a mental break, I turned on my nature music and stared at the bridge picture at the foot of my bed, meditating about the present moment and the possibility of becoming the student commencement speaker. I envisioned myself standing at the edge of the dock. Then, the dock transformed into a stage at the old Boston Garden. Speaking with confidence and conviction to a sea of excited graduates, proudly wearing their graduation gowns, hats, and tassels, I conducted the audience into embracing their overwhelming pride. I could hear the applause of friends and family members swelling to a roar in the auditorium.

In that moment, I saw myself singing in my speech. I jumped up from bed. That was it! I needed to start my speech by singing like Maya Angelou had my freshman year! After nine years of singing in high school and college, and singing musical selections at karaoke and during the last call for alcohol at the local watering holes, I knew I could carry a note or two. My only obstacle now was that I did not know what song to sing, and more importantly, how I would connect the song to my speech.

The next day I called my mother to tell her that I was chosen as a finalist for the student commencement speaker, and I told her about my daydream about opening my speech by singing. Ma was very supportive.

"Douglas, that is so great," she said. "I told you that one day all of those music lessons would pay off. Yes, you should sing for them. No one else will do that."

"Yeah, Ma, I think singing will set me apart from the others, but the only problem is I don't know what song to sing," I replied. In the long, silent pause on the phone, I could tell my mother was thinking.

"If God inspired you to sing, then I am in agreement with it, and I'm positive that He will give you the song. Just spend some time praying, and God will reveal it to you."

This response soothed me, as I had come to know it as her default anytime we came to a crossroad in life. My mother always trusted in God for direction, and nine times out of ten, God responded.

I worked on my speech for hours. "Day-O (The Banana Boat Song)" by Harry Belafonte kept coming back to me. But I couldn't figure out how this Jamaican calypso folk song could tie it all together. Sure, it was a fan favorite at the karaoke bars at the end of the night. The song is widely known as a work song, as it's sung from the point of view of dock workers who spend all night loading bananas onto ships, and when daylight appears, the shift is over and they want their work to be counted up so they can go home. Even though the connection wasn't clear, I had to trust that the song kept returning to me for a reason. I was determined to find a way to connect it to my story.

Then, an inner voice—what my mother calls the Holy Spirit—spoke clearly and directly to me: *Home, daylight come and me want to go home. When you were a senior in high school, you were homeless and had no place to stay. Slow the melody of the song down, and sing it from a place of being homeless—as if you were recounting the days you spent on the streets, in the motel, couch-hopping from friends' homes, and sleeping on the floor at Joe's place.* I heard these words whispered into my ears and my heart, so right away I worked on revising my speech to connect the metaphor. I was certain this was the direction I needed to take, but I wanted to try it out in public before my audition.

I went back to the training department at John Hancock and

asked Steven Bell and his team to give me some constructive feedback, and they graciously agreed to serve as my panel of friendly critics. I felt very nervous but told myself that if I couldn't do it in front of less than twenty familiar faces, then how could I do it in front of thousands of not-so-friendly faces? With the confidence of a lion, I roared the opening bars of the Banana Boat Song from a place of being homeless, and in that moment, I saw the eyes well up on the faces of those staring at me. It was the first time since being homeless that I had emotionally put myself back in that situation, and it took everything inside me to finish the song and the speech without breaking down.

"Wow, Doug, what a voice," one person said, and then others chimed in.

"Why that song and why did you change the melody that way?"

"Oh, I loved the song, but I would sing it this way."

"What a story, Doug. I never knew you were homeless; you are such an inspiration to so many others . . . keep going."

"There are some areas that need work, but I think you are onto something."

Their responses were both encouraging and constructive—and the group was unanimous that opening my speech by singing was the best way to do it. In the back of my mind, I kept thinking of Ms. G and her pep talks about singing from my heart and using music to tell my story. She never knew how impactful her teaching and mentoring was for me, but I felt that winning this competition was a way for me to let her know.

By the day of my audition, my speech had undergone multiple iterations and had been reviewed by over a dozen critical friends who provided feedback, guidance, and constructive opinions. I felt that what remained was my very best work. It was out of my hands and in the hands of the judges.

I arrived fifteen minutes early, just as Coach Miller had taught me when I was ten years old. I checked in and sat down in the hallway, fiddling with the paper on which my speech was written, so much so that it lost its crisp and neatly prepared shape. There I sat, alone in the hallway, and I couldn't help recalling the experience of living on the street less than five years prior. Regardless of the outcome, I had already won. There was nothing for me to be ashamed of. I had accomplished so much more than I ever thought was possible.

A voice called out from the other end of the hallway. "Doug Luffborough!"

"Yes," I replied, jumping up from my seat.

"We are ready for you," the voice came back. As I walked down the hallway, I heard a bell go off in my head from the Rocky movie, and I knew there was no turning back. I gave myself a silent pep talk. *Let's do this. This is my Whitney Houston, one-moment-in-time chance to let them know what Doug Luffborough is all about, and I will never get this type of opportunity again, so let them have it.*

When I walked into the room, I introduced myself to a panel of five people staring at me with blank, expectant faces. Three were faces of faculty members that I vaguely recognized, and the two others were student leaders on campus—but I did not know or have personal relationships with any of them. After I introduced myself, I handed out an updated speech. The judges seemed amicable to the change, so without any second thoughts, I put my head back, rolled my eyes back in my head, and took a deep and powerful breath. I opened my mouth with confidence and sang.

"Day-O, Day-O . . ." And just like my pre-audition with my coworkers at John Hancock, when I opened my eyes and looked at the judges, their eyes were welled up with tears. I could see that they were doing everything they could to fight off the emotional connections the song was making with them, just like what happened to me five years earlier with Maya Angelou's speech. It was then that I thought, *I might just get this thing.*

When I finished my speech, the judges still seemed to be fighting back tears, but they maintained the same stoic demeanors they displayed as I entered the room. One member of the panel said, "Thank you, Doug. We have five finalists, and we will make our decision in about a week. Regardless of the outcome, you will hear back from us. Thank you for coming in."

Outside the building in the quad area, I felt the weight of all that pressure had lifted. There was no trace of the stuttering impediment that plagued me in the third grade and throughout most of elementary and middle school. It was not an overnight transformation, but this was when public speaking became natural to me, as natural as breathing. In one way or another, I wanted to become a professional speaker and move others with my words.

Before I knew it, a week had passed and I received the phone call I had been waiting for.

"Doug, I want to start off by congratulating you for being chosen as our next student commencement speaker for Northeastern University."

"Wow," I said, in total amazement. "I am so excited and honored to win this distinction and to represent my class." In that conversation, I learned that I needed to meet with the president of the university, who would assign a speech coach to work with me, but that bar none, my speech was the best and the most creative. I had put myself out there by singing, but my motto in life was swiftly becoming "Go big or go home." God knew what He was doing, and I immediately called my mother to tell her the good news. I went to my bedroom and lay on my bed to make the call, and as the phone rang, the boardwalk picture at the foot of my bed caught my attention.

"Ma, you are never going to believe this, but I did it! We did it! I was chosen as the student commencement speaker for my graduation!"

"Praise God," she replied. "I knew it! I knew you could do it. Thank you, Jesus. Yes!"

I added to her excitement. "I don't know who the keynote speaker will be at this point, but usually it's someone famous, and I will be sharing the podium with that person. I cannot believe that they chose me!"

"Well, whoever it is, it will be someone that complements you, son. Now is your time, and I have a feeling that whoever speaks will be moved with what you have to say," Mom said confidently.

They picked me, they picked me, I do have something to say! I said to myself after getting off the phone.

The next week, I started working with my speech coach. To my surprise, he did not cut up the speech or rewrite it. The only thing we worked on was my delivery, formalizing certain comments and phrases, and slightly condensing the speech to fit within a seven-minute window that had little wiggle room.

After my speech was polished, I went to my meeting with John Curry, who was then president of Northeastern University. He was a very warm and welcoming person. He wanted to know more about my family and me, and he reviewed my transcript.

"So, Doug, tell me a little something about yourself."

"Well, sir, I grew up in Worcester, the oldest of four and the first person in my family to go to college." The words flowed freely from my lips as I continued. "I had a tough upbringing but have learned to take my disadvantages in life and turn them around."

Next, Mr. Curry shared his story, and as he was talking, I realized that this was a bigger deal than I expected. He looked at me with serious composure and asked, "Is there anything in your past that I need to know about that could reflect negatively on the university?"

I got nervous, not wanting to self-sabotage this once-in-a-lifetime opportunity, yet I also wanted to be as transparent as possible.

"I have nothing to hide, President Curry. My story is true. I grew up without a dad, had challenges in school, was involved in a breakdance gang, and was homeless my senior year of high school. That's it. I have never been arrested and really want to make you, my mother, my mentors, and the university proud. This is an opportunity of a lifetime, sir, and I'm not trying to mess it up."

Assured by my confidence, President Curry nodded and said seriously, "Good, because the spotlight will certainly be on you and the university. Our keynote speaker for your graduation will be President Bill Clinton."

I grabbed the desk with both hands. *Excuse me? The president of the United States will be the keynote speaker?! No pressure there.* My internal sarcasm competed with my enthusiasm, but shock won out. I felt like I blacked out for a couple of seconds, and chills went down my spine as I envisioned preceding the president of the United States of America. If there was ever a time to step up to a challenge, now was it. For most of my life, I had sought shadows instead of spotlights, and now I would share my story and the stage with the president of the United States while my mom, Mr. Cott, Coach Miller, Mrs. Quinn, Ms. G, Pam Boisvert, Steven Bell, and the rest of the world watched.

The news travelled fast, and students came up to me saying things like, "Wow, how did you get that?" and "Are you ready to speak before the president? What an honor." The team that had helped me with my speech at John Hancock was ecstatic. Every time I passed one of them in the hallway, they looked at me as if to say, "That's my boy!" Pride gleamed from them.

The sessions with my speech coach went great, and the speech became more and more natural for me. The local news stations picked up my story and the fact that President Clinton was going to be the keynote speaker, and I did several interviews just two weeks before graduation. During the interviews, I shared my challenges of growing up, being homeless, and applying to college despite my guidance counselor's negative recommendations. To my surprise, my high school principal called my mother to express her disappointment that I would talk about the help I was denied by my guidance counselor, who was still on the job and was probably telling other students who were in my situation that they were not college material. The principal went so far as to schedule a meeting with my mother, the guidance counselor, the principal, and me, encouraging me to retract my story and share the positive aspects of the advice he did give me. *Sure*, I thought. *After blowing me off for most of my senior year and telling me that I was not college material, now, as I prepared to graduate from my first-choice university, he wanted to meet with me.* Unfortunately, he was five years too late. I was not in high school anymore and no longer needed to bow down to him, or anyone else for that matter. I decided not to drive back to Worcester from Boston to help cover up his image. The microphone was now in my hand, and he had no control of what I was going to say.

I received a great deal of press in the weeks leading up to graduation, and the momentum was building, along with some great expectations. One part of me was intensely anxious, wondering if I could really do it, but, the other part of me was fearless, casually sounding off positive self-talk with the likes of "Bring it on," "Let's do this," and my personal favorite, "I was made for this day."

The week before my graduation, I received a phone call from a staff writer at *USA Today.* The paper wanted to do a story on me in preparation for my graduation. The story would run just two days before the ceremony and would be featured on the front page of the education section of the newspaper. This was no small success in my mind. *USA Today* has one of the widest circulations of any newspaper in the United States, and it was then that I realized how much bigger this was than I had even imagined. The nation was going to know me, my story, and my journey to graduate from college—up close and personal. My hope was that it would inspire other kids who grew up the way I did, as well as single moms sacrificing themselves to raise their children. I wanted them to realize that if my mother and I were able to do it, they could do it, too.

Chapter 15

Lights, Camera, Action!

I must tell you, ma'am. There are a lot of people of great and famous achievement who will never know the pride you must have felt when your son stood up here earlier today. I thought it was unbelievable, and I appreciate what you did.

—Former President Bill Clinton

The night before graduation, my entire family came up from Worcester to stay with me in my residence hall apartment. The buzz was so high about my graduation speech, and the pressure mounted all around me. *Can I really pull this off?* I wondered. *Did they pick the right person?*

I wanted to run away from the pressure, just as I ran out of my high school classroom when the teacher wanted me to read aloud. However, my mother represented my security blanket, ironing my clothes the night before and praying relentlessly every waking moment throughout the night. Much like she had many nights when I was growing up, she alternated between talking with me and talking to Jesus.

My mom could feel the pressure as well. She rubbed the sweat off her forehead as she paced from one side of the room to the other, asking me questions that she had asked just moments prior. Finally, I had to tell her I was going to sleep. And just like I'd asked Ma to wake me before work on my Frito-Lay route, I asked her if she would wake me up around four the next morning so that I could have time to review my speech before getting ready.

As I lay down on my bed, I looked at the boardwalk picture—as I had done every night and every morning—and in my mind, the bridge had been built further out across the water, not too far off from the mountains. It served as a visual metaphor that I was making progress in my life and that this speech would be a turning point. Going forward, I would live out of the convictions of my heart and not the fears that might come into my head. I tossed and turned all night, and by all accounts, pulled an all-nighter as I performed my speech over and over and over again in my head.

Around three o'clock, I decided that I could not sit in bed and stare up at the ceiling any longer. As I opened my door, I saw my mother bent over on her knees, praying.

"Ma, did you get any sleep?" I whispered so as not to wake up my other siblings.

Mom looked up at me, joy and presence of mind dancing in her eyes. "No, baby, this is a big day for you and for our family, and I have been praying all through the night for you. You are going to do great. God is for you, so who can be against you. This opportunity is going to change the trajectory of your life for the better. I'm so proud of you," she said, closing her Bible.

"Ma, God has prepared me for this moment, and I thank God he gave me you as my mother. People will never look at us the same after this," I said with confidence as I made my way to the bathroom. When I opened the door and turned on the light, I was overwhelmed by a sea of yellow sticky notes covering the mirror. I couldn't even see my face through them. My mom had been up all night, copying down verses from the Bible that she thought would inspire me, and neatly placing them on bright yellow, sticky squares of paper that would eventually cover every inch of the bathroom mirror.

You can do all things through Christ who strengthens you.
You are the head and not the tail.
Greater is He that is in me than he that is in the world.
You're blessed when you come in and you're blessed when you go out.
No weapon formed against you shall prosper.
Fear not, for I am with you. Be not afraid, for I am your God.
For I know the plans I think toward you.
If My people who are called by My name will humble themselves, and pray and seek My face, and turn from their

wicked ways, then I will hear from heaven, and will forgive their sin and heal their land.

Scripture filled the mirror from top to bottom, and I felt my mother's love in her effort to inspire me, bless me, and strengthen me against the potential onslaught of public scrutiny or judgment. The depth and seriousness of what I was about to do hit home as I read each note over and over again until I believed and received what I was reading. This was it. I had lived my entire life for this moment in time.

"Douglas, before you leave, can I pray for you?"

"Yes, Ma, I would like that," I replied. We clasped our hands and bowed our heads together.

"Lord, I pray your mercy and favor over my son, and give him the courage and boldness to say what you will have him say today. And thank you, Father God, that you receive the victory today in Jesus' name, Amen."

"Amen, Ma. Thank you . . . and I will see you later," I said as I took my cap and gown off the ironing board and left the room. In the bathroom, I paused to catch my breath, to take in the moment. I stood in front of the mirror covered with sticky notes, wearing my cap and gown and beaming with pride. This was the day I had dreamed would come true. I stared at my silhouette, remembering the dream I'd had when I was homeless and living in the motel. I had dreamed of graduating from college, and now, in six hours, that would come to fruition. I would be a college graduate.

I spent a minute in the bathroom silence with the lights off to say one last prayer: "Father God, thank you for showing me what is possible. I pray that you will anoint the words that come out of my mouth to reach those who need to be reached. In Jesus' name, Amen."

After quietly getting ready and a final prayer of encouragement from Ma, I made my way to the front door, out of the building, and to the train—the T—that would take me to North Station and to the Boston Garden. On the T, the only people I saw were the early morning janitorial and housekeeping staff traveling to or from one of the many hotels in Boston. The train stopped at Park Street (a couple of stops from North Station), and a dark-skinned, clean-cut and shaven African-American man boarded and sat exactly across from me. His Polo cologne wafted throughout the train car, and I noted that he was dressed in a matching dark gray top and bottom, with black athletic sneakers.

As the train began to move, I could feel him looking at me, *staring* at me. On the heels of the breath I inhaled with my decision to make eye contact with him, he spoke.

"Hey, man . . . are you the guy I saw on television who was homeless and is now graduating from college and speaking before the president?"

Shocked that my face was recognizable, I stuttered, "Uh . . . ah . . . yeah, that's me. I'm heading to the Garden right now for my graduation and to make my speech," I smiled, and my body tensed with anticipation.

"I know you don't know me," the stranger said, "but I'm proud of you, brother. I know you will be great today, and never forget where you came from, young blood." I shook my head as if to say *I'm with you, man, and much respect.* For the remainder of the ride, we both sat there, looking around and avoiding eye contact in solemn solidarity. It seemed to me that we both knew that words could not express what I was about to do, and still, I knew it would change the course of my life forever.

"Next stop, North Station!" the conductor announced over the intercom. I got to my feet, re-centered myself, and straightened my clothes. Just before the doors opened, I looked back at the man I had been talking to.

"Thanks, man, I appreciate our conversation."

In response, he just looked at me as if to say, *Do your thing, brother . . . do your thing.*

The Boston Garden was an ocean of caps and gowns—a constant and powerful reminder that today was our day. As the student commencement speaker, I had a special invitation and directions to meet in a large conference room underneath the stage with the valedictorians from each of the university's colleges. President

Clinton was going to do a meet-and-greet with the fifteen featured students, including me. In such a small setting, I knew that I would get the chance to personally meet the president and perhaps ask him if my mother and I could visit him at the White House.

Prior to the president's arrival, while we were still mingling nervously, an official from the university approached me.

"I thought your mother would be coming with you," he said, holding his clipboard above his belted walkie-talkie. "President Clinton specifically requested that she be here."

"I didn't know that!" I exclaimed. "I know where she will be sitting, and if someone can go get her, that would be great."

The man took down the information and went off to get her. About ten minutes later, my mother was escorted into the room, her face beaming with pride and awe at the VIP treatment. She was the only non–university official and non-student in the room. She carried herself like royalty, floating around the room as she mixed and mingled with my classmates—who all happened to be valedictorians. It was such a contrast to watching her struggle year after year, cleaning homes and raising a family from the ashes.

The jovial mood shifted when Secret Service, dressed in black suits, starched white shirts, matching ties, and Ray-Bans infiltrated the room. They demanded our names and identification cards to check off their security clearance list. Everyone cleared but my mother.

"I'm sorry, ma'am, but your name is not on the list," one of the Secret Service agents said. "You cannot stay down here. You must return to your seat."

The woman who, only minutes before, had floated around the room with grace and ease came crashing down like a jackhammer. Ma put her head down as if she were talking to her housekeeping clients.

"No problem, sir," she said quietly. "I will go back to my seat."

Not wanting my mother's joy to be smothered, as it had been all her life, I stood in between the Secret Service agent and my mother and said, "A university official told her that the president wanted to meet her. That's why she's in the room, sir."

Another student spoke up. "Yeah, she is the mother of the

student speaker and hasn't done anything wrong. Let her stay." Others started to get involved, and quickly the mood shifted again . . . this time away from our impending graduation to what started to resemble a civil rights rally. Being the compliant diplomat that she is, my mother gracefully stayed silent, smiled, and quickly left the room without saying another word. I became angry and could see my attention turning from getting ready to make my speech to wanting to get back at the Secret Service agent. If anyone in the room had the questionable background, it was me—not my mother. Ken, one of the valedictorians, approached me.

"Hey, Doug, don't let this incident throw you off your game. Let it motivate you to do better." I knew Ken was right. I could not let this episode with the Secret Service agent stop me from making one of the biggest speeches of my life. And like water poured over a duck's back, I decided to let the incident roll off of me. What I had to say to the nation was more important than what I had to say to the Secret Service agent who was just trying to do his job.

The next thing I knew, more and more Secret Service agents filled the room, double-checking everyone and everything. I stood in the center of the room, keeping to myself as the agents cleared it for safety. Then, like noon on a grandfather clock, when the president of the United States, Bill Clinton, walked in, we pointed our focus on him—whether we wanted to or not. His *presence* commanded our attention. He smiled, dressed impeccably in a suit, and surveyed the faces in the room. Then he met my eyes and walked directly up to me.

"I know you, young man," he said. "You are our student commencement speaker, Doug Luffborough, right?"

"Yes, sir!" I said in shock. I thought, *How did he know it was me?* Out of all the students in the room, he approached me first. The enormity of what was happening consumed me. I felt that I needed to step up my game because I would precede the president of the United States on live television with the world watching me.

I snapped out of my zombie trance. "Mr. President, it is a pleasure to meet you. Would you be so kind as to sign my commencement speech for good luck?"

"Well, from what I learned about you, I don't think you will need any luck . . . but sure. Let me sign it for you," the president conceded. In the top right-hand corner of my speech, he wrote: "To Doug; Congratulations on your outstanding achievement. Bill Clinton." He handed the speech back to me and said, "Hey, I thought your mother was going to be here. Where is she?"

Out of the corner of my eye, I watched the guilty Secret Service agent fidget with nervous energy as he heard the president's question to me. I responded, "Mr. President, your Secret Service staff said she was not on the clearance list and could not be here."

President Clinton looked around and smiled again, genuinely happy. "Well, at least they are doing their jobs right. Heck, I'm not even sure *I'm* on the list." This elicited a spray of chuckles and laughter from all who heard it, demonstrating his political appeal and talent at winning a crowd—even a small one. He closed the conversation. "Well, I hope to meet your mother someday, and please give her my best. She did a great job with you, and I can't wait to hear you speak."

The president moved throughout the room, meeting other students with charm and enthusiasm. Our time together concluded with a group picture with the president. I was on one side of the room and the president on the other. Once the first picture was taken, Ken, who was standing right next to me, said, "Would the president be so kind to take another picture with the students on the other side of the room?"

The room erupted in laughter as the president gracefully made his way to the other side of the room. In the second picture, the president stood right in between Ken and me, and our faces beamed with joy. We felt right at home with one another. President Clinton has a way with people; making them feel as if they are the only ones in the room is a big part of it.

The time was upon us . . . we were to start our procession, which would kick off graduation. We lined up, the valedictorians first. I was the last student in line, right before President Clinton. As we made our way down the hallway to the main entrance of the Boston Garden, excited noise filled the arena. Many people I had never met gave me a pat on the back or high five as I stood in line.

When our school band started playing "Pomp and Circumstance," a wave of chills went down my spine. Not only was I graduating from college and making one of my dreams come true, but I was also conquering my fears of public speaking and stuttering as the student commencement speaker. The moment was surreal.

The doors to the auditorium swung open, and the sweltering heat inside the non–air conditioned Boston Garden hit us like a sauna. People fanned themselves with the graduation program, and some had purchased handheld portable fans for relief from the hazy heat that filled the immense space. The crowd erupted, cheering as if they were witnessing a championship game, as we made our way to the stage. There was no turning back now; it was game time.

I saw many of my friends and classmates as I followed the procession, and many of them greeted me with open arms and cheers of encouragement. However, some of them simply stood in amazement or shock that I was the featured student speaker. The looks on their faces were priceless, as if to unanimously say, "How did he get picked to be the student speaker?"

But I did not say anything. I didn't need to. I was going to let my speech answer their lingering questions.

We climbed the stairs to the stage, and I found the seat that had my name on it: Doug Luffborough, Student Commencement Speaker. As I sat down, I realized that I was among the top politicians in our state. Seated next to President Clinton was Senator Ted Kennedy, and not too far from him was Senator John Kerry. Next to Kerry was the former governor of Massachusetts, Mike Dukakis. There I sat, among men who had given decades of their lives to public service, and I knew my life, my story, represented what they fought for: access to higher education for low income, first-generation college students, access to financial aid and student scholarships, and access to college-to-career opportunities through Co-op programs at Northeastern. There was no coincidence that I was seated among these men. I, too, was meant for something greater than my past.

Right next to me, a Secret Service agent was dressed in cap and gown, but he stood out like a sore thumb. He wore an earpiece and spoke quietly into his wrist every time the president engaged in conversations with others. From my seat on the stage, I could see my mother, sister, and two brothers, nestled close to one another in their seats. I could not believe what was happening and was more than ready to speak. After the color guard presentation finished and everyone sang the national anthem, President Curry took to the podium to introduce me:

"Ladies and gentlemen, Douglas Luffborough III represents what Northeastern University is all about. Access to college regardless of economic station, access to academic excellence for bright and talented young people, access to good professional jobs during college and afterwards. A double business major in management and human resources, Doug will next week begin full-time work at John Hancock Financial Services, where he has worked under our co-operative plan of education over the last two and a half years. I am proud, ladies and gentlemen, to introduce to you your student speaker, Doug Luffborough!"

While my introduction was being read, instead of fear or nerves, what ran through my mind was that *this* was the moment I had waited for my entire life—a chance for my voice to be heard.

I stood up and went straight for the glass of water I saw just beside the podium. My speech would open with a song, and with the steam-room heat, the talking and the laughing, I did not want my voice to crack. As I tasted the refreshing, cold water, I noticed that my thumb covered over the emblem of the White House, and then it dawned on me that the water was not intended for me, but for President Clinton. I could not believe that I just drank the president's water . . . but making sure that I stood proud in front of 14,000 people on live television was my number one priority.

My classmates immediately made me feel comfortable and at ease, and I looked across the audience to locate my mother and family. In the rafters, Secret Service snipers had their semi-automatic rifles pointed in my direction. I was just a few feet from the president of the United States, and security was *their* top priority. I closed my eyes, found my pitch, and inhaled the first breath for my speech, which began with singing "Day-O." At first, the audience joined me, but after a few bars, they listened closer to see how the song would end.

When I finished the song, the auditorium erupted in cheers and applause. For an instant, I thought, *Yes! This is exactly what I was hoping would happen!* The energy in the Boston Garden was electrifying. I had them!

After the applause quieted, the silence was reverent—I could have heard a pin drop when I started speaking. And while I knew that everyone there wanted to hear President Clinton, I wanted them to know about Doug Luffborough, too. I couldn't pass up the opportunity to address students, both past and present, who were just like me, who struggled in life to get to college. I wanted my story to encourage other students and parents to believe that what seems impossible *can* be possible.

It seemed as though everyone there, including the president of the United States, was on the edge of their seats with anticipation of each word, each phrase that I had prepared. I thought about my trials and tribulations during my speech and looked at my mother several times out of respect for all she had done in my life. When I finished speaking, over 14,000 people rose to their feet, including the president of the United States, who greeted me at the podium. He shook my hand, bringing us closer together. "Great job! Where is your mother?"

I wanted to point, but the president held my hand firmly with both of his, so I tried to explain where she was, which was difficult in a room full of thousands of proud parents. I could see the Secret Service snipers in the ready position because I was right next to—and touching—the president. Fortunately, my directions worked, and he was able to see where my mother was sitting. I then made my way back to my chair, sighing in relief. *I did it*, I thought. *I nailed it.*

President Curry returned to the podium beaming with pride, obviously moved by my speech. After that, the focus shifted to the keynote speaker, President Clinton. As he took the podium, the reality of what I had just done hit me. I felt like I had just woken up from an uplifting dream. At that point, I could not focus on his speech; I was dwelling on what I had just done and the courage and confidence it required. Especially with what I had endured in the third grade, with my challenges with stuttering and reading out loud in public, with the lack of support from my guidance counselor—but now, my inferiority complex and personal insecurities were shattered in front of the entire nation. Then, one part of Clinton's speech caught my attention:

"I can also tell you that I was deeply impressed by Doug Luffborough, and if I could sing like him, I would not be up here today as president." The audience laughed as President Clinton went on. "I read an article about Doug and his mother and his family, and his trials and working his way through college before I came here. And, in the article, he said he plans to invite himself and his mother to the White House. Well, I'm going to beat him to the punch . . . I would like Doug and his mother to come to the White House. If any man in America knows what having a good, hardworking, strong, loving, and disciplining mother can mean, I certainly do. I know it can make all the difference in the world as it did for Doug and as it has for me, and I think it would be appropriate, just sort of as a symbol of all the parents who are here, if Doug's mother, Mrs. Elsa Luffborough Mensah, would stand up!"

As my mother stood to her feet, I stood as well, to honor the woman who endured pain, physical abuse, and disappointment after disappointment, but who did not let the negative circumstances around her change her positive outlook on life. One by one, others stood to honor the housekeeper and single parent who raised four kids on her own, and who was now being honored by the president of the United States of America. One of my life goals has always been to make my mother proud, and on that day, I knew she was. She had every right to be proud that the nation recognized her for her journey, and the sacrifices she made for her children.

Chapter 16

The White House

You are carrying the future of America in your heart and your mind. So live your dreams and remember, whatever you choose to do with your life, you must also be a citizen of your country, your nation, and our interdependent world. Because while our differences make life more fascinating, our common humanity matters more.

—Former President Bill Clinton

As I wove through the crowd to meet my family, I was overwhelmed with the number of people cheering me on and patting me on the back.

"Way to go, young man!" someone shouted, and everyone I looked at had either tears of joy in their eyes or big smiles on their faces. I was amazed at the impact my speech made. A group of my friends and I rented a nearby restaurant for after the graduation, but our celebration was a blur. My mind raced back and forth, reliving individual moments in a frenzied, disjointed way. My memory tells me that I had a true out-of-body experience; as soon as I was introduced, I went on autopilot. I waited my entire life for that moment and rehearsed my speech hundreds of times in my mind—*and it paid off.*

Back at the residence hall, my family collected their belongings and headed back to Worcester. Since I had graduated, I would soon need to pack up my belongings and move to an off-campus apartment. But for that evening, I sat down to watch TV, and every news station covered the graduation and played and replayed me singing and President Clinton's personal invitation to the White House. I vividly remember washing dishes with my basketball clothes on and hearing my own voice coming from the television. I had to do a double take. Seeing myself on television was so awesome. I wondered how many people were watching with me.

Later that night, I went out with a couple of friends to some of the bars near Fenway Park. At the first bar, people immediately came up to me and started singing: "Day-O, day-o, daylight come and me want to go home!" As a novelty, I thought it was flattering, and I smiled and shook people's hands. After the tenth drunken Day-O singer, I looked sternly at a friend of mine who sat next to me at a squat bar table and gave him the look that said everything: enough already.

From one bar to the next, I became known as the *Day-O Guy*! And by the end of the night, I had received a lot of attention from quite a few flirtatious women, all asking me questions about the graduation and the experience of meeting President Clinton.

That weekend, I took my time packing up my belongings to move to my off-campus apartment. I wanted to enjoy getting ready for the next phase of my life: my first week as a full-time employee at John Hancock Insurance Company. I knew some of my colleagues from my previous Co-op assignments, and I also knew my new manager's name was Diane.

That first morning I was off to work, dressed in a blue suit, white shirt, and red tie. I wore my black wing-tip Bostonians and carried a black briefcase, trying to assimilate into the mainly white, male-dominated corporate environment. I still lived near Northeastern, so I decided to walk to work for the exercise and scenic views. It felt incredibly empowering to be decked out in my business attire, my hard-top briefcase in hand, and walking among other business professionals. I tried to make eye contact with as many people as possible, greeting them with a *good morning* and a *have a nice day*.

When I arrived at work, I went down to the breakfast kiosk in the lobby, and as I stirred creamer into my coffee, one employee after another congratulated me on my speech and commented on what President Clinton said about me. People were particularly thrilled about my personal invitation to the White House.

"Hey, aren't you that guy that sang that song, Day-O?" one asked, then, "Yeah, didn't you get a personal invitation to the White House?" Another followed up with, "Wow, I thought you'd be working at the White House by now, and not for John Hancock!" At the breakfast kiosk, I was the topic of conversation.

A woman in her forties approached me tentatively.

"Hi, my name is Gloria. I watched you live on television last week and want to let you know that you totally inspired me and my son. He's in high school and wants to go to college one day. If it's not too much trouble, would you be kind enough to give me your autograph and write something to my son?"

I put down my bagel, mid cream-cheese-spreading, and made eye contact with Gloria, who was smiling now. Returning her smile, I said, "Sure, Gloria, I would love to. What's your son's name?"

"Marcus!" she enthused. I grabbed a nearby clean napkin and took out my gold-plated Cross pen from my suit jacket and wrote the following on the napkin: "Marcus, you have a great mother who is very proud of you. Wishing you the best on your quest to go to college and remember that if you believe it . . . you can achieve it!" and then I signed my name. As I handed the autographed napkin to Gloria, her eyes welled up.

"You don't have any idea how much this means to me. Thank you so much!" And with that, we parted ways. The feeling I was left with was contentment and happiness that I was able to brighten this person's day. I also felt hopeful that maybe I *had* made a difference in a kid's life. That felt powerful.

At the elevator, even more employees recognized me from the graduation. The elevator doors opened and we all crammed in like well-dressed, nice-smelling sardines. When the doors closed, we stood silent through the awkward moments between floors. After two stops, in the perfect silence, a baritone in the back of the elevator broke out in song: "Day-O!" Everyone in the elevator—including me—burst up laughing, which erased the awkwardness of being in such close proximity.

As soon as the laughter subsided, the elevator doors opened on my floor. I stepped out, and without turning back, I sang "Day-O!" The folks in the elevator graciously responded in kind with a "Day-O" echo. En route to my department, I passed several colleagues who stopped to talk about the graduation and sing my praises, but some people seemed less than enthusiastic about my success. They ignored me when we passed each other, even avoiding eye contact. The looks on their faces was a familiar one, one I saw in my third-grade teacher, one I saw in the assistant baseball coach, and the one I saw in my high school guidance counselor. As I walked into my new supervisor's office, she glanced coldly up from her paperwork and shot pure negativity at me. "Celebration time is over. I hope you are ready to get to work!"

In that moment, my eyes, my head, and my heart dropped. "Sure, Diane. Of course I'm ready to work." My enthusiasm was deflated as I tried to stand tall.

"Good. Then let me walk you back to your cubicle so you can get started." She walked past me, indicating that our brief meeting was over.

At my desk, Diane introduced me to Paula, a tall Italian woman with long black hair and big brown eyes. Paula had joined the department right out of college and would train me. She was maybe five years older than me, so I felt comfortable taking the lead from her, and she seemed very competent. On the other hand, I was shocked by how cold Diane had been. She had to have seen my graduation speech, but instead of it inspiring her, it appeared that she might've been jealous—or possibly annoyed—that I would be working for her after all the fanfare. It was a reality check and a reminder of what I had experienced all of my life: not everyone was going to celebrate my success.

I knew doubt and discouragement. I lived with them on the streets when I was homeless, and I was not going to downgrade my experience at graduation to pacify those who got their kicks by limiting others. As I sat at my desk and processed my new job duties, the question that lingered was whether or not Diane would be open to me going to the White House when the plans were confirmed.

That first day at work, I focused on learning everything to make my transition as smooth as possible. The next day, I dove right in, and received a message from President Curry that he wanted to give me my diploma and discuss plans to go to Washington.

When I arrived at his office the next day during my lunch break, I was excited to be back on campus. The moment I walked through President Curry's doors, his secretary stood up and greeted me.

"Doug, you did such a great job at graduation! We are just so proud of you." Her response was the polar opposite from what I had received from Diane. She added, "Please have a seat. I will get you some water and let President Curry know you are here."

When President Curry came out of his office, he greeted me with open arms and a big hug—as if I was being reunited with the father I never had. It made me feel validated to know how proud he was of me and that I had exceeded his expectations during graduation.

"Hey there, Doug. Thank you for coming." We moved to our own seats, him behind his desk and me across from it, and as we settled in, he continued. "I have to say, you did a great job at graduation, and all of us at the university are so proud of you. We are working with the folks at the White House as we speak."

"Wow, that's great! I didn't know that the trip would be so soon," I replied. My voice jumped with excitement.

"Yes, we want to take advantage of the offer while we have it, so I have many people getting things set up for us. I believe it will happen next week. I know you just started your new job at John Hancock, but I hope they will let you off for a couple of days. I'm also hoping your mother will be able to join us for the trip." As I looked at President Curry in his dark blue pinstriped suit, matched by his white shirt and light blue silk tie, I was in awe. Here I sat, with the ear and the heart of the president of Northeastern University, and he wanted *not just me* to go to Washington, but also my mother. I felt proud and honored for the invitation, and time felt like it slowed down.

"I'll discuss it with my supervisor and also my mom and get in touch with you as soon as possible. I have to ask you what *you* thought about President Clinton's speech and how the graduation went, as a whole?"

Without a pause, his face brightened with joy. "Your graduation was by far one of the best we have ever had at Northeastern University and not just because of having President Clinton, but because of you. You truly represented what Northeastern is all about." He was beaming with pride, and by this time, so was I.

"Northeastern has been good to me, sir, and I wanted to do my best." After that simple exchange, President Curry and I confirmed some of the logistics for the Washington trip, and then I was back at work before I knew it.

The week flew by, and nothing particularly exciting happened, though I did share the news with Diane about my trip to Washington. Not surprisingly, she seemed reluctant to approve my short-term leave.

"Doug, I understand that if the president of the United States invites you to the White House, you need to go, but, you are also starting a new job, and you do not have any time accumulated to take off."

I swallowed hard and held my ground. "Well, I don't want to let this opportunity go by and would appreciate your understanding." I was fearful that she would block my invitation to the White House, but I wasn't going to let her take that away from me.

"Perhaps someone you work with can transfer their days off for you to go. Why don't you try that first and then let's see what happens," she said, trying to avoid yielding to my request.

I left her office confused about the whole encounter. At my cubicle, I explained the situation to Paula.

"I was invited to the White House and we are scheduled to go next week, but I don't have enough days in order to take the time off. Diane wanted me to ask others if they had two days I could use in order to go, but I don't know that many people in the department yet. Who could I ask?"

Without hesitating, Paula made me an offer. "I can give you two of my days if you need them. This is an opportunity of a lifetime, and you need to be there." She had become one of my biggest fans, supporting me in my new position, which made the cold shoulder from Diane somewhat manageable.

Over the weekend, I went to Worcester to talk with my mother about our upcoming trip. When I arrived at her house, I found out that my brothers Darrell and Derrick had been in a fistfight, and my mother was worried that the fight was not over.

When I asked her what happened, she sat down at the kitchen table with a glass of water and a heavy heart. "Darrell and Derrick were playing basketball, and Darrell kept pushing Derrick's buttons, so Derrick fought back and hurt Darrell, and now Darrell wants revenge. Derrick is afraid to come home and I haven't seen him since."

I felt angry and irritated, and I was afraid their fight would sabotage the trip for my mother. "This is crazy. The plans are being made for us to go to Washington, D.C., next week and they want you to go with me."

"Douglas, I'm not sure if I feel comfortable leaving Darrell, Derrick, and Danielle alone." She shook her head from side to side and lowered it at the prospect, her face hidden, but the quiet in the room reflected her conflict. For Ma, her children and their safety always came first.

"Ma, the president of the United States invited us to an all-expenses-paid trip to Washington, D.C., and the White House, and you're going to tell him you can't go because your other two grown-ass sons are fighting with one another like little kids? You have to be kidding me."

"Just give it a couple of days for the dust to settle. If I need to be there, Douglas, I will go with you, but I need you to talk with Darrell and Derrick about this," she said.

I breathed deeply, trying to understand her reasoning, but I was upset in a way that I hadn't been since Ma had called the police after Joe beat her up and Darrell and I stepped in to defend her. My heart was pounding and it took everything in me to remain steadfast in that moment. This disappointment felt like a deep wound to me; each time our family received good news, it always came with more bad news. I was determined not to let my brothers ruin this time for my mother and me, which was a win for our entire family.

First, I talked to Derrick, then fifteen, to get his side of the story.

"Douglas, we were just playing basketball and Darrell kept taunting me and egging me on, so I threw one punch that gave him a bloody nose and knocked him to the ground. When he fell down, I got scared and ran off. That's what happened. I don't want to fight him anymore . . . I just wanted him to stop picking on me."

When I talked with Darrell, who was just one year younger than me, he was still angry about what had happened, but I couldn't hold back my own anger at his immaturity anymore.

"Why are you picking on Derrick?" I yelled. "He's younger than you. What's wrong with you?"

"Shut up, Douglas, this has nothing to do with you. It's between me and Derrick." Darrell's words were thick with vengeance.

"No, Darrell, it has everything to do with me and with Ma. Both of us have to go to D.C., and Ma needs to know that no more drama will go on while she's gone. You need to squash your beef with Derrick and that's it. Seriously, Darrell. Touch Derrick while I'm gone and see what happens." I stood over him, intentionally invading his personal space.

"Oh, is that a threat? Are you threatening me?"

"No, it is a promise," I replied. Our eyes met, ready to fight, when the voice of our five-year-old sister chimed in, begging me to take her outside to the park. This distracted me enough to let down my guard and move on, but I had said what I needed to say.

We left for Washington the following Wednesday. President Curry arranged for my mother to be picked up at her home in Worcester and dropped off at Logan Airport in Boston. We were met there by a sea of reporters and photographers; the flashing lights and shouting questions were like a swarm of celebrity paparazzi. The attention was overwhelming. I felt nervous, and my mouth went dry at the sight of the buzzing crowd—and it was all directed at me. Less than five years earlier, I felt anonymous. But now it appeared that I was living my life under a microscope, with beaming lights zeroed in on my every move.

As my mother and I greeted each other, a reporter from the *Boston Herald* interrupted our embrace. "Okay, now smile for the camera."

Then another reporter shouted, "Turn this way so we can get a picture as well."

Mom also seemed overwhelmed. "Come on, Douglas, let's just head directly inside so that we can check in and get to our terminal."

Even at the ticket counter, we were in the limelight. "Hey, you're the Day-O guy I saw on TV a couple of weeks ago! Oh my God, is this your mother? Are you guys going to Washington, D.C., to see President Clinton?"

"Yes, I'm the Day-O guy, this is my mother, and yes we are going to see the president," I replied, shifting my weight from foot to foot and smiling politely.

"I see that you guys are in coach and not first class," the agent frowned.

"Well, ma'am, the university is covering all the costs, and we'll take whatever seats we can get." I could still see flashes from the photographers outside the corridor, and I wanted desperately to speed up the process.

"Wait for a moment, please . . . I will be right back," she said. Five minutes later, she was back with someone who appeared to be her supervisor. She took one look at me and immediately recognized me.

"Hey, you're the Day-O guy I saw on TV a couple of weeks ago!"

"Yes, ma'am, that's me," I said, and smiled at her.

The supervisor clicked around in the computer system and in another minute, she looked up at us, a grin on her face. "Well, today, Mr. and Ms. Luffborough, you will be guests in our first-class cabin. We will board both of you now, before everyone else, so that we can provide you with some refreshments."

In unison, Mom and I thanked the agents, and then Mom added another nicety. "May God bless both of you for your kindness." And she meant it.

Everything, from the empty jet bridge, to sitting in the first-class seats 1A and 1B . . . we felt like rock stars, especially since it was the first time either of us had flown first class.

As each passenger filed in, they greeted us like we were distant relatives seeing each other for the first time. We stood, hugged, signed autographs, and kissed lots of babies—and we were glad when the plane was full and everyone had found their seats.

The smile on my mother's face, the dignity with which she sat down in her first-class seat and pulled out her own flower tea cup and saucer set, refreshed me. Dressed in her favorite deep-purple glittery scarf, sipping tea and taking small bites of the airport cookies . . . she looked like royalty. This is how I always envisioned my mother—a figure like the sophisticated former First Lady Jacqueline Kennedy. This moment felt like redemption for a life of obscurity and second-class-citizen treatment. Finally, she was being treated with the honor, respect, and admiration she deserved.

I stifled a laugh as the president of Northeastern University and other university officials walked past us in first class to sit back in the main cabin.

Midway through the flight, the intercom came on. "Ladies and gentlemen, this is your captain. We want to thank you for flying with us today, and we are excited to have Doug Luffborough and his mother, Elsa Luffborough Mensah, with us in our first-class cabin. Please join us in congratulating both of them as they are on their way to Washington to meet with President Clinton in the Oval Office." The entire plane cheered, clapping as if we had won a gold medal at the Olympics.

As the plane descended for landing, I looked outside my window and saw the Washington Monument as a reminder of our country's history and our freedom. I felt myself inhale with pride at being part of the fabric of this country, and I could hardly wait for our adventure in our nation's capital to begin.

At baggage claim, we were met by Secret Service agents—our escorts for the duration of the trip. I had hoped that the agent who had given me such a hard time about my mother during graduation would be there, but I was out of luck on that one. We had a police escort from the airport to our temporary residence at the St. James Inn. At the time, I didn't know what a big deal it was that we were staying at the St. James Inn, which is a historic Washington, D.C., hotel for elected officials and guests of the president. Mom and I had adjoining rooms, and when we opened the shared doors, our smiles were as long as the Potomac.

My suite was immaculate and smelled as if I were the first person to ever sleep there. A fruit basket sat on the coffee table, wrapped in a big red bow with a small card inside, and perched in front of the basket were two large books, also wrapped in ribbon. The card in the basket read: *On behalf of the St. James Inn, we would like to welcome you to Washington, D.C.*

I grabbed a couple of strawberries and stuffed them into my mouth with one hand and thumbed through one of the books about Washington, D.C., with the other. Just before I finished skimming the pages, I heard a knock on the adjoining door, from Ma's room. I picked the fruit basket up in one arm and put the books in the other to show off my presents, and when I opened the door, my mother was standing tall, with a St. James robe draped over her clothes, holding a dozen multicolored roses and a box of Godiva chocolates.

"Douglas, can I interest you in a chocolate?" Her eyes sparkled with joy.

"Wow, Ma, is this great or what? And a far cry from the motel we stayed in when we were homeless, right?" I invited her in and sat on the couch, putting my feet up and grabbing one of the chocolates from the box she placed on the coffee table.

"Douglas, this is awesome, just awesome. God has answered all of my prayers, and I'm as excited as all get-out!"

We sat there for what seemed like hours, eating fruit and chocolates and reading the books with one another, trading stories from the past and from the journey travelled that got us to that moment. When evening came, we ordered room service and turned in early. We had a busy two days planned.

The next morning, we had breakfast at the St. James Inn and then went to the Capitol building to meet with the two senators from Massachusetts, John Kerry and Ted Kennedy. The first stop was Senator Kerry's office. I was overwhelmed with all the pictures of the senator with former presidents and dignitaries from all over the world. We spent most of our time talking with the aides but did get to spend ten minutes with the senator.

"Honored to meet you, Senator."

He reached out his hand and shook mine, looking me in the

eyes and smiling. “Are you kidding me? The honor is mine. You had one hell of a speech at Northeastern, and I’m happy to see that our president came through on his promise. Mrs. Luffborough, you must be so proud of your son.”

“Yes, Senator, I am very proud of Douglas’s accomplishments.”

Senator Kerry looked at us both and gestured to the wider landscape of the city. “I hope you enjoy your time visiting Washington. And Douglas, you really did a great job with your speech. You have a bright future ahead of you with whatever you decide to do, but don’t stop here. Keep going.” The senator’s words of encouragement inspired me, and I nodded and assured him that I would.

We then walked down the hall to visit with Senator Kennedy. My mother enjoyed meeting Senator Kerry but she was *elated* to meet Senator Kennedy, since the Kennedy name is a household one if you’re from Massachusetts. In fact, in most homes in the Bay State, you’re sure to find two pictures on the walls: one of Jesus Christ and one of John F. Kennedy. When I was growing up, my mother talked highly about the Kennedy family and the work they did for the poor and for people of color. My mom was a true fan of the Kennedy clan. When we walked into the senator’s office, she was mesmerized by the display of family pictures on the walls.

One picture specifically caught her eye. “Douglas, come here and look at this picture. I was a young teenager when this picture was taken. Look . . . it’s Senator Kennedy with his two older brothers, Bobbie and Jack, when all three of them were in politics together. It’s a shame what happened to Bobbie and Jack Kennedy . . . God bless their souls.” Her face reflected the deep sadness she had about their assassinations.

I tried to shift her attention toward the present moment, one of meeting a Kennedy face-to-face. “It’s okay, Ma. We are going to meet with Senator Kennedy in a few minutes . . . Can you believe it?” I rested my hand on her shoulder, and she touched it lightly before turning away from the wall of memories.

Then, from the other side of the room, a baritone voice with a noticeable Massachusetts accent called out to us.

“Hey there, Luffborough family. Welcome to Washington, D.C.

I'm Ted Kennedy, and I'm delighted to have you here. Douglas, you almost upstaged the president of the United States with your speech at Northeastern, and it was great to be there to see it all in person." Senator Kennedy was large in stature and personality, and his voice took up the whole room as he naturally belted out an impressive volume.

"It is great to meet you, Senator. I loved your brothers, Bobbie and Jack," my mother blurted out.

"I loved them, too," the senator retorted with a big smile on his face as he looked back and forth at the pictures of Bobby and Jack. He then added, "I know you have a busy couple of days planned in Washington, and I wanted to meet you personally, as your senator, to tell you how proud I am of your son for representing Northeastern the way he did. It will go down in history as one of the greatest graduations the university has ever seen. You did a great job raising him and it showed." He looked at her gracefully, waiting for her to respond.

"Well, thank you, Senator. I tried to model how I raise my kids after the Kennedy family and the way you all were raised."

The senator chuckled. "So, where is your next stop?"

"We will be touring the city, stopping at some of the monuments, and just sightseeing for most of the day," I shared. As we left the senator's office, the senator's aide took a picture of the three of us, and to this day, it's hanging right next to my mother's pictures of Jesus Christ and former President John F. Kennedy.

Secret Service agents led us to our police escort, who took us to many of the famous sites in Washington. Though some of our favorites were the Vietnam Memorial, Arlington National Cemetery, and the Lincoln Memorial, the most moving one was the Holocaust Memorial Museum that had opened a short three months before our visit. As I walked into the lobby, the souls of the innocent reminded me that others had paid the price for me to be where I was that day. I felt a strong sense of freedom and liberty wash over me in a wave of gratitude. For over two hours, I walked three floors of the museum, taking in everything I saw. Tears streamed down my face as I read about the millions of Jews killed and tortured at the hands of the Nazis for no legitimate reason. The tremendous loss of human life was too much to bear, and by the time I reached the last room, my heart had broken apart. The walls were carved in a rotunda, with all of the names of the deceased engraved on them. In the middle was a stone statue with the following scripture from Deuteronomy 4:9:

> *"Only be careful, and watch yourselves closely so that you do not forget the things your eyes have seen or let them fade from your heart as long as you live. Teach them to your children and to their children after them."*

The sun beamed through the windows, and I sat down on the concrete bench by myself, trying to process everything I had witnessed. I was convicted to never forget what I saw and experienced at the Holocaust museum, and going forward, to ensure that my children would one day understand their history.

As we were leaving, I turned to my mother. My gratitude was overwhelming me, and my heart felt wide open. "Thank you, Ma, for all you do for us! Your sacrifice was not in vain."

Mom smiled. "Thanks be to God, son, thanks be to God." We both were wiped out with everything we saw and experienced, and we wanted to go back to our hotel and rest because the next day's visit to the White House and meeting with President Clinton was our primary purpose for the trip. The ride in the car was filled with *did you see that?* and *how about that?* We could not stop talking about the final rotunda room with the thousands of men, women, and children's names engraved into the slabs of concrete—people who ended up at the wrong place at the wrong time in our world's history. Even though it was a conversation filled with wonder, it was also a somber one.

Later that night, I said goodnight to my mom and went back into my room. I lay down on my king-sized bed, complete with marshmallow pillows, and thought about how radically my entire life had shifted before my eyes: from a homeless teen my senior year in high school to graduating from college and meeting the president of the United States five years later. Out of comfort, I put on my Jim Brickman music and quietly thanked God for this once-in-a-lifetime opportunity as I drifted off to sleep.

The next morning at the White House, we felt like foreign dignitaries meeting with the president, since everyone treated us as VIPs. Naturally, our Secret Service escorts guided us, and I was amazed at how keenly aware they were of their surroundings at all times. I felt a deep admiration for the way they did their job, as unique as they were to devote themselves in that way.

As we turned down Pennsylvania Avenue, numbness washed over me from head to toe. Intermittently, I heard Mom mumble to Jesus, but it was silent aside from that. Once past the inner security gate, I reached across my seat and grabbed her hand. My excited smile aimed to break down the wall of fear that had enveloped the backseat of the Lincoln Town Car during our drive.

"Ma, this is just awesome. We're going to the kickin' White House and meeting with President Clinton. You did such a great job raising us kids, and today, Ma, you will be honored by the president of the United States for being an example of what all parents need to be for their children."

Ma smiled, looking through the dark glass of the window that showed her silhouette against the White House in the background. "God heard my cries, He heard my prayers, and today He is living up to all of His promises. To God be the glory!" For a moment frozen in time, she stared, motionless, with tears streaming down her cheeks. Moved by my mother's emotions, I turned and looked outside the window on my side of the car. In contrast to the White House's majesty, I noticed a small group of homeless men living in the park across the street. Here we were, a formerly homeless family, now receiving access to the White House and meeting with the president in the Oval Office. The irony of the moment consumed me, and the silence in the car was the loudest kind—a silence that only reverence and gratitude know.

As we stepped out of the car, we were met by President Curry from Northeastern, Senator Kerry, and Liz Walker, the first woman of color to anchor the news on a Boston television station. She'd travelled from Boston to cover our story.

A college-aged, conservatively dressed White House tour guide greeted us just outside the doors of the North Portico, which led into the State Floor. Right away, my mom and Ms. Walker hit it off, because they were both distinguished-looking African-American women around the same age who were single parents raising young men on their own, beating the odds against them.

"Ms. Walker, we look like we could be sisters," Mom said as she approached her.

"Well, on this trip, Mrs. Luffborough, we *are* sistas!" Ms. Walker's mood and warmth broke any tension that had previously clouded our space, and I could palpably feel our comfort increase.

My mouth fell open at the beauty of it all: the large chandelier glittering with light, the marble and ivory columns that separated one room from another, the intricate oil paintings of former U.S. presidents with red patterned velvet chairs placed up against the walls, the ruby-red carpet with golden trim that filled the entire hallway. Instantly I felt like I was somebody, which was the feeling I had been searching for all of my life—the feeling of being noticed, of being wanted, and of being valued and appreciated by others. We then toured the East Room, Green Room, Blue Room, Red Room, and the State Dining Room. Our guide pointed out that the Green and Red Rooms were personally designed and refurbished by former First Lady Jacqueline Kennedy. At this, Ma perked up with excitement, just as she had at Senator Kennedy's office.

She leaned toward the guide with a half-joking-half-serious candor. "Are you guys looking for a housekeeper?" she asked, followed by, "How long does it take your housekeeping staff to clean this part of the White House?" Her questions went along with her expressions of approval at the former First Lady's color and design scheme in each room. My only response was an eye roll, and I put my head down and chuckled as I watched her act as if we were in our own home.

We toured the museum-like public access part of the White House for an hour and then walked back outside, along the White House lawn, toward the West Wing—the entrance to the Oval Office. There, a single U.S. Marine stood expressionless and opened the door for us. I felt very official with the U.S. Marine posted outside the door. As we walked in, my palms began to sweat, and my knees threatened to buckle as our guide shared that when the president is working in the West Wing, a single U.S. Marine stands sentry outside the north entrance on thirty-minute shifts until the president leaves the West Wing. I was ecstatic with heart-pounding excitement to see the president again, now on *his* turf. In the West Wing reception room, where visitors wait to meet with the president, well-known politicians walked past us, sharing hellos or smiles. In the hustle and bustle, we saw Vice President Al Gore, former U.S. Surgeon General Charles Everett Koop, various members of Congress, foreign dignitaries, and other world leaders I had seen on television. After twenty or so minutes, we were escorted down a hallway just outside the doors of the Oval Office and were told to stand there until someone came out to get us. Everyone in our group was full of excitement and reverence for the situation. Although there was commotion, talking, and lots of activity all around us, we became observers, not saying a word.

White House Communications Director George Stephanopoulos opened the doors of the Oval Office, and the breeze it created brought with it the same confidence that came over me at the podium during my graduation speech. With his clipboard in hand, Mr. Stephanopoulos addressed us all.

"The president of the United States is now ready to see you." Those words were music to my ears. *The president of the United States will now see me.* In that moment, I felt that if the president would give me the time of day, as he was right now, then the world was my oyster . . . I could do anything.

Mr. Stephanopoulos turned to the president. "Mr. President, I would like to present to you Doug Luffborough and his mother, Elsa Luffborough Mensah; President John Curry from Northeastern University; and Senator John Kerry from Massachusetts."

The mystique of the Oval Office covered me, and it was just like it looked in the movies—but it was *real*. I was first to cross the threshold, and President Clinton greeted me and handed me an autographed photo of us from my graduation.

Right behind me was my mother, who by this time felt so at home that the first thing out of her mouth was, "Mr. President, it is nice to meet you, but my throat is dry from today's tour, and I wonder if you would be so kind as to get me a glass of water?" Her straight face and polite demeanor incited laughter from everyone in the room, and an aide quickly met her request. My insides leaped in momentary humiliation that the first thing my mother did when she met the president of the United States in the Oval Office was ask him for a glass of water, but even though all formality was out the window for her, she was in her element, so I let her have her moment in the sun. After the life she lived, why not!

The president walked me over to his desk and told me that when he was sixteen years old and a part of Boys Nation, he met former President John F. Kennedy.

"That was the first time in my life that I knew that one day, a boy from Hope, Arkansas, would also become president. In fact," he went on, beaming, "when I became president, I found out that each president has a choice of using another president's desk during his term, and for me, only one desk would do. I chose the famous JFK Resolute Desk, recognized in the historic photograph of the young JFK Jr. peeking out from its panel. See!" He pointed out the details of the picture, and being so close to modern history sent another wave of amazement through me. I vowed then to keep giving life my best.

After the exchange, we all sat down to visit, but I was so mesmerized that I can't remember much of our conversation. A short time later, we gathered in the front of the Oval Office as what seemed like a drove of Associated Press staff filled the back of the room for a formal press conference.

Right on cue, the president commanded the room. "Hello, everybody. Those of you who travel with me regularly will, I think, recognize the young man on my right, Mr. Doug Luffborough. He was the student speaker at Northeastern University in Boston the other day. This is his mother, whom I introduced and got a big hand. They're here with President John Curry of Northeastern and Senator John Kerry, his senator. I invited Doug and his mother to come visit me in the Oval Office, so they didn't wait long to take me up on the invitation." The president paused as the room filled with laughter, and then added, "I'm glad to see them here today.

"You may remember also that he brought the house down. He not only gave a great speech, but he sang at the beginning of his speech. I thought to myself, if I could sing like that, I wouldn't be giving speeches today."

Compelled to say something, I blurted out, "Well, it was a wonderful opportunity for me and a wonderful opportunity for my family and especially for my mother. I've been waiting for an opportunity like this, and I'm just really thrilled. And I'm really glad that Northeastern was the place you decided to come. It's been a pleasure and an honor to be here today. Thank you."

Ms. Walker, the news reporter from Boston, chimed in. "Mr. President, what was it about Doug that impressed you so much?"

Without skipping a beat, the president eloquently answered her. "Well, first of all, that he had come from such humble circumstances to go to college and to stay in college and that he had made the most of it. He obviously never felt sorry for himself. He obviously had a mother who helped him to believe in himself, as many others do. And the fact that his fellow students picked him to be the spokesperson for their class showed that they identified with the values and the inner strength and drive that took him to the success that he enjoys. I was very impressed. And I just thought it would be neat if they could come down here and see me."

After the president finished his statement, Mr. Stephanopoulos ushered the press out of the room and we said our goodbyes. I had hoped to have more time with the president, but I also understood how busy he must have been, and I knew that these moments would be some of the most memorable in my entire life.

President Clinton turned to shake my hand. "Thanks for coming to see me. By the way, Doug, have you ever thought about a career in politics?"

"Not at this time, Mr. President, but I'm open to where my career will take me," I said before I turned to leave the Oval Office.

The president smiled and nodded, pursing his lips in a satisfied smile, which I took as approval for my politically correct response.

It was hard leaving the White House because I knew the realities I faced back at work. My supervisor, Diane, would be the pin to burst the White House visit bubble. However, deep down, I knew how real this experience was for me and my mother, and I knew that we would never forget it. To this day, I'm appreciative of President Clinton's public invitation to visit him in the Oval Office. He honored my journey from being homeless to graduating from college in less than five years, but what impressed me the most was the way he treated my mom . . . like the queen that she is and has always deserved to be.

Chapter 17

City Year

Everybody can be great . . . because anybody can serve. You don't have to have a college degree to serve. You don't have to make your subject and verb agree to serve. You only need a heart full of grace. A soul generated by love.

—Martin Luther King Jr.

It seemed like the minute we left the steps of the White House, the reality of our common life crashed down upon us like a hailstorm. The attention I had twenty minutes earlier as I stood in the Oval Office went back to *Doug who?* interactions in the world at large. At the airport, the fanfare, reporters, and photographers did not show up as they had in Boston. There was no first-class seat on the way back; my mom and I sat in the rear of the plane near the bathrooms.

"Well so much for the rock-star status, Ma," I teased as I buckled my seat belt and tried not to breathe in the odor that came in waves whenever the bathroom door was opened.

My mom smiled. "It is what it is, Douglas. But know that I'm so proud of you, with or without any cameras around."

We were both exhausted and slept the entire way back. When we arrived in Boston, the driver greeted us with a smile and helped us with our bags. The plan was for him to drop me off at my apartment not too far from Northeastern and then take my mother back to her home in Worcester.

When we got settled in the van, the driver asked about our visit. "So how was it meeting the president of the United States?"

My mom and I looked at each other. I was sure we were both thinking, *Where do we start?*

"It was awesome," I said finally. "The White House is something to see and an amazing experience."

"The place was so clean, I mean spotless," Ma added. "I would love to work in the White House as a housekeeper one day . . ." she trailed off, I'm sure reminiscing about falling in love with the Green and Red Rooms. We talked about the trip until we arrived on my street, when I had to collect my belongings and say goodbye to Mom.

"Ma . . . this was awesome, but now I have to get back to the real world. I'm so glad you were able to come on this trip with me. Please let me know if you have any problems with Darrell or Derrick when you get home." I hugged her tightly, grabbed my suitcase out of the back of the van, and headed toward the steps of my apartment. I turned in enough time to watch my mom disappear down the road. I inhaled deeply and knew that this trip, this moment, would remain with me for the rest of my life.

I lugged my bags up the stairs, and when I opened the door, my roommate, Keith, was drinking a beer on the couch. He looked up, and his eyes met mine. "Day-O!"

Dropping my bag in the doorway, I kicked off my shoes and grabbed a beer from the fridge to join him.

After I opened it, Keith confessed. "They aired the Oval Office press conference . . . it looked cool. How was it, *really*?"

"Awesome, Keith, just awesome. I can't believe I was actually there."

"How was Clinton?" Keith persisted.

"A natural politician, but very nice, and he treated my mom like a queen," I replied. For the next hour and a half, I recounted every step, every experience while we were in Washington. Eventually, I retired to the one bedroom we also shared. Even as my head, exhausted and full of a paradox of possibilities and my current reality, hit the pillow, my thoughts shifted to going back to work. I would have to face Diane and the mindless job I had of administering employee death claims and retirement plans, and signing up former employees for COBRA coverage. The contrast could not be more stark.

The next morning, I was still amazed by the trip, but my chest felt tight with anxiety about the barrage of questions Diane would have for me when I got to my cubicle.

True to form, there she stood, tapping her foot. When I was within earshot, she looked at her watch. "Well, good morning, Mr. Celebrity. Glad to see that you showed up to work on time this morning." She wasted no time doling out my orders. "Once you get settled, can you please update me on the work you are doing and the status of your projects?"

"No problem," I replied as I opened my briefcase. I sorted through the work I had taken with me.

Looking over our adjoining cubicle, Paula waited until Diane was gone. "Wow, she is totally giving you a hard time."

I put my hands on my head. "I know . . . this whole celebrity thing is killing her. I don't see myself in this department long, Paula. I think I need to transfer to another department where the manager supports me—or at least is not always dumping on me."

Even though I had been there for no more than two weeks, it was already clear that I needed to get out of there.

My visit to the White House had received national exposure, so I got anywhere from five to eight inquiries a week while I was at work to come speak at various schools, organizations, churches, and other random places, but I had to turn down the ones that were during work hours. There was no way in hell that Diane would let me off work to promote my motivational speaking debut. I had originally thought that working for corporate America was what I wanted for my life, but I saw my passion for motivational speaking developing.

I joined the Toastmasters organization at John Hancock and besides enjoying it, I found that giving speeches was natural for me. When my schedule did allow me to accept a speaking engagement, it made me incredibly happy because it confirmed that the speech I made at Northeastern actually had an impact on others. I bought books on public speaking, listened to motivational speakers like Les Brown and Anthony Robbins, and practiced my speeches in the mirror daily.

Even though the majority of people who wanted to meet me, have dinner with me, hire me, or have me sing to them were insurance brokers, dreamers, or entrepreneurial multilevel marketers, one man turned out to be different: Fred Davis. Fred was in his seventies, tall, heavy-set, and of Irish descent. He dressed in dark, deeply creased suits and was the president of the Freedom Trail Foundation. Fred was a graduate of Harvard Business School and called me out of the blue one day when I was at work at John Hancock.

"Hello there. My name is Fred Davis. I watched your graduation on TV and saw your interview from the White House. I wanted to ask if I could meet you in person, perhaps take you out to lunch to hear more about your experience . . . I'm interested in knowing more about what you want to do in the future." I had received so many calls asking me to do all sorts of things, but no one ever asked me what I wanted to do with my future.

"Well, if you could meet me in the lobby of the Hancock building for lunch, I think I can do that," I agreed. We set a time to meet later that week.

When the day came, we met in the lobby of John Hancock and walked to the closest coffee shop for our introductory meeting. Our time was short but productive and was more of a getting-to-know-you exchange. We decided to meet again the next week, and this time he invited me over to his office near the Charlestown Navy Yard.

During my lunch break on the day of our second meeting, I took the T to meet with Fred: the Green Line to Park Street and changed to the Red Line closer to the Charlestown Navy Yard. Even though we did not know one another well, I trusted the process of meeting him and seeing what that would bring. I needed people in my life to direct me towards my next step, and I felt like Fred was put in my life to do that. As I exited the train to walk to Fred's office, I noticed that the address he gave me looked like a house and not a traditional brick-and-mortar office building. I got a little nervous and thought to myself, *I sure hope this guy is really who he says he is and not some type of child molester or something.* But the chance to meet someone who could help me was more powerful than the thought that this guy wanted to hurt me. I knocked on the door and heard a familiar voice on the other side say, "Just a minute." When the door opened, it was Fred, dressed in a dark blue suit, white shirt, and red tie . . . as sharp as a politician.

"Hey, Doug, come on in. This is an old, fully restored home from the early nineteen hundreds that has been converted to half office space and half part of the Boston National Historic Park Museum. There's a lot of Boston history in these walls." I looked around me and wondered how I would have been received as an African-American male if I had been there in that era. To the left of the entryway was Fred's office. We walked in together, talking about my visit to the White House, and Fred showed me to my seat.

As he made his way around the big mahogany desk that took up much of the room, he said, "Doug, thanks for making time to come to see me. I really admire you for everything you've overcome, and after our meeting last week, I've been wondering who is mentoring you through all of your overnight success?"

"Well, to be honest with you, my mom has been my mentor for most of my life. She helps me out when I need it," I replied.

Fred put down his pen and looked at me. "You know, Doug, you have a lot of talent, and if you don't have the right mentors in your life, I'm afraid that people and organizations may take advantage of you. When I saw you on TV, I knew I needed to get in touch with you and be that safe voice to help guide you through the whirlwind of success you are experiencing. No strings attached."

I listened intently but remained silent until Fred continued.

"I came out of retirement to run the Freedom Trail because of its long history, and I wanted to revitalize the experience for the next generation. I have been married for over forty years and have children older than you . . . even *grand*children," he chuckled. His experience as a husband, a father, and a grandfather made me feel at ease. I was open to finding someone to help me navigate life, so I was hopeful that I could find a mentor like Fred to guide me.

"Thank you, Fred, for sharing. I would love a mentor like you. You know, not everyone celebrates my success and brief time in the limelight. The other challenge I have is being able to discern who is legit and who is selling me a bag of baloney," I confessed.

We went back and forth, building up trust for our impromptu mentoring relationship. I didn't know what an accomplished, Harvard Business School, retired, Irish Catholic family man saw in a fatherless, formerly homeless, recent college graduate African-American male, but I really didn't care, as long as he was a man of his word. Fred became the mentor that I needed. We met many times over the next few months while I was at John Hancock. His advice was always timely and appropriate.

One time we met after work for dinner at the Ritz-Carlton in Boston. Fred took me to the most expensive and classy places in Boston to expose me to a different type of living. That night over dinner, he shared his thoughts about my work situation.

"Douglas, your boss at John Hancock does not want you to succeed. For some bizarre reason, she sees you as a threat. The best advice I can give you is to transfer to another department, or you may need to leave John Hancock altogether. You have so much raw talent that it's hard for others to know how to manage and lead you. Keep speaking on the weekends, keep looking for greater opportunities," he advised. As much as I wanted to fit into the corporate environment, I always felt like a square peg trying to fit into a round hole.

Another time we met for drinks during happy hour at the Copley hotel bar and traded martinis and stories with one another. During that evening, he shared another equally valuable piece of advice.

"Doug, I have been around a long time. I grew up with white privilege, and the best advice I can give you is to learn the game of golf. The greatest deals in America are made on the golf course, and the groups of people I never see on the course and in these meetings are inner city African-American males like yourself. So therefore, you and others are left out of the conversations and miss out on the opportunities you need and are looking for."

Until Fred said this, I hadn't considered golf that way. For starters, it's an expensive and exclusive sport, which can be difficult to both learn and play. And given the hard environments urban African-American males develop within, golf is not usually an option. Although it was a risk, I was willing to take it to meet new people and to avoid missing out on future business opportunities. I picked up the game of golf shortly thereafter, and the most important lesson I learned was the importance of golf etiquette—something you can only learn on the course. And Fred was right. The greatest deals in America *are* made on the golf course.

One time I went to play golf in the neighboring town of Framingham. My coworkers at John Hancock spoke about it often, and I thought one Saturday morning that I would head over there to play the course. As I arrived, the setup looked private and exclusive, but I pushed through the stigma of only seeing white men and no people of color around me. All the men around me were in their forties and fifties, drove expensive cars, and smoked long, thick cigars. I made my way to the Pro Shop, feeling like all eyes were on me because I was this twenty-something recent college grad trying to network with others outside of my element. Because I was a player of one, I was linked up with three other guys who were already on the first tee and seemed to know each other. I hurried to join them.

"Good morning, gentlemen! My name is Doug Luffborough, and it looks like I will be joining you today. I must warn you I'm not the best player, but I am a great conversationalist. If my game starts going south, I will just pick up my ball so I don't slow you guys down." The guys laughed with relief that I would not ruin their experience and welcomed me on the team. True to form, I followed the etiquette of the game and kept our conversations going for the four hours we were out there. We talked about family, education, business, politics, and even religion. After we finished, I joined the group in the clubhouse for some drinks. One of the guys was the CEO of a waste management company in Boston.

"Doug, you are a great conversationalist and have a super personality. I could use someone like you at my place. If you ever want a career in waste management, here is my card. I would love to talk more with you."

Flattered, I took his card and wrote on the back of it: "The greatest deals in America are made on the golf course!" and signed it *by Fred Davis.*

Off the golf course, my working relationship with Diane grew worse. It escalated to where I did not want to go to work at all, and when I was there, I looked for every excuse not to talk with her.

I worked the networks I had built up over the years as a Co-op student, and inquired about other positions throughout the company. From senior vice presidents to managers to employees, I talked to anyone who would meet with me. I knew that the company was a small place, and word would travel fast about my displeasure with Diane, but I tried my best to imply that dealing with death benefits was a dead-end position for me.

The overwhelming resistance I had from working in Diane's department became so big that I started getting anxiety attacks. Toward the end of my first year, Diane and I met to review my performance and to discuss if I would be getting the annual raise most employees received each year. The awkwardness of both of us being alone in her office was so uncomfortable that we met standing up.

"Well, Doug, I want to say that I am disappointed by your performance this first year in our department. I believe that you exhibit poor time management skills, and you procrastinate with getting things done. I will be putting you on formal probation and giving you six months to turn your performance around. I have recommended that you not receive a raise this year, and I want you to start tracking a thirty-minute time log to help you stay focused with your job responsibilities. I will need you to turn in your time log once a week for my review. Do you have any questions for me?"

With glazed defeat in my eyes, I conceded. "No, I have no questions for you." And just like that, my performance evaluation was over. As I walked out of the office, I knew that this was the straw that broke the camel's back. I would implement the time-tracking, work hard, and at the same time, aggressively pursue work elsewhere. Fred was right: Diane did not believe in me, support me, or want me working for her. My trip to the White House, graduation success, and prior Co-op experiences were too much for her to deal with, and if I wanted to follow my own success, I was not going to do it on her watch.

Once back in my cubicle, I sat in shock, terribly upset by what I had heard. A procrastinator with poor time management skills? Really? I would not have been there if it was not for my proactive approach to life. My job at John Hancock rested on the fact that I had managed my time wisely enough so that I had a job offer *before* I graduated from college. The thoughts bounced around in my head, creating heat and energy. I recounted going from homelessness to being a college graduate, despite my guidance counselor's negative recommendation. None of these triumphs matched up with Diane's description of my work performance. After the blurring frustration, I settled on what I knew to be true about me: I always tried my best to use *every* opportunity in my life to better my life and those around me. With the odds stacked against me, I came out on the other side thriving, and I was not going back. I would not slip back into depression, doubt myself, or belittle my life experiences and accomplishments. Diane was a new face, but her tactics were familiar to me. With my jaw set in a firm line, I rejected her opinion of me that day but did everything she asked until another opportunity came along.

One day after lunch, I was walking back to the office and ran into one of my former Co-op advisors from Northeastern. Janice had recently left the university to work for an organization called City Year. Michael Brown and Alan Khazei, roommates at Harvard Law School in 1988, founded City Year because they felt strongly that young people in service could be a powerful resource for addressing America's most pressing issues. Together they built City Year with the conviction that one person can make a difference; and since its inception, City Year has promoted the vision of service as a common expectation—and a real opportunity—for citizens all around the world. City Year's vision is that one day the most commonly asked question of a young person will be, "Where are you going to do your service year?" Currently, City Year is serving in twenty-five cities across the United States and in three international affiliate sites located in Johannesburg, South Africa; Birmingham, England; and London, England. They are known for their red jackets, sense of idealism, and strong organizational culture. Many times on my way to work, I saw over fifty energized and enthusiastic young people with bright red jackets, khaki pants, and boots doing morning military-like calisthenics on Copley Plaza. Rain or shine, wind or snow, they were out there. I was inspired by their spirit, discipline, purpose, and pride for the work they did throughout the community and thought City Year might be a better fit for me. I liked the image of working in a corporation, but I also wanted to work within the community helping the poor and other kids who grew up the way I did.

My former Co-op advisor introduced me to a woman named Nancy Routh, who was the director of Human Resources at the time. Nancy was looking to grow her HR department, and my generalist position at John Hancock and my HR degree from Northeastern were a perfect match. Almost six months later, before my next formal review with Diane, I resigned from John Hancock and accepted a position with City Year. I would be working with Nancy in Human Resources, making more money working in a nonprofit than I was receiving at John Hancock. The pay surprised me, but Nancy shared that City Year was looking to recruit top talent and was willing to compete with the for-profit sector to get the right people on board. Without looking back, I walked away from John Hancock, leaving the start of my corporate insurance career and Diane's iron fist of poor leadership behind.

The move to City Year felt right; the staff I worked with appreciated the skills I contributed. Not long after being hired, Nancy offered me a lateral move to become a Team Leader, overseeing and managing six to eight corps members.

"Doug, I have been watching you since you started here, and I'm impressed with your attention to detail and professional sense of urgency. I think the role we have you in is great but will not get the best out of you. I would like to provide you with an opportunity where you can utilize your leadership skills and work more directly with our young people in the community," Nancy persisted. This would be my first formal supervisory role and would give me greater exposure in the company as a burgeoning leader. It was hard to believe that Diane had told me at John Hancock that I was a procrastinator and had poor time management, and now in my new job, I was being asked to play a greater role. *If Diane only knew,* I thought.

Being a Team Leader was more challenging because I worked with young adults, ages seventeen to twenty-four, who were working on their GED, had a high school diploma, had some college experience, or were college graduates. The young adults had different maturity levels, work experiences, and intellectual capacities.

With nervous enthusiasm, I spoke. "So, hi, everyone. My name is Doug, and I will be your new Team Leader for the rest of the year."

The team looked at me with blank stares plastered on their faces; it was clear that we did not all share the same excitement. On cue, the team looked toward Jonah—the pseudo–Team Leader.

He recognized the attention, stood, stepped forward one foot, and spoke. "You are the third Team Leader we've had in the past four months. I guess we are glad to have you, but I'm compelled to ask: will you be with us for the remainder of the year?" His voice was steady and stoic, but he wore an apprehensive and nervous look on his face, as if to say he wasn't convinced I was there to stay.

"I can tell you that I just joined City Year, and I don't plan on going anywhere, so I hope you guys will at least give me a chance."

The team looked up to Jonah and trusted him, so I knew very early on that in order to make progress with the team, I had to get Jonah on my side as quickly as possible. City Year was an organization that believed in order and structure and had strict policies regarding being on time, wearing a neat and clean uniform, and wearing your nametag on the top right side of your shirt. If corps members or staff showed up late, were out of uniform, or forgot their nametag, they were written up. After three write-ups, corps members and staff members would be put on probation and risk being released by the organization. The first week, I wrote down infractions but did not formalize them. It was my way of showing the team that I meant business but that I wanted to make sure we were all clear on the expectations before I upheld existing parameters.

The second week was a different story. At physical training, or PT, that Monday, I noted two members who arrived after we started. Once the exercise was complete, I pulled the team aside and explained the rules, the process, and my detailed notes regarding the previous week.

"Someone once told me that if you are fifteen minutes early, you are on time. If you are on time, you are late. And if you are late, you are fired. After today, if you are going to be late you need to call me. If you don't, I will mark you down as a no-show, no-call, and you will be written up."

Immediately, there was push-back by Jonah. "Written up? You just got here and already you are trying to be Mr. By-the-Book Team Leader? Give me a break . . . I'm out of here!" He turned on his heel, his chin in the air, and walked off.

I called after him. "Fine, Jonah. If you walk away, I will have to write you up for insubordination and for leaving our team circle." But Jonah kept walking.

I turned my attention to the rest of the team. "Does anyone else want to leave?" To my surprise, no one else left, even though they acted like they wanted to by looking in Jonah's direction; some rolled their eyes while others huffed with a sigh of frustration. It was then that I realized that their alliance was not as strong as I thought it was.

Later on that evening, after I ate dinner and had some downtime, I decided to give Jonah a call. Not really wanting to deal with the confrontation, I sat at my kitchen table and slowly dialed each number, and then took a deep breath when I heard the call go through.

"Hello, Jonah, this is Doug. I find it ironic that you questioned me about walking out on the team and then you walked off when you heard something you didn't like."

"Well, you became our third Team Leader and then within a week, you went on a power trip. You don't even know who we are," Jonah fired back.

I cleared my throat, careful about the words I would use. "Listen, I just started working here, and I'm following the rules set in place by the organization. Our team needs order, structure, and accountability, and it is my role to make sure that happens. You can either help me or you can leave the team, because there is only room for one Team Leader."

Jonah's frustration was palpable through the phone. "Is that a threat?"

"No, it is a promise. But . . . I hope you will work with me to lead the team, because I need your help, Jonah. Give me a chance and see what I can do by backing me, bro. Can you do that?" I protested as the seriousness of the conversation lifted me out of my chair to a standing position. The tone of my voice was firm yet hopeful that Jonah would join me.

Dead silence paused our conversation for so long that I wasn't sure if the phone had died. "Hello, Jonah. Are you still there?"

His voice dropped, an unhappy reconciling with the reality of accountability confronting him. "Yeah, I'm still here, but I have a lot to think about tonight to see if I want to still do this."

I exhaled relief. "Okay, I can respect that and want you to have that time. If I see you tomorrow, I will consider that you are with me on this. Thank you for taking my call." And with that, we hung up. When I set the phone down, a lump filled my throat. I wondered if Jonah would be willing to work with me. He was a leader, and I really wanted to work with him—growing our previously leaderless team *and* him. Even though I was on the verge of strong emotion, I was confident I could do it with the right people surrounding me. I went to bed that night dreading the worst—that Jonah had called the other team members after our call and that no one would show up for work the next day. Despite my confidence that I handled it the best possible way, I tossed and turned, questioning whether leaving John Hancock was a wise career move. I realized that being in a leadership position is one thing, but *becoming* a leader is another. I was starting to learn that being a leader might also mean being misunderstood.

The next morning, there were no messages from him or any of the other members. Right away, I concluded the worst: that they had bailed and that I was down to a team of one: me. At work before the morning program, other teams huddled and stretched together, but I stood alone. I replayed the conversation I'd had with Jonah the night before until it was a broken record. Was I off target with what I shared with him? Was I wrong to push him so hard? I sat down on the cement staircase and questioned my leadership and fit with City Year, the lump from last night returning to my throat. I looked up and shaded my eyes to avoid the beam of sun on my face, and off in the distance, Jonah clipped his way towards me, each team member behind him in single file. I sat there motionless and smiled on the inside, but my pride would not allow me to show it. The image of him leading the team towards me was a sign of the changing of the guard. My words *had* impacted him, and he now seemed receptive to letting me lead. I stood up, and when he was within a few feet, I first extended my hand to him, looking him directly in the eyes, and and then pulled him to me to show gratitude for him trusting me.

I said good morning to each team member and gave them each a hug, too. Then we circled up.

"Thank you guys for coming this morning! It means a lot to me. Now let's get to work!" The big smile covering my face from ear to ear made the team smile and laugh, too.

Our team worked at two different sites each day. In the mornings, after we finished all organizational affairs, we headed to Boston City Hospital where we worked in various departments. In the afternoons, we worked at an after-school program called the Shelburne Community Center, serving as tutors, mentors, and recreational aides. We ran a homework assistance program, and once homework was completed, we led various athletic activities such as basketball, dodgeball, kickball, volleyball, and capture the flag. We had a two-hour break to travel from one site to the next via public transportation and ate lunch along the way. During the travel time between both sites, I gained the best insights on each of my team members.

At Boston City Hospital, our main contact was Reggie, a graduate of the Harvard Graduate School of Education. He was in charge of managing volunteers at the hospital and working with organizations like City Year to help us manage our projects. Though we did everything from warehouse work and clearing out storage areas to working directly with doctors and patients throughout the hospital, working in the maternity ward with high-risk mothers and babies in the prenatal unit truly changed my heart.

Most of the babies we took care of did not make it, or they developed major complications that persisted for the rest of their lives.

But even so, they needed someone to care for them, hold them, and pray for them and their families. I grew to love working there—holding, feeding, and rocking these sick angels to sleep. The more I was there, the more my heart expanded for children born into this situation. Inside of one week, I worked with a newborn baby born with crack in his system, another born with fetal alcohol poisoning, and two others that were born prematurely and severely malnourished. On that Friday at the end of our shift, our team walked into Reggie's office, and I couldn't hide that my heart was heavy.

"Sometimes it is so hard to come here and hold these babies who, through no fault of their own, are in these situations. It makes me so angry at the parents . . . what in the hell were they thinking?"

Reggie drew in a thoughtful breath. His weathered, dark skin reflected the emotions he felt day in and day out at his job. "Thinking, that's just it Doug. They *weren't* thinking, and as a result, they gave birth to a child who is sick and needs a lot of medical attention. But don't lose hope. The more bonding you can do with them, the more love you show them, the better off they will be." Reggie's voice cracked in a few places with his passion. "That's why we appreciate your team here. You may think that all you do is hold sick babies, but what you guys *really* do is give these babies another chance at life. Because of you, these babies feel caressed, held, and comforted."

Out of nowhere, Jonah spoke. "To be honest with you, this is the best part of my City Year experience. It feels much better to give love than receive it, and each one of these babies needs love." Tears streamed down his face, and other team members teared up.

I still held a tiny baby in my arms, and I looked everyone in the eyes. "Tonight when you go home, remember that you made a difference to this one." Holding up the baby to the entire team, I whispered with my voice cracking to fight off the tears. "What other young people your age can say they are making this type of an impact on another human being?"

Another team member, Francis, burst into tears. "I can't deal with this. It's just too much for me. These babies did nothing wrong and don't deserve this." It was harder for some members on my team, though we always had interesting and often sad conversations with one another once we left the hospital. For me, it was a great birth control lesson.

One time, Jonah shared with the team on the bus while in transit to the Shelburne Community Center: "I have a whole new outlook on what it means to become a father and my role in taking care of a child. Through this experience, I realize I'm not ready."

The Shelburne Community Center, where we spent our time in the afternoons, was in the middle of Roxbury, in the hub of the community. The center supported kids and families living in and around the neighborhood, and it was a great place for teens to go after school because it held recreational activities for the entire family. Our contact there was named Ms. Crystal. My team members warned me that she had a strong personality and was not a fan of City Year because of past broken promises and rapid leadership turnover. I thought to myself, *How bad could it be*? That was until I met her.

When we opened the doors to the center, we were met by Ms. Crystal—an oversized African-American woman dressed like a tomboy, wearing a button-down flannel shirt, overalls, and a turned-backwards baseball cap.

"Oh, it's my City Year team. Are you guys here to work today or just passing through?"

I stepped to the front. "Hi, Ms. Crystal. My name is Doug Luffborough, and I'm the new Team Leader."

Turning her cap from side to side, Ms. Crystal looked past me to Jonah. "Is this fool for real?" The team laughed at this, but thankfully Jonah came to my defense.

"He is our new Team Leader, Ms. Crystal. He's cool."

Stepping towards me with her hand extended, she said, "Well, anyone cool with Jonah is cool with me, but you better come strong up in here, or we're going to throw your ass out like your predecessors." Even though I knew she was joking, her face relaxing into a semi-smile, I was not smiling. I couldn't help but see the parallels between Ms. Crystal and Diane at John Hancock. In this moment, when Ms. Crystal was leading us to that day's activity, I had an epiphany: these types of people are everywhere, and I would have to learn to live with them. I sighed in the realization, knowing that this time, I was willing to give it a try, but I knew I had a lot of work to do. Winning Ms. Crystal over would be a herculean feat, but somebody was destined to stand on top of that mountain. Why shouldn't it be me?

Progress was steady, but day by day, month by month, Ms. Crystal eventually trusted me. I followed her lead, did what I said I was going to do, and stayed later to help with the center. My direct supervisor at City Year, Ernest, was impressed with my relationship with Ms. Crystal, and one afternoon when I was completing paperwork, he approached me about an idea.

"Hey Doug, I want you to ask Ms. Crystal if we can host our kids' and teen camps at the Shelburne Center during the next school vacation coming up—maybe for Easter break or summer?"

"Okay," I said, curiously looking up from my paperwork. "And who will take the lead in running the camps?" I wondered if Crystal would approve such an appointment, and I knew I had to give her as many details about the request as possible.

"Why . . . you will!" Ernest fired back, looking me directly in the eyes.

I was taken aback, shook my head, and put both my hands in the air. "Me? Ernest I just got a handle on managing my team, and now you want me to be the camp director? I am going from leading a team of six to leading a department of sixty people. Are you serious? I can't do that!" Anxiety overrode all my other calm senses. I took a few breaths, trying to quell the rushing nerves, but it wasn't happening. "You are crazy . . . I can't do it!"

"No. Actually, you *have* to do it, Doug. Crystal will not let us do it if you are not leading it. Over the weekend, put your plan together, and share it with me on Monday." Put off with my resistance, he raised his eyebrows, shook his head, and marched out of the room. The first thing I did when I left work that night was head straight to the bar for a tall, stiff drink. I contemplated resigning and going back to John Hancock to beg for my job back. I tossed and turned in bed Friday and Saturday nights, running different scenarios through my mind. Should I stay or should I go? If I left, I would be walking out on a team that had been walked out on many times before. The decision was tearing me open from the inside out, so I sought advice: I called Jonah.

When he picked up the phone, I didn't waste any time. "Jonah, Ernest wants me to be the camp director and lead camps for our entire department at the Shelburne Center. How can I do that?"

"Well, the team's got your back! Tell us what you want us to do and we will do it." Jonah encouraged and assured me that I was not alone. "If you want, I can even meet with you over the weekend to help you, but I think you have to do it. You are the leader we have been waiting for, and what a great way to show everyone what you're all about," Jonah added, his words lifting both my spirits and my confidence that I could do it.

After a bit more deliberation—my sincerest uncertainties floating to the top, I conceded. "Alright, if we can do this as a team, I'll do it. Can you call the rest of the team and get their support as well? I will take the rest of the weekend to lay out the plan. When I have it finished, can we get together to go over it?"

Without missing a beat, Jonah jumped at the idea. "You bet. It's in the bag!"

After I hung up, my fears subsided because I knew that I was not alone. I had a support team behind me that believed in me and that made all the difference.

I met with my team, went over the plan, and got their feedback for running the camps before I presented a revised plan to Ernest. Taking a brief pause after he reviewed the documents, Ernest sent me to get Ms. Crystal's approval that afternoon. Surprisingly, her only caveat was: "This only gets approved if you and your team are leading it. If so, then let's do it." I immediately clenched my fist in the air as to say "Right on." I had climbed that mountaintop.

The first day of camp, I was so stressed that I developed a teenager's breakout on my face . . . but even so, I breathed deeply and smiled a lot, trying hard to not let my stress show. I followed the plan that I created and led one of the best camps during that time. The kids were happy, the parents had nothing but great things to say to Ernest, the staff worked as a team and grew closer with one another, and Ms. Crystal gave me the first smile and hug I had ever received from her. I had everything I needed to run a successful camp—I just needed to believe in myself. The experience restored in me the confidence I had lost when I was working for Diane. And I learned that having the right team behind you is what makes any dream work.

Our team made it through the year together, and their graduation from the program was bittersweet. On one hand, I was elated for my team members that were graduating, but I knew that they would be moving on and leaving City Year. Reggie and Ms. Crystal came to graduation to support the team, and I felt immense pride and relief that I had been able to bring the team together, strengthening our relationships with each other and with our community partners.

Since then, the City Year service model has evolved in high-poverty communities to bridge the gap between the support the students in the communities actually need and what their schools are designed to provide. In doing so, City Year helps to increase graduation rates across the country, and changing the lives of the students they serve.

During that summer, Nancy continued to mentor me, and she offered me a promotion working in the recruitment and admissions department, serving as the head of recruitment for City Year, Boston. Nancy wanted me in this position to increase my scope and visibility, as well as to expose my charisma, leadership qualities, and ability to get things done in the organization as a whole. She saw the same raw talent that Fred Davis saw during our encounters. My primary responsibility would be to recruit the following year's corps of three hundred in less than one year's time. I graciously accepted the position and dug my heels in to get to work. I loved everything about the job, and by that time, I had a reputation as a producer. Although the stakes were high with reaching my recruitment quota, I saw the task as a challenge I could meet.

One day, while I was compiling a list of recruits to follow up with, Nancy called me into her office. "Doug, a local advertising agency called Austin Knight will be working with us on recruitment. I want you to call Claire at their agency and get started."

I jumped on the phone right away. "Hi, can I please speak to Claire?"

"This is she."

"Hi there, I'm Doug Luffborough with City Year. Nancy Routh asked me to give you a call so that we can meet about our ad campaign to recruit next year's corps. When would be a good time for me to come by and meet you?"

With a charming and professional manner she replied, "I have some time next week. Call me on Monday, and we'll confirm."

That next week, I followed up with Claire and set a time to go down to her office for our initial meeting. I arrived at her building just steps away from the T stop at Government Center.

I walked into the lobby, the cool marble floors and walls reflecting my shined shoes. "Hi . . . I'm here to meet with Claire Navarro."

"I'm Claire," she said. We shook hands, and Claire's Asian beauty caught my breath. She had fair skin and wore a brightly colored scarf tied around her neck. We made our way to their conference room and got right to work.

"So what do you know about City Year?" I started.

"Well, I know that you work with seventeen- to twenty-four year-olds who commit to a year of community service work. My boss Jen is good friends with your boss Nancy, and she wanted us to do some pro bono work for a nonprofit organization, so Nancy recommended City Year." Although this was a lead that had been prearranged by someone other than her, she seemed relaxed and content to work together on the project.

"That's great . . . all right, I think we should start with our founding stories." For the next twenty minutes, we talked about what we do, figuring out the message we wanted to promote throughout the community and staying focused on the task at hand. After talking her ear off, I left her office. We both agreed to meet again the following week to work more on our message, branding, and strategy for the advertising and recruitment campaign. We had one purpose: to develop a successful marketing and recruitment campaign to reach the corps recruitment and admission numbers for the next year.

For the next nine months, Claire and I developed a very close relationship, even hanging out after work together. We went out to eat, went dancing at clubs, and bar-hopped through the streets of Boston—but it was just friendship. Towards the end of the year, with her help, I recruited over three hundred corps members in less than eight months; we won an award for recruitment that year.

When the project was over, I still wanted to see Claire and didn't want to think of our time together as over. One day after the awards ceremony, I called her up to see if she wanted to have lunch with me. We met at the same bagel shop we met at during the project.

As we sat down and shared some small talk, I met her eyes with determination. "So . . . Claire, the project is complete, but I still want to hang out with you. Would you be interested in going out to dinner with me to celebrate?"

"Sure," she said, smiling. "Just let me know when and where you want to go, and I would be happy to."

Later on that week, we spoke again over the phone and picked an evening that worked for both of us. We decided to meet outside at a restaurant in Faneuil Hall, not far from where she lived in the North End. As I was getting dressed, I picked hip-like clothes as if I were going out on a date. Claire and I had spent a lot of time working together and kept our relationship professional, but now that the project was over, I was interested in developing the personal side of our relationship. I assumed she was interested by her willingness to say yes anytime I wanted to get together with her, but I was not sure as to what degree she liked being with me.

When she showed up at the restaurant, she was dressed up and wore full make-up . . . and she walked right up to me and kissed me on the cheek. I swallowed hard and smiled back, the scent of her skin washing over me. I was surprised at Claire's gesture—that had never happened before, so I took it as a good sign.

We sat down for dinner and then talked and laughed all night until it was time to go home. As we left the restaurant, I looked at her and asked, "Can I walk you home?"

She shook her head politely. "No, I'm okay."

"Are you sure?" I persisted. I simply didn't want the night to be over—yearning for even another block walking with her.

"Yes, I'm sure. I don't live that far from here. I can walk home," she smiled.

I sighed, accepting her response. "Okay . . . well, I had a great time tonight. I hope we can stay in touch with one another, you know, if you are interested."

Claire smiled even brighter. "Yes, I would like that," she replied, and just before we parted ways this time, I grabbed her hands and pulled her close to me and kissed her on the cheek.

Chapter 18

Harvard

Oh, my goodness, I'm at Haaaaaavard! Not too many girls from rural Mississippi have made it all the way here to Cambridge. I consider today to be a defining milestone in a very long and blessed journey.

—Oprah Winfrey, 2013 Harvard University Commencement Speaker

The difference I made at City Year was life changing; working there gave me the opportunity to lead and make an impact in the lives of others. Throughout my life, I had developed a strong desire to serve others, and I felt particularly compelled to help families in poverty and with dysfunctional dynamics, much like mine had been. And very early on, I knew that education was the key to getting out of poverty.

When I finished school at Northeastern, my life didn't magically transform on the outside. However, on the inside, I felt wealthy—full of knowledge and wisdom, and having a solid plan for my future. Money still wasn't growing on trees, but for the first time in my life, it was not something I had to focus on or worry about the way I had most of my life. I had food at home and could even go out to eat without worrying. When I was homeless, my dream was to go to college, but now that I had graduated, my mind wandered to graduate school. I wasn't sure what I wanted to study or where I wanted to go, but I had seen how transformative higher education was, and I wanted more of it.

After some research, I decided to stay in the nonprofit sector but still wasn't certain whether I wanted an MBA or a master's degree in education. I learned that the founders of City Year had met at Harvard Law School, where they came up with the idea. City Year staff members always seemed to pursue advanced degrees, so there was constant positive peer pressure drawing me down the same path.

After graduating from Northeastern, I was confident that I could get an advanced degree. I had the discipline and motivation to go to graduate school, and I was willing to work hard, put in the time, and show myself worthy of doing graduate-level work.

One day, I was browsing the magazine shelves at Barnes & Noble when I came across a copy of a *U.S. News and World Report* "best colleges" edition that ranked the highest-performing schools in the nation. I decided to purchase the magazine and take it home to read it from cover to cover. I lay on my bed, dissecting schools and potential majors that matched my skills and passion to serve and help others. A part of me leaned toward an MBA, since my undergraduate degree was in business, but the power of my education engaged me in educational policy issues that impacted urban environments. After hours and hours of research, I narrowed my focus to align with my passion: education.

With education as my primary concentration, I thumbed through the pages of *U.S. News and World Report*, only to find that the number one school for education administration was the Harvard University Graduate School of Education.

I closed the magazine at once. *Harvard! Really, Harvard! Could I go to Harvard?* I sat on the edge of my bed, looking at the familiar boardwalk picture that had carried me through my undergraduate experience. Was God speaking to me? Was that my next adventure? Part of me felt foolish for even thinking about it, but, the other part of me was saying *Why not me? Why not now?* With everything I had been through in my life, Harvard seemed to represent the pinnacle of my journey. I just needed to go for it.

I spent the next few days tempering my growing ambitions to apply to the Harvard Graduate School of Education because I was still building my own confidence in my ability to apply. Finally, I called the highest human voice of motivation: Mama Luff. When she picked up the phone with her usual cheer, I launched into my excitement.

"Ma, this is Douglas! I was thinking about going to graduate school to get my master's degree in education. I want to help other kids and families that live in situations like how we grew up . . . and the number one graduate school for education administration in America is at Harvard. Do you think I should apply?"

Mom broke out in laughter. "Douglas, why not Harvard, why not you? If they say no, you will be right where you are today, and that is not bad at all. But what if they say yes! If God put this thought in your heart, then follow through by at least applying."

That was all the advice I needed to hear. Every time I thought about applying, my chest pounded, and my body tensed up with enthusiasm . . . I faced the possibility of attending an Ivy League school. On a whim one morning, and because I lived so close, I took the T to Harvard Square to walk the campus and pick up more information from the admissions department.

The T conductor's voice belted over the speaker. "Haaaaaavard Square."

I jumped from my seat, each movement like an out-of-body experience. I stepped off the train and climbed the stairs to Harvard Square. With each stride, I remembered a bit of my journey up to that point in my life. Everything went in slow motion, and the movie in my mind allowed for the right timing and soundtrack to accompany my ascension.

The first step symbolized my struggle of growing up in poverty; the next signified overcoming the absence of a father or father-like figure in my life; the next was seeing my mother get mistreated as a housekeeper; the next was the paralyzing fear of being bullied in elementary school; the next step was my uncontrollable stuttering impediment developed through the alienation and condescending remarks of my third-grade teacher; the next was for my Little League assistant coach, who told me that I suffered from delusions of grandeur; the next was former friends that discounted my gifts; the next was my high school guidance counselor, who told me I was not college material; and the last step was for Diane at John Hancock. With each stair I climbed, I remembered how I overcame that obstacle, ultimately arriving at the Harvard Yard. Mama Luff's words rang through my mind as I walked the uneven cobblestone sidewalks. "If not me, then who? If not now, when?"

The doubt and insecurity that I'd felt when my third-grade teacher asked me to read out loud among my peers paralyzed me briefly as I reached out to the double doors of the Education building, but the momentum of graduating from Northeastern and my visit to the White House pushed me through.

A kind voice behind a plain cubicle-like secretary desk greeted me immediately.

"Hello, welcome to the Graduate School of Education. How can I help you?"

I froze, overwhelmed by Harvard and tradition, but it only lasted a second. "Yes, hi, my name is Doug . . . Doug Luffborough. I would like some information about the Ed school, and I'd like to pick up an application, please."

To my surprise, the secretary did not ask any other qualifying questions: my GPA in undergrad, what qualified me to apply, or what my parents did for a living were non-issues in that conversation. She simply went to the back of the room and returned with a full application packet.

Without realizing it, I blurted out my next request. "I'm sorry, but can I have two applications? I have someone else that I need to get one for as well." I thought of my brother, Darrell. He was only one year younger than I was and had done well in high school and college. Out of the two of us, Darrell was stronger than I was academically, so I wanted to include him as well.

Without balking, the secretary agreed, and I left the office with two applications, guarding them like a bank security guard. The glossy printed covers had embossed lettering that spelled out Harvard University Graduate School of Education: HUGSE. Reading the front made a smile spread across my face uncontrollably. The thought of both of us even applying thrilled me, and I felt a rush of excitement in my heart, like fizzing soda and sunshine. If anyone had overcome major obstacles to go to Harvard, it was certainly Doug and Darrell Luffborough.

That weekend, I went to Worcester to see my mother and personally give Darrell his application. I felt nervous talking to him about it, because growing up, we used to tease each other with names like *stupid-ass* and *dummy,* which became his pseudonyms for my real name. A part of me felt that Darrell had a better chance than I did of getting into HUGSE, but I wanted to see at least one of us get in to the school. While the entire family was hanging out in the living room and Darrell was watching ESPN, I leaned over his shoulder and asked him to join me in the kitchen in the back part of our apartment. As he entered the kitchen, I pulled out a chair and asked him to sit down. Hovering over him, I said, "Darrell, sit down—I need to talk to you about something," I said. "You may think I'm crazy, but I think we should both go back to school—graduate school. I did the research, and the number one school of education in the nation is at Harvard. I picked up two applications, one for you and one for me, and I think you should apply with me."

"Harvard?" Darrell burst out laughing. "Harvard! We can't get into that school! You are crazy, Douglas." For a moment, I laughed with him in agreement to his response, but then I sharply switched to stating my case about why we should apply.

I squared my shoulders, determined to get his attention. "Look, I know I'm not Einstein, but Darrell, I believe that *you* could get in, and if you did, it would be a win for you, for our family, for Ma, and for our community. How many gang-involved, formerly homeless, African-American males from Tatnuck Square do you know who have gone to Harvard? Exactly. Come on! Plus, if we don't get in, we will be just where we are right now, and that's not too bad, is it? We are already college graduates, so what do we have to lose? Nothing!" I was fired up, ready to fight him over it; the winner would choose.

We argued back and forth, escalating until Ma stepped in. "Lord, have mercy! My boys are going to kill each other over applying to Harvard! We really have come far as a family, but I want both of you to just calm down. Douglas, you have done your part. You gave Darrell the application, and it is up to him if he wants to apply . . . we support you, too, if you want to apply. Considering the road less travelled, Harvard is new territory for us, but, God is able!" After Ma spoke, our confrontation ended.

Over the next couple of weeks, I worked daily on the application and called my brother to see how he was doing with the process, but we never went into too many details about it. In addition to sharing that I'd overcome gang involvement, low expectations, and homelessness, I also shared my graduation experience at Northeastern and our visit to the White House. I felt that if anybody had used education as a platform for success, it was Darrell and me. Also, my experience at City Year gave me a passion for educating children within an urban context because I had lived it.

As the deadline approached, I tapped in to some of my mentors for feedback on how I could strengthen my application. Just one day before the deadline, Darrell and I completed our applications, and together we went to HUGSE and dropped them off. Our shoulders rose up, our heads lifted with a big sense of accomplishment, and Darrell and I decided to celebrate by going out to eat in Harvard Square. We had a little celebration but knew that even though we had done our parts, the rest was out of our hands. Because I feared friends would discourage me, similar to how my third-grade teacher had, I did not share my application process with them.

Months passed without incident, and on April Fools' Day in 1996, I received a large envelope in my mailbox. The return address said: Harvard University Graduate School of Education.

I remembered similar large envelopes showing up when I was in high school and applying to college, and it meant one thing: I must have gotten in. And despite this knowledge, I couldn't find the courage to rip the envelope open to see for myself. I set the envelope on the kitchen table and paced back and forth until I thought my heart might beat out of my chest. I grabbed the envelope and ripped it open.

"Congratulations! You have been accepted into the Harvard University Graduate School of Education." I rubbed my eyes to make sure I was seeing clearly, and I read the words over and over again. Like a leaky faucet gasket, ready to explode, I burst into tears of joy, covering my face with my hands as saliva filled my mouth and leaked onto my hands.

I panted, barely uttering my words. "Thank you, God, thank you, God, we did it!" At that moment, I knew it was God's will for my life, that it had been *we* all along. I went to my room, looked at the infamous boardwalk picture, and saw my silhouette on the other side of the mountain. I stood there staring at the picture, talking to Jesus and wailing until my eyes were bloodshot red, irritated, and sore from rubbing them. Not only was I college material, but I had been admitted into the number one Ivy League graduate school of education *in the world*. I had to compose myself because I knew I had one very important phone call to make.

"Hello? Darrell, this is Douglas. Did you get anything in the mail today?" My voice was still recovering from the weeping, but I was full of joy.

"Yes," he said, not giving off any indication of the outcome.

"Well, what did they say?"

Instead of answering my question, he fired one back at me. "Did you find out anything?"

Now it was my turn. "Darrell, did you get a small envelope or a large envelope?"

The pause on the line was almost imperceptible. "I got . . . I got a large envelope." His voice was confident, certain, happy. I went numb; I was beside myself with disbelief of what we were able to pull off. Not missing a beat, I replied.

"I did too!" I wailed again like I had done just twenty minutes before. Both of us yelled and screamed into the phone as if we had won the lottery. Between the two of us, we recited every happy proverb we could remember. The one repeated most often, above the shouting and whooping, was "All things are possible for those who believe."

Darrell and I agreed that we would share the news and our acceptance letters together with Mama Luff. We met outside Mom's apartment, immediately reaching for each other's letter to see for ourselves that the information was true. Leaning up against my car, we pored over those letters like internal investigators checking for authenticity. The letters were identical: same letterhead, same introduction, and same instructions on what to do next. Everything was the same except that one letter was addressed to me and one to Darrell. We embraced like we never had before.

We decided to play up the great news. Darrell went in first, waving his letter in the air, and I followed in a somber mood. When Ma saw Darrell and read his letter, her eyes lit up with joy, but when she saw my long face, her attention went from congratulating Darrell to consoling me.

"Ma? Would you mind reading my letter, too?" I sauntered up to her and put it in her free hand. With both letters, Ma went back and forth between them. The puzzled look on her face contorted her eyebrows and she put one wrist on her hip.

"Okay, now I need you boys to help me out. From what I am reading here, both of you got in to Harvard! Am I missing something?"

I beamed with pride. "No, Ma. We thought there must be some type of mistake, but it looks to us like both of your sons are going to Harvard!"

In the middle of the kitchen, Ma fell to her knees. Tears streamed down her face, and she held both letters high in the air. "God does not make mistakes, son! God does not make mistakes! Thank you, Jesus! Thank you, Lord! My boys are going to Harvard!" Darrell and I stood there, tearing up like proud soldiers returning from the battlefield. Indeed, we were victors over adversity, just as our mother had prayed for all these years.

That summer flew by, and when the multicolored leaves fell from the trees, it was the start of fall in New England. One of the first things we did was register for classes. When we were issued our Harvard IDs, which was truly the icing on the cake, we were officially Harvard University Graduate School of Education students. When the first day of school came, the early morning dew and the dawn of a new day for Darrell and me kept our attention as fresh as it could be. We went to Harvard's bookstore, called the Coop, to get the latest Harvard attire and books, and to make sure we were ready for our first day of classes.

Darrell and I had the same major and took many of the same classes while we were at Harvard. Our very first class was educational policy. Darrell and I were dressed up with shirts and ties. As we sat in the front row, I scanned the other students in the class. The sound of chalk drew my attention back to the front of the room where the professor wrote his contact information . . . and it hit me. This was not a dream. This was the real deal.

Each student had to choose an advisor who would be his or her support faculty member and help make sure all course requirements were met. I chose Dr. Charles V. Willie, the only African-American male professor at HUGSE. Dr. Willie grew up in Texas and graduated from Morehouse College with Dr. Martin Luther King Jr. He was an old-school brother from a tough time in our nation, where he'd faced discrimination and civil unrest to reach his status.

Dr. Willie was serious about teaching at Harvard and expected all of his students to go on to do at least one of three things: (1) become a school board member and create effective educational policy that supports the hardest-to-serve students; (2) work in Washington, D.C., at the U. S. Department of Education on equity and access educational policy issues; or (3) start school systems that challenged the traditional public education school paradigm by providing social service components to help students and families when they get out of school. I wasn't sure how my dreams for myself would manifest in one of these, but my excitement for the support and possibility was almost more than I could bear.

Before I knew it, I finished my first semester at Harvard. When I reviewed my grades, I was proud of the A- and B+ I received in my other classes, but my heart sank when I saw that I had received a B in Dr. Willie's class. On my final paper, he'd written a note that read: "Please make an appointment with my secretary so we can discuss your paper."

I felt awful. The last thing I wanted was to flunk out of Harvard and not be supported by my faculty advisor. I moved quickly on his recommendation and made an appointment with his secretary for the next day. As I stood in the lobby of the Gutman Library waiting for the elevator (appropriately dubbed *Waiting for Godot* because it notoriously takes way too long to arrive) to meet with Dr. Willie, I thought to myself, *This is no big deal . . . he is my faculty advisor*

. . . *he is here to help me . . . don't trip!* I kept up the positive self-talk in the elevator and as I exited.

When I walked into his office, he had a serious look on his face, and he was clutching a copy of my paper, which was covered in red ink.

"Douglas, I am going to get right to the point. You need serious help with your writing if you want to graduate from this school. I have edited your paper, and it is not up to par with where we expect our students to be. I advise you to seek assistance at the writing center on campus. I have also assigned one of my Ph.D. student teachers to work with you. I cannot have a student in my class, especially another African-American male, failing Harvard!"

Failing! He said failing! Failing at Harvard! Heck no! I thought. *This guy does not know me and the struggle and sacrifice it took for me to be here.*

But in that moment, I also realized that my elementary, middle, high school, and college experience at Northeastern did not prepare me for the academic rigor of Harvard. The pressure of high quality and the sheer volume of writing got to me. Soon, words blurred together and I would have severe bouts of writer's block. Getting started was the hardest because when I saw a blank sheet of paper, my mind went blank.

The next week, I started going to the writing center and working with my assigned student teacher. I also asked my brother Darrell to review every paper before I submitted it. Darrell was a better writer than I was, but I was a hard worker. I remembered what my mother said when she found out both Darrell and I got into Harvard: "God does not make mistakes, son! God does not make mistakes!" I felt like I was in the Super Bowl of my destiny, and losing was not an option. I started staying up for twenty-four hours sometimes, studying, reading, and writing, writing, writing. At least once a week, I pulled an all-nighter, but unlike my high school years, I studied and spoke life into myself through the word of God and positive affirmations during these hours. When other students were fooling around, I had my head in a book, often waking up with ink on my cheeks. I re-wrote the paper as Dr. Willie recommended (with the help of the writing center, the student teacher, and my brother), and the next week in class, he handed it back to me with a note that read: "Now this is much better." The final grade was a B+.

Dr. Willie did not mince words. I got As and A minuses in all of my other classes, but Dr. Willie never gave me a grade higher than a B+. I worked harder in his classes for the Bs I received than the As I received in all of my other classes. I began breaking out in golf ball–sized boils all over my face because of the pressure and expectations. I even spent a couple days in the hospital getting treatment for the boils and the anxiety attacks, which were related to my overwhelming stress. Despite knowing where the attacks came from, I kept having them, and they were exacerbated by the lack of sleep and the fear that showed up like an unwanted ex-girlfriend every time I stepped inside Dr. Willie's class. Some of the other students of color had a difficult time as well, because the education they'd received before coming to Harvard fell short of preparing them—some even dropped out of the program. Getting kicked out scared me, but dropping out was the farthest thing from my mind. I thought, *If you can handle being abused as a child, growing up hungry, being homeless, living on the streets or in motels, and attempting suicide, then finishing Harvard is a cakewalk.*

I took Dr. Willie's comments to heart so much that I remember them clearly to this day, even as I write this book. His harshness caused me to not be satisfied with the level of education I had attained, and it pushed me to pursue my own Ph.D. in Leadership Studies. I learned from him that sometimes the people who push us hardest are the ones we come back and thank because they allowed us to be better than we were.

Another benefit at Harvard was the opportunity to cross-register for my elective classes. I took one class at the Divinity School and two classes at the Kennedy School of Government. It was great to see that even Harvard had culture and expectation differences from one school to another. In one of my classes, one classmate was a prince from somewhere in the Middle East. Like a scene from Eddie Murphy's movie *Coming to America*, on the first day of class during my second semester, this guy showed up with an entourage of bodyguards and personal assistants, who smothered him and catered to his every need. Despite his money, he was in America for only one reason: to get his Harvard degree and go back to his nation to one day take over the throne. All I could think when I saw him was how great God was. The world measures man by what he has and what he looks like on the outside, but God measures a man by who he is inside. Up until then, to the world, I had been a poor, gang-banger-turned-homeless teen. I was told I was not college material, but on the inside, God saw the king in me; He brought me all the way to Harvard and had me sit right next to a real prince. Even though I left the class to take public transportation back home while the prince left in his limo by motorcade, greatness swelled inside of me, and I knew my journey to Harvard was only a training ground for what would later come.

Taking classes and studying under some of the greatest minds in academia—like Dr. Charles Willie, Dr. Marshall Ganz, Dr. Preston Williams, Dr. Richard Elmore, Dr. Gary Orfield and others—was awe-inspiring. But, by far Harvard's most valuable assets are its students. Never in my life had I been surrounded by such bold world changers . . . the best and the brightest minds and public servants combined. Each day, I left inspired by what my fellow classmates were doing, both in and outside of the classroom.

I observed that many of the students I went to school with were important figures *even before* they went to Harvard . . . Harvard did not make them who they were. Harvard just complemented the attributes they already possessed. I met students of color who grew up like me but were from East Los Angeles, Oakland, Detroit, and the Bronx; they had decided that the life they lived prior to Harvard would not define them. Just like me, they defeated the odds stacked against them.

One classmate who embodied this was a Native American guy named Hawk, who received a free ride from the Apache Nation in Texas. Hawk was paralyzed from the waist down and lived his life in a wheelchair. He had much pride and honor for his people and the role Native Americans played in the United States. He was at Harvard so that he could go back to the Apache Nation and run their independent school system as superintendent of schools.

"Doug, I am so blessed to be here at Harvard," he told me. "I am the first person from my tribal community to be at HUGSE. I am representing my elders and the next generation and serving as the bridge from the Apache Nation to the halls of Harvard. That's why they sent me here." You could feel his presence of greatness just being around him. He made you want to step up your game. Hawk was in many of the same classes as Darrell and I, and he, too, got to class early and sat right in the front row, ready to learn and ready to contribute to the classroom conversations. His strong sense of purpose and optimism about life was amazing. His soul was amazing, and every time he spoke, wisdom laced each word he shared. Even though he was still in his twenties, he spoke like an elder who had "been there and done that" years earlier. He had a fearless attitude and did not let being in a wheelchair stop him from doing anything. In one class, we were discussing educational policy issues and concerns regarding urban education, and Hawk declared: "We talk so much among the scholarly elite about our plans and ideas to develop policy to better urban education, but we miss one very important piece—we forget to talk to those we are seeking to liberate to understand their perspective."

One time on a Friday night, Darrell and I received word that a group of students had decided to go out dancing. We decided to have Chinese food at the Hong Kong restaurant and club in Harvard Square. When we arrived at the front door, we stumbled into Hawk, who was also waiting to go dancing. We entered the restaurant and decided to eat before going upstairs to the dance floor. If you walked by, you would have thought that we were all brothers, the way we were going back and forth with one another, trading jokes and stories from our time at HUGSE. After we finished eating, the rhythmic beat from upstairs signified that the dance club was open, and we were eager to show off our moves.

As we made our way to the stairs, my brother Darrell asked the hostess where the elevator was so that Hawk could join us. She looked at us, puzzled, and told us that they did not have an elevator. Darrell and I looked at each other, determined to figure it out.

Hawk interjected, "Well, I guess one of two things will be happening now: either I will jump out of this chair and crawl up or both of you big guys are going to carry me up in my chair . . . but I'm getting my dance on, so which one will it be?"

Darrell and I smiled at one another as we each reached for one wheel on Hawk's chair.

"Ready, one, two, three!" And off we went, both hugging the walls as we lifted Hawk up in his wheelchair and took him to the top of the stairs in the dance club. Without skipping a beat, the three of us headed over to the dance floor and got our groove on, socializing with other students who had decided to join us.

Hawk was a social butterfly who could work a room. He wheeled from one side of the room to the other as if he worked there. He never let his disability stop him and maintained an attitude of gratitude the entire time I knew him at HUGSE.

Despite the cold weather and the sting of winter that kept us indoors more, Darrell and I headed out to class one evening. About one hundred yards ahead of us, Hawk struggled to push himself in his wheelchair through the snow and iced-cobble stone streets and uneven sidewalks.

I watched as, one by one, other students and professors walked by Hawk as he fought to move from one side of the street to the other. I was so upset that no one stopped to ask him if he needed help, no one offered to push him, to clean off the snow on his sneakers or even offer him a jacket or gloves in the single digit weather. I turned to Darrell.

"Look, that's Hawk up there, and look at how many people are walking by him and not offering to help. Let's go help him."

Darrell agreed, and when we caught up with Hawk, puffs of foggy breath filled the air between us.

"Hawk, let us help you get out of this crazy weather." We reached for the back of his chair, each taking a side to push.

"I had been hoping that someone would stop," Hawk said, "but no one said a thing."

I took off my hat and covered his ears with it, and Darrell placed his gloves on Hawk's hands. And just like we did at the Hong Kong, each of us grabbed a wheel and lifted Hawk up off the snowy streets and to his next class. I often wondered why Hawk and I were so much alike even though we grew up in two different communities. Our stories were the same—overcoming poverty, overcoming fear, and overcoming educational barriers to be at HUGSE, and I could always feel our kindred spirits.

"Thank you guys for looking out for me," Hawk said as he cleared off the snow that was packed on his wheel chair. "It never ceases to amaze me that people see what they want to see and block out others who appear unseen." I looked at Hawk and understood what he was saying. During my senior year in high school when I was homeless, I felt invisible to the world and as though my cries for help fell on deaf ears.

"I hear you, Hawk. But because we see what others can't see or choose not to see, we must succeed despite the limiting beliefs that others have about who we are inside," I said, stamping the snow off my shoes.

During the spring, I had an epiphany when sitting in my educational policy class. The professor posed the question: "How do we fix urban education?" And it hit me that Darrell and I were greater assets than we were liabilities at Harvard. If they wanted to figure out how to fix urban education, Darrell and I had the answer because *we were the answer.* We had grown up out of the urban context, and therefore our lives were a representation of how urban education could be fixed.

Later, what seemed like an infinite education came down to just a couple of hours before our commencement address began. Beaming with pride and standing next to each other in our Harvard caps and gowns, we smiled for every photo opportunity that came our way. To my knowledge, two African-American brothers have never graduated from HUGSE at the same time with the same degree.

As we stood in line, "Pomp and Circumstance" once again filled the courtyard, along with the sense of accomplishment that graduating from Harvard held. While we stood in line, waiting for our names to be called, I looked out among the audience of proud parents and relatives. There, toward the back, dressed in her favorite purple scarf and white-brimmed church hat with matching white gloves, sat Mama Luff. On her face was the same stoic look she wore during my Northeastern graduation and our visit with President Clinton in the Oval Office. The pride she must have felt with both of her boys graduating from Harvard was surely overwhelming. I was next to Darrell, and when I heard them call his name, I shouted with great joy.

Then I heard my name: *Douglas Edward Luffborough III.*

I walked across the stage with a sense of purpose, a calling, a reason for my life. Darrell stayed in the middle of the stage, and we embraced each other tightly, proudly displaying our Harvard degrees together. All my life, I had felt as if I was not good enough, as if I did not measure up to those around me. That I was not going to be anything or anybody. I was even told that I was not college material and had tried to end my life. But standing on that stage and holding my Harvard degree, I realized there was a purpose for my pain, and that in the midst of my pain, I had found my greatness. I learned that each tear, each disappointment, was a setup for something better in my life. Nothing was ever wasted.

A new revelation was occurring to me as I walked off the stage: *you get there when you get there.* And all I could say as I re-entered the rows of graduation-capped students was, "Thank you, Jesus!" Just as my mother had known from the beginning, I had never been alone on my journey.

I never will be.

Douglas E. Luffborough III

As the son of a housekeeper, Doug grew up in an impoverished environment. He was thrown into the role of father figure to his three younger siblings at an early age, while lacking a strong male role model for himself. Doug's greatest ambition was to become the first member in his family to attend college—a dream challenged when his family became homeless during his senior year in high school. Despite homelessness and discouragement from guidance counselors, Doug aggressively pursued his dream and was accepted into Northeastern University in Boston, Massachusetts.

Five years later, he was chosen as the student commencement speaker for his class and preceded then-president of the United States Bill Clinton at the podium. President Clinton was so impressed with Doug's leadership, tenacity, and grit that he invited him and his mother to the White House.

After directing a national community service organization, Doug went back to school to receive his master's degree from the Harvard University Graduate School of Education with a concentration in administration, planning, and social policy. He was also chosen to receive a fellowship degree from the Center for Social Innovation at the Stanford University Graduate School of Business, Executive Program for Nonprofit Leaders. Currently, Doug is a PhD candidate at the University of San Diego School of Leadership Studies with a concentration in leadership and consulting.

Doug has spent over twenty-five years working with organizations as a heart-inspired motivational speaker, social entrepreneur, and advocate for social change. Extremely devoted to youth development and family empowerment, he has created and directed social service programs throughout the United States and Asia.

Doug was recently recognized as a recipient of the esteemed San Diego Channel 10 Leadership Award as a caring resident "who goes above and beyond to make San Diego a better place to live by improving the quality of life for those who need it most." His core values and belief in faith, discipline, action, and hard work led to special appearances at the Fleet Center (formerly the Boston Garden), the White House, the John F. Kennedy Library and Museum, and the Crystal Cathedral's "Hour of Power" television broadcast, among others. Doug's life is a tale of inspiration and hope for the American dream that has impacted hundreds of institutions and thousands of people around the world.

Today he lives in Chula Vista, California, with his wife and five children. Currently, Doug serves as an elected school board member, professional heart-inspired motivational speaker, and leadership consultant with dougluff.com. In his spare time, he also founded a nonprofit organization called Watch Me Rise Social Services, whose mission is to help those who have been knocked down in life get back up.

To book Doug Luffborough for a speaking or consulting engagement, please email him at dougluff@gmail.com.

Doug and family

Mama Luff

S&S Landscaping/Orange Crush Little League Team with Coach Miller

Doug, President Curry, Senator Ted Kennedy, and Mama Luff

Mama Luff with Liz Walker

To Douglas Luffborough
Best wishes for the future,

You were great on this day! Bill Clinton

To Doug, Congratulations on your outstanding achievement Bill Clinton

Graduation Speech

Northeastern University Class of 1993

Douglas Luffborough III

Day O, Day O, Day Light Come and Me Wanna Go Home. Day, Me Say Day, Me Say Day, Me Say Day, Me Say Day, Me Say Day O. Day Light Come and Me Wanna Go Home!

DURING MY FIRST WEEK AT NORTHEASTERN I WAS SO SCARED, THE ONLY THING I WANTED TO DO WAS GO HOME. I ASKED MYSELF, "WHY AM I HERE?" BUT THEN I REMEMBERED THAT COMING TO COLLEGE WAS A DREAM I HAD ALWAYS ENVISIONED. WHEN I WAS A HIGH SCHOOL SENIOR, MY MOTHER WAS PREGNANT WITH HER FOURTH CHILD, MY FATHER WAS NOWHERE TO BE FOUND, AND WE WERE HOMELESS WITH NOWHERE TO LIVE. MY MOTHER CLEANS BATHROOMS, WASHES WINDOWS, AND TAKES CARE OF OTHER CHILDREN TO CREATE A LIFE FOR HER OWN CHILDREN. SHE GAVE ALL SHE HAD TO FIND A WAY TO GET MY

BROTHER AND ME TO COLLEGE/AND SHE DIDN'T STOP UNTIL SHE'D FOUND A SCHOOL/AND A SCHOLARSHIP TO PAY FOR IT/THAT'S HOW I GOT TO NORTHEASTERN. (Pause)

MR. PRESIDENT, PRESIDENT CURRY, FACULTY, FRIENDS, AND CLASSMATES:

THOUGH YOUR STORIES MAY BE DIFFERENT FROM MINE/YOU HAVE ALL HAD OBSTACLES TO OVERCOME/TO GET WHERE YOU ARE TODAY/ BUT NOW THE QUESTION IS/HOW CAN WE AS GRADUATES/ USE OUR EXPERIENCE AT NORTHEASTERN/TO BETTER THE WORLD?/ WE CAN START BY DOING SOME OF THE SAME THINGS MY MOTHER DID FOR ME/ LIKE CHALLENGING OTHERS TO WANT NOTHING BUT THE VERY BEST OUT OF LIFE AND HELPING THEM TO TURN THEIR LIVES AROUND.

BECAUSE NORTHEASTERN HAS GIVEN US THE OPPORTUNITY TO WORK SIDE BY SIDE WITH LEADING PROFESSIONALS FROM ALL OVER THE WORLD, WE ARE NOW PREPARED TO BECOME THE FUTURE LEADERS OF OUR COUNTRY. LIVING AND WORKING IN BOSTON HAS EXPOSED US TO DIFFERENT PEOPLE, CULTURES AND IDEAS. BUT THERE ARE SOME THINGS WE HAVE SEEN THAT WE NEED TO CHANGE, LIKE POVERTY, RACISM, DRUG ABUSE AND BAD SCHOOLS. WE CAN CHANGE THESE THINGS BY APPLYING WHAT OUR EXPERIENCE AT NORTHEASTERN HAS TAUGHT US — RESPONSIBILITY AND ADAPTABILITY. BUT IF WE WANT CHANGE, WE NEED TO START WITH OURSELVES. AND THEN WE NEED TO REACH OUT TO HELP OTHERS BECAUSE IF WE DON'T, WHAT WILL THE FUTURE HOLD FOR THE GENERATION THAT COMES AFTER US?

MANY OF YOU HAVE ALREADY BEGUN/IN A SMALL WAY/TO DO JUST THAT BY CONTRIBUTING TO SENIOR CHALLENGE '93. THOSE SCHOLARSHIPS WILL MAKE A DIFFERENCE IN THE LIVES OF THE STUDENTS WHO FOLLOW US/ BY GIVING THEM A FUTURE HERE AT NORTHEASTERN/ BECAUSE PROVIDING EDUCATIONAL OPPORTUNITY IS THE MOST IMPORTANT STEP IN MAKING THE WORLD A BETTER PLACE. (Pause)

AND LET'S NOT LEAD LIVES FILLED WITH I SHOULD HAVE/ I COULD HAVE/ IF ONLY I HAD; LET IT BE I CAN/ I WILL/ I DID/ TAKE THE TIME TO MAKE EACH DAY COUNT/FOR GETTING SOMETHING ACCOMPLISHED/ AND REMEMBER/NO ONE GETS TO THE TOP WITHOUT STUMBLING/AND BY MAKING MISTAKES/WE FIND OUT HOW TO DO THINGS RIGHT. SO DON'T BE UPSET IF YOU HAVE FAILED

TO CHANGE THE WHOLE WORLD; INSTEAD, BE INSPIRED IF YOU HAVE BROUGHT HOPE INTO JUST ONE PERSON'S HEART FOR ONE MOMENT AND I'D LIKE TO DO THAT RIGHT NOW FOR MY FRIEND AND OUR CLASSMATE SCOTT DAVIS, WHO LIES IN A COMA IN THE HOSPITAL. (Pause)

NORTHEASTERN HAS GIVEN ALL OF US A CHOICE AND A CHANCE — A CHOICE IN THE WAY WE WANT TO LIVE OUR LIVES AND A CHANCE TO REACH AND EVEN EXCEED OUR GOALS. TODAY I ASK MYSELF ONCE AGAIN: "WHY AM I HERE? WHY ARE WE HERE?" WE ARE HERE IN PART BECAUSE WE HAVE EARNED IT. BUT EACH OF US ALSO OWES THIS DAY TO THOSE WHO HELPED US GET HERE. THANK THEM! THANK THEM FROM THE BOTTOM OF YOUR HEARTS.

FOR ME IT WAS MY MOTHER'S ENDLESS DEVOTION TO GIVE EVERYTHING SHE HAD — NO MATTER HOW LITTLE — TO HER

CHILDREN/SO WE COULD MAKE SOMETHING OF OUR LIVES/ MY MOTHER ALWAYS TOLD ME/"DOUGLAS, SET YOUR DREAMS AS IF THEY WERE IN THAT CORNER RIGHT OVER THERE/ AND NEVER TAKE YOUR EYES OFF THAT CORNER/ NO MATTER WHAT YOU DECIDE TO DO/NEVER STOP REACHING FOR YOUR DREAMS/AND DON'T LET ANYTHING OR ANYBODY STOP YOU."/ THAT'S THE CHALLENGE FOR ALL OF US/ AND IF WE MEET IT/ONE DAY/EVERYONE ALL OVER THIS COUNTRY/AND ALL OVER THE WORLD/WILL BE ABLE TO SEE THEIR DREAMS IN THAT CORNER RIGHT OVER THERE OR WHEREVER THEIR CORNER IS/AND/— ONE DAY/— EVERYONE WILL BE ABLE TO SEIZE THOSE DREAMS AND MAKE THEM COME TRUE. (Pause)

CONGRATULATIONS, CLASS OF 93, AND MAY YOU NEVER STOP REACHING TO BE THE VERY BEST YOU CAN BE.

44838189R00163

Made in the USA
San Bernardino, CA
24 January 2017